Twelve Great Books that Changed the
University, and Why Christians Should Care

Twelve Great Books
that Changed the University,
and Why Christians Should Care

. . . .

EDITED BY

Steve Wilkens and Don Thorsen

CASCADE *Books* · Eugene, Oregon

TWELVE GREAT BOOKS THAT CHANGED THE UNIVERSITY, AND WHY
CHRISTIANS SHOULD CARE

Cascade
An Imprint of Wipf and Stock Publishers
199 W. 8th Ave., Suite 3
Eugene, OR 97401

www.wipfandstock.com

ISBN 13: 978-1-62032-739-5

Cataloging-in-Publication data:

Twelve great books that changed the university, and why Christians should care /
edited by Steve Wilkens and Don Thorsen.

xvi + 200 p.; 23 cm—Includes bibliographical references.

ISBN 13: 978-1-62032-739-5

1. Civilization, Western—History—Sources—Study and teaching (Higher)—United
States. 2. Humanities—Study and teaching (Higher)—United States. 3. Science—Study
and teaching (Higher)—United States. I. Wilkens, Steve. II. Thorsen, Don. III. Title.

CB245 T88 2014

Manufactured in the USA.

To our colleagues
who seek to integrate their passion for learning
with their passion for God

Table of Contents

Foreword

BY MARK STANTON

IT SEEMS TO ME that a book must have a compelling purpose in order to find its place in the overwhelming flow of information in contemporary society. The book must fill a unique niche. It must provide a perspective not otherwise available if it is to rise to the top of the heap of books, articles, and media that pile up daily, asking us to spend precious time reading or reviewing them. So, why read *Twelve Great Books that Changed the University, and Why Christians Should Care?*

Robert Bellah, in *Habits of the Heart,* suggests that social coherence requires a recovery of tradition and an understanding that genuine tradition exists in continuous development and revision. He urges us to "learn again from the cultural riches of the human species and to reappropriate and revitalize those riches so that they can speak to our condition today."[1] *Twelve Great Books* presents reflections on the contribution of influential works in the academic disciplines and notes their impact on the academy and broader society, with the additional value of providing a Christian perspective on these works. This book is truly "value added" and grist for academic discussion as these works are considered today with a fresh generation of university students.

A Christian perspective should not be understood as superimposing some artificial evaluative rubric on the original texts of the authors. The chapters in this book counter the stereotype of a narrow Christian mindset that is dogmatic and exclusionary. Instead, they reflect the epistemological awareness that "all truth is God's truth"—an argument and quotation adapted from Aristotle and suggesting the underlying coherence of truth rooted in God and represented in the statements and "discoveries" of people. It is the role of the Christian scholar to consider how prominent

1. Robert N. Bellah, *Habits of the Heart* (New York: Harper & Row, 1985), 283.

texts in one's discipline demonstrate truth, identifying persuasive insights but challenging questionable elements. This involves holding (or even embracing) the ideas of the author and reflecting, interacting, responding, and reacting critically in light of Christian faith. It is not sacrilege to endorse ideas from a secular or avowedly non-Christian author when one sets out in pursuit of God's truth. In the same fashion, there is no renunciation of one's discipline when a scholar questions or challenges ideas inconsistent with one's understanding of Christian theology and God's truth.

In a previous book entitled *Everything You Know about Evangelicals Is Wrong (Well, Almost Everything)*, Wilkens and Thorsen counter the caricatures of evangelical Christianity, including the ideas that evangelical Christians are necessarily mean, dogmatic, or endorse monolithic views on controversial matters. This volume is an extension of the unifying spirit identified in that earlier volume. It brings together authors from disparate disciplines (from education and economics to physics and politics) and diverse theological orientations within the evangelical mosaic. But they are all committed to critical thinking about their discipline within the context of Christian faith. In my opinion, this is the role of Christian higher education. At Azusa Pacific University, faith integration is at the core of our identity and purpose. It is defined as "the informed reflection on and discovery of Christian faith within the academic disciplines, professional programs, and lived practice, resulting in the articulation of Christian perspectives on truth and life in order to advance the work of God in the world."[2] All faculty are expected to engage in the integration of their faith and discipline. This book is an example of that endeavor, and I believe it will be useful to Christian academics and students who seek to do likewise.

Finally, this book brings together disparate and often disconnected disciplines in the academy to remind us that academic pluralism and attention to the details of an individual discipline may be enhanced by placing them cogently under one umbrella at times. The book provides some content specific to the interests and concerns of scholars in a particular discipline, but it stretches us all to reflect on the contributions of neighboring and distant disciplines that enrich our understanding of our chosen discipline. This is at the core of education in the liberal arts and sciences. It can be refreshing for those of us who become isolated in our disciplinary literature to come back to the broader foundation; this work provides that opportunity.

2. *Azusa Pacific University Faculty Handbook* (Azusa, CA: Azusa Pacific University, 2013), section 8.3.

Acknowledgements

We want to acknowledge those who have helped us in the completion of *Twelve Books that Changed the University, and Why Christians Should Care*. First we want to thank our editor Rodney Clapp at Cascade Books for his wisdom and encouragement in completing this publication. He has been a longtime colleague and friend.

We want to thank the authors who contributed chapters to this book. They are all colleagues of ours at Azusa Pacific University, and they are experts in their respective fields of academic study. We benefited from their professional insights as well as from how they integrate their Christian faith in relationship to the great literature from their respective areas of scholarly expertise.

We thank the support of Azusa Pacific University for its contribution to our scholarship. Both Steve and Don benefited from the Writers Retreats, where we first framed the book project. In addition, many of the contributors were provided the opportunity to direct uninterrupted time to their chapters as a result of the Writers Retreats. We also benefited from Accomplished Scholars Awards for release time in order to complete our work. Finally, Steve received a Faculty Research Grant, which aided in expediting the publication of the book.

Our Provost Mark Stanton graciously agreed to write the Foreword to this book, and Paul Gray supported us through his Deanship in the University Libraries. Our colleagues in the School of Theology also provided insight, encouragement, and humor—though not necessarily in that order.

Finally, Steve thanks his wife Deb and his children, Zoe and Zachary, for their support and patience with Dad's late-night writing and editing forays at McDonalds. Don thanks his daughters Liesl, Heidi, and Dana, who continue to indulge his passion for writing with a filial forbearance that warms his heart.

List of Contributors

Roger B. Conover, Ph.D., teaches courses in Economics and Religion, Microfinance and Microenterprise Development, and Comparative Economics at Azusa Pacific University. His research studies the integration of environmental and development economics with Christian missions work, as well as the conversation between economics and theology on such issues as scarcity, competition, and value. He currently serves on the Board of Directors for GMI, Inc., a Christian organization doing strategic missions research and the mapping of linguistic, cultural, and economic data.

David D. Esselstrom, Ph.D., is Professor and Chair of the Department of English at Azusa Pacific University, where he teaches creative writing, composition, and literature. He has published fiction and journalism, as well as written extensively for the stage and screen.

Bradley Rainbow Hale, Ph.D., is Associate Professor of History at Azusa Pacific University, where he teaches courses on the Enlightenment, modern Europe, Africa, and the humanities. He specializes in French colonial history, especially French missionary activity in Algeria in the twentieth century. His research interests also include the global revolutions of 1968.

Anita Fitzgerald Henck, Ph.D., serves as Dean of the School of Education and Professor at Azusa Pacific University. She previously held administrative and faculty positions at American University and Eastern Nazarene College. She is a graduate of Indiana University (B.A., Psychology) and American University (M.A. in Higher Education Administration, and Ph.D. in Education). Henck's primary areas of teaching, writing, and consulting relate to organizational culture and change, focusing on schools, churches, and nonprofit organizations.

Nori Lowe Henk, Ph.D., is Assistant Professor of Sociology at Azusa Pacific University. She received her doctorate in Sociology at Loyola University Chicago. Her areas of specialty are sociology of religion, social movements, and qualitative research methods.

Andrea Ivanov-Craig, Ph.D., is a Professor of English at Azusa Pacific University, where she teaches a number of undergraduate courses, including World Literature. Her expertise is twentieth-century American Literature and Film, and she is currently writing a book on the Catholic short story writer Andre Dubus, on whom she has previously presented and published. She also serves as the Far Western Regent of Sigma Tau Delta, a collegiate international English honor society.

Joshua Morris, Ph.D., is Associate Professor of Biology and Chemistry at Azusa Pacific University, where he teaches courses in genetics, developmental biology, and scientific ethics. He received his doctorate in Molecular, Cell, and Developmental Biology from the University of California, Los Angeles. His current research project explores the development of termite eyes in a variety of species native to Southern California.

Mark Stanton, Ph.D., is Provost at Azusa Pacific University, and Professor in the Department of Graduate Psychology. He was the 2005 President of the Society of Family Psychology of the American Psychological Association, and the Editor of *The Family Psychologist* (2002–2007). Stanton was recently elected to serve as President of the American Board of Couple and Family Psychology (2011–2013), a constituent board of the American Board of Professional Psychology. He is coeditor of the *Handbook of Family Psychology*, with James Bray.

Don Thorsen, Ph.D., is Professor of Theology and Chair of Graduate Theology and Ethics at Azusa Pacific University. He is author of more than ten books, including *The Wesleyan Quadrilateral, An Exploration of Christian Theology, Everything You Know about Evangelicals Is Wrong*, and *Calvin vs. Wesley: Bringing Belief in Line with Practice*.

Theresa Clement Tisdale, Ph.D., is Professor of Graduate Psychology at Azusa Pacific University. She earned her masters and doctorate in clinical psychology from Rosemead School of Psychology at Biola University. She is currently a third year candidate at Newport Psychoanalytic Institute and maintains an independent practice in Glendora, California. Her academic, clinical, and research specialties are psychodynamic psychotherapy, spirituality and spiritual formation, and the integration of spirituality/religion in clinical practice. She has presented and published on each of these topics.

Rico Vitz, Ph.D., is Associate Professor of Philosophy at Azusa Pacific University and a member of St. Peter the Apostle Orthodox Church in Pomona, California. He is the editor of *Turning East: Contemporary Philosophers and the Ancient Christian Faith* (St. Vladimir's Seminary Press), as well as author of *Reforming the Art of Living: Nature, Virtue, and Religion in Descartes's Philosophy* (Springer), and of a number of articles on the work of David Hume.

Jennifer E. Walsh, Ph.D., is Associate Dean and Professor of Political Science at Azusa Pacific University. Walsh earned her M.A. and Ph.D. degrees in Political Science from Claremont Graduate University and has scholarly interests in American government, public policy, crime and punishment issues, and constitutional jurisprudence. Her research on the California Three Strikes law has been disseminated broadly and referenced in reports issued by state and national lawmakers and the New Zealand Parliament.

Leslie Wickman, Ph.D., directs the Center for Research in Science at Azusa Pacific University. Her current projects include research on global climate change and national security issues, assessment of current and future space mission technologies and applications, human factors issues in extreme environments, and sustainable water reclamation systems. Wickman holds masters and doctoral degrees in Engineering from Stanford University. She earned a bachelor's degree in Political Science, graduating with honors from Willamette University, Oregon.

Steve Wilkens, Ph.D., is Professor of Philosophy and Ethics and Faith Integration Fellow for Faculty Development at Azusa Pacific University. He has authored and edited several books, including *Hidden Worldviews: Eight Cultural Stories that Shape Our Lives* and *Beyond Bumper Sticker Ethics*.

INTRODUCTION

Twelve Great Books and the Christian Faith

BY STEVE WILKENS

The Desire to Know: Christianity and the University

"ALL MEN BY NATURE desire to know."[1] Aristotle's words remind us that we cannot avoid the pursuit of knowledge; the desire to know is part of the human DNA. Indeed, at the most basic level, learning is a necessity of our existence since *homo sapiens* (Latin, "wise man") is blessedly deprived. While other species have deeply ingrained instincts that allow them to navigate basic survival tasks such as securing food and shelter, human beings have to learn these skills. Lacking these instinctual capacities, we do not simply want to know and learn. We *need* to know.

Reflection upon this basic difference between human beings and other species quickly leads to another distinction. We are not satisfied with a learning process that terminates in survival and security. We also want to know things such as the moral implications of our survival and security processes, understand why we find certain sounds beautiful or grating, analyze the meaning of our social structures, predict the future in view of technological trends, and—as we will do in this book—reflect upon our educational endeavors.[2] To put it in the traditional shorthand, human

---

1. Aristotle, *Metaphysics,* ed. Richard McKeon, trans. W. D. Ross (New York: Random House, 1981), 980a.

2. The givenness of this distinction is evident in the fact that every reader will assume that "we," in this sentence, excludes all living entities other than members of the human species.

1

beings are perennially interested in knowing the *meaning* of the life we seek to sustain.

Although it is not the only venue in which human beings reflect on life's meaning, the university came into existence precisely for the purpose of intentional and sustained reflection on the host of questions that ultimately crystalize into the meta-question: "What does it all mean?" Thus, it should not surprise us that whenever a society achieves a level of prosperity and security sufficient to venture beyond the basic demands of existence, institutions of higher learning emerge. In other words, we find a direct progression from Aristotle's statement that "all men, by nature, want to know" and his founding of the Lyceum, usually considered the second forerunner of the modern university (late fourth century BCE)—after Plato's Academy (mid fourth century BCE). History confirms what Aristotle affirms: what the university seeks to know is not simply an optional activity within the range of human capacities. It is intrinsic to the structure of human existence.

This book is an exploration of the human desire to know as it has manifested itself in twelve books that explore life's most profound questions. Each book represents a specific discipline taught at virtually every institution of higher education and has been selected because it is a generative text within that field, even if it was not specifically written with academia in view. Two preliminary observations about the disciplines and representative texts are in order. First, we recognize that these choices are not uncontroversial. Additional areas of study could have been selected and, most certainly, different pivotal works within those disciplines could have been chosen. We will have more to say about our selection of representative texts later, but the disciplines we examine in this book are mainstays within the broad range of the liberal arts and sciences. It is within this segment of the curriculum that we most consciously reflect upon the profound questions of life.

This allows a segue to the second observation. The existence of these disciplines as discrete entities within the university system may give the impression that they are arbitrary divisions. Upon closer inspection, however, we recognize that they parallel our initial statement about the natural human desire to know. The disciplines are simply an efficient manner of referring to the various dimensions of the human life about which we seek to know. In other words, to be human is to be a political, economic, spiritual, social, aesthetic, and historical being. Thus, the pursuit of knowledge, not just as a generalized desire to know but as an endeavor to know in and about every dimension of our personhood, is a naturally emerging human activity.

While this book is interested in higher education as a naturally emerging human activity, it is also curious about how higher education is (or should be) related to the Christian faith. Our initial comment on this relationship is that formal educational institutions were late arrivals to the "meaning of life" questions. Religion existed long before Plato founded his Academy, and it has always been concerned with the same matters of transcendence and meaning that gave rise to the university. Thus we find that Christianity, from its inception, has offered its answers to the same big questions investigated within the university. In light of this shared interest, the question is how the two should be understood in relation to each other. Are they allies that should share their unique resources in a joint quest for truth and purpose, natural enemies that both lay claim to the same contested territory, or something in between?

Obviously, neither the university nor Christianity has been unified in how the question above should be answered. Indeed, the debate about the appropriate relationship between Christianity and the academy runs through almost every book surveyed in the following chapters, although usually at the subterranean level. However, at the core of this book is the observation that, from its very beginning, Christianity has produced scholars. Whether it is the Apostle Paul engaging the philosophers on Mars Hill, the philosopher Justin Martyr (c. 100–165) who retains the philosopher's tunic and founds a school after his conversion, or any of a vast number of believing intellectuals who followed them in subsequent centuries, a significant segment of the church has viewed engagement of the big ideas as entirely consistent with faith. Moreover, this engagement was not merely a matter of personal interest by maverick believers. Instead, higher education was, and continues to be, embraced at the institutional level of Christianity as a task central to the church's mission in the world. In fact, if we ignore the role of Christianity in the history of Western higher education, we must excise most of the timeline. It is to that role we now turn.

The Place of the University within Christianity

Secular education has rather decisively divorced itself from Christianity. Thus, Christian scholars often wonder whether Christianity has a rightful place in the academy. We will get to that question in short order. However, a lack of historical perspective often obscures the fact that the more salient question throughout most of Western history was not whether Christianity belonged in the university, but whether the university had a rightful place within Christianity. Because Christianity was the dominant force in Western culture, the variable was not whether it would have an influential role in social structures. Christianity's place was the given. Throughout much of the last 2000 years, it was higher education's place that was in question. Indeed, if Christianity had not embraced formalized education as an expression of its ministry, our universities, and our world, would look very different today.

One of our surveyed texts, Gibbon's *Decline and Fall of the Roman Empire*, chronicles the seismic shifts caused by the demise of the Roman Empire. Gibbon observes that as the empire's instability increased, the availability and rigor of Rome's educational institutions waned. During the same period, however, educational endeavors took root in Christianity's monastery and cathedral schools. These survived Rome's fall, proliferated, and became the bastions of education for centuries.[3] The learning offered in these schools varied greatly. The rules of most monastic orders assumed basic literacy skills, making minimal grammatical and musical skills a necessity for monastic or clerical vocations. However, some schools required regular reading of classical works, and out of this often came a robust study of the liberal arts and sciences that preserved the classical education in the trivium (grammar, logic, and rhetoric) and quadrivium (arithmetic, geometry, music, and astronomy).[4] In such cases, our two earliest texts surveyed in this book, Plato's *Republic* and Augustine's *Confessions*, would have been widely read. Study of the classical poets was viewed as important preparation for rhetorical skills and creation of liturgies. In addition to those preparing for the priesthood and monastic life, many students were the sons (and less frequently, daughters) of well-to-do families whose education employed philosophical, historical, and political texts in preparation for

---

3. See particularly volume two of Gibbon's work, which outlines the establishment of Constantinople as an important center of learning and the provision for the erection of cathedrals, particularly under Constantine. Cathedrals allowed for the centralization of Christian efforts, education included. See Edward Gibbon, *Decline and Fall of the Roman Empire*, 6 vols., ed. Hans-Friedrich Mueller (New York: Modern Library, 2003).

4. Christianity's educational impulse received an added boost during the Carolingian Renaissance with Charlemagne's decree in 787, which required each abbey to have a school.

roles in government and law. However, many orders also viewed it as their mission to provide elementary educational opportunities for the poor.[5]

While the scope and depth of learning within the early medieval institutions varied, two general statements are possible. First, education was never an end in itself, but a means and expression of devotion to God that was placed in the context of community worship. Second, regardless of how "dark" one believes the so-called "Dark Ages" to have been, the Christian church kept the flame of teaching and learning alive through this period and fanned this light into a highly visible fire in later times. Moreover, without the important work of preserving and copying classical texts undertaken by scriptoria (literally, "a place for writing") linked to these schools, our knowledge of the ancient world would be greatly impoverished, not to mention the new intellectual wealth generated in the texts, art, music, and literature produced in these venues during the post-Roman period.

The cathedral and monastery schools provided the seedbed for the great universities of the high scholastic period. One did not displace the other; instead, the university supplemented the continuing work of the earlier institutions. This co-existence was not without tension. The cloister schools were often critical of high scholasticism's focus on dialectic and complex metaphysical speculation, believing the heavy focus on disputation was counterproductive to the devotional purposes of learning.[6]

The emergence of Renaissance humanism led to strong growth in both the number and prestige of the European universities. In 1400, twenty-nine universities had charters; by 1625, this number had increased to seventy-three.[7] While individual universities gave differing levels of emphasis to the four faculties of arts, medicine, law, and theology, numerous elements were common to the curricula of these schools. Almost universally, students would receive instruction in the classical poets, the medicine of Galen and Hippocrates, Aristotelian logic and science—all in Latin. Even

5. For a useful overview of monastic education, see Jean Leclercq, *The Love of Learning and the Desire for God*, 2nd ed., trans. and ed. Catherine Misrahi (New York: Fordham University Press, 1974).

6. For a summary of this tension, see C. H. Lawrence, *Medieval Monasticism*, 3rd ed. (Essex: Pearson, 2001), 137–45. However, this tension should not be absolutized. In some cases, universities worked closely with monastery schools that supplemented their instruction, especially in theology.

7. Paul F. Grendler, "The Universities of the Renaissance and Reformation," *Renaissance Quarterly*, 57, no. 1 (Spring, 2004) 1–42. Grendler's article offers an overview of the university system during this period.

in the universities that lacked numerically strong theology faculties, theology was acknowledged as the "Queen of the Sciences,"[8] and the theologian Peter Lombard's *Sentences* and courses in Bible were curricular mainstays. This reflected the conviction that all learning, if properly apprehended, led the student back to the source and *telos* (literally, "purpose" or "goal") of knowledge—God.

Ironically, the same university system that was the glory of Catholic learning was also essential to the birth of the Protestant Reformation. It was from universities such as Cambridge, Heidelberg, Oxford, Marburg, Leiden, and mostly significantly, Wittenberg, that the ideas central to Protestantism were born.[9] Students trained at these schools became the pastors who propagated the Reformers' message throughout Europe. As a result of the schisms of the Reformation and Counter-Reformation, Protestants assumed control of many universities, which led to deep changes in the theological ideas taught at these institutions. Despite this, the curricula of these universities remained almost indistinguishable from their recent past, and the theologians retained the methodology of earlier ages and developed Protestant forms of Scholastic Theology.

While the longevity of the university structure provided ballast that largely preserved the curriculum and methodologies of scholasticism through the Reformation's upheavals, other forces would create decisive changes in Western higher education. Some of those impulses are hinted at in texts examined within this book. For example, Cervantes' *Don Quixote* provides a portrait of the ambiguities felt as the old ideals of chivalry and the medieval period's social structures began to wobble. In addition, *Hamlet* captures the ambiguities of a populace caught in the struggle between Catholicism and Protestantism.

While the ferment largely runs beneath the surface in such literary sources, it emerges clearly in Bacon's *Novum Organum*. Bacon's work directly contests the scientific methodology of a university system that had all but canonized Aristotle's *Organum*, and establishes an experimental and empirical approach to natural philosophy (what we now call the natural sciences) that later reshapes the social sciences. From a different trajectory, Pietism's emphasis on vital, individual faith challenged what seemed to be

8. This expression of theology's status within the curriculum is usually traced to the thirteenth century theologian, Bonaventure, although the idea certainly precedes this particular phrase. See Christopher M. Cullen, *Bonaventure* (New York: Oxford University Press, 2006), 30.

9. Grendler, "Universities," 14–23.

the detached lifelessness of both Catholic and Protestant Scholastic Theology. Groups inspired by Pietism actively founded schools and academies that, although they lacked charters that allowed them to grant degrees, drew faculty from the universities and maintained academic rigor. The Thirty Years' War (1618–1648) was an important catalyst for changes coming to the university. Besides draining the human and financial resources that had maintained academia in past centuries, it also undermined confidence in the theological underpinnings of higher education. In short, Western society was ready for something new, and the university reflected this openness.

The Marginalization of Christianity within the University

The Enlightenment university arose in the midst of this social and religious ferment and challenged traditions of the past on every level. Because so many of these traditions led back to the church, theology's role—previously immune from scrutiny—was under attack. While few Enlightenment figures directly rejected Christianity, they were highly critical of the sectarian theological claims that had led to political and social upheaval during the Thirty Years' War. The "Queen of the Sciences," which was supposed to be the unifier of all knowledge, appeared to be a divider instead.

Early Enlightenment figures had no intention of forfeiting the long-established ideal of the unity of knowledge. However, they modified the terms of the deal. Philosophy, grounded in the rational faculties shared by all human beings, displaced theology as the final arbiter of truth and the center around which all knowledge coalesced. Christianity had its place in the discussion, but could not claim authority when its pronouncements went beyond the boundaries imposed by reason. The title of Kant's *Religion within the Limits of Reason Alone* summarizes the mood of the Enlightenment well.[10]

10. While those within the universities were the strongest critics of the older order, the institutional structures often slowed changes in the intellectual milieu. As an example of this lag, scholars often cite the University of Berlin as the university that best expresses the shifts. However, by its founding in 1810, it was only a short time before its educational assumptions would be challenged by new forces. For an account of the importance of Berlin, especially for the role of theology within the university, see Thomas Albert Howard, *Protestant Theology and the Making of the Modern German University* (New York: Oxford University Press, 2006).

Reason's new role as truth's gatekeeper is reflected in John Locke's *Second Treatise on Civil Government*. In its challenge to divine right theory of the monarchy, it also, by extension, undermined the claims of special revelation used to prop up this theory's view of political rights. Locke's alternative, the idea that government legitimacy requires the consent of the governed, is rooted in natural law. Natural law, the idea that God's truths are invested in the universe's operations and are rationally discernible by empirical means, reflect the Enlightenment's optimism that reason, not special revelation, will yield social order and tranquility.[11]

In a similar manner, Gibbon's *Decline and Fall of the Roman Empire* challenges the tradition of interpreting historical movements through the lens of God's ultimate purposes.[12] Enlightenment assumptions are apparent in his commitment to examine only "secondary causes" that could be publically verified by documents, artifacts, and historical record. The effect of this approach is obvious in current historical methodology.

A third Enlightenment era text in our survey is Adam Smith's *Wealth of Nations*. Smith mirrors Gibbon's focus on secondary causes by speaking, not of the divine will in the distribution of economic resources, but of the observable effects that ensue when the market itself governs the flow of resources in comparison with distortions produced by the imposition of external forces. Moreover, when *Wealth of Nations* is placed beside Smith's other famous work, *The Theory of Moral Sentiments*, the contrast presages the fact/value dichotomy that would later reign within the university. In *Wealth*, Smith emphasizes the descriptive intent of his work; he describes market operations without offering moral and spiritual prescriptions for how they *should* function. In *Moral Sentiments* Smith finds certain sentiments (values) to be morally binding but keeps these moral obligations separate from his later work on economics (facts).

As the university moved to North America, the various institutions planted there were an interesting hybrid. On the one hand, these colleges

11. Locke maintains that there are revealed truths known by faith that are "above reason." Even so, he effectively subordinates special revelation to reason by arguing that the latter must determine which claims to authority on matters "above reason" are to be trusted. See John Locke, *An Essay Concerning Human Understanding*, 2 vols. (New York: Dover, 1959), IV.18.8.

12. The paradigm of this approach is Augustine's *City of God*, which views history as the coexistence of two "cities." The "City of Man" sets itself against God by establishing itself on pride. However, the "City of God," as a demonstration of divine sovereignty, flourishes in the midst of the earthly city's upheavals and ultimately prevails.

were established by denominational groups for the propagation of their theological tradition, and the majority of their early graduates from most of these colleges were clergy. On the other hand, many of the faculty had absorbed Enlightenment ideals that, over time, moved these schools away from their denominational and Christian roots. The secularization of the great universities of the United States has been recounted from a number of different angles.[13] However, by the middle of the nineteenth century, they were caught up in many of the decisive forces reshaping, once again, the universities of Europe.

For our purpose, three closely related changes are worth noting as the modern university emerges in the West. First, philosophy's reign as the unifier and arbiter of truth was short-lived, and it was rapidly being over-shadowed by advances in the natural sciences. These advances prompted other disciplines to abandon philosophical orientations and apply scien-tific methodologies to their subject matter. Second, science's methods were directed toward the investigation of specific problems, not generating an overarching "theory of everything." Thus, the ideal of the "unity of truth" progressively moved toward specialized knowledge of various *worlds*, not *The World*. Finally, as science displaces philosophy as the measure of truth, the university increasingly edges toward a fact/value dichotomy in which the "sciences" pursued concrete facts, while the "arts" engaged the expres-sive world in which individual or group values—which could not be veri-fied or falsified—were communicated. These three elements converge in the sudden proliferation of new departments and majors within the univer-sity structure, each with their domain of specialized knowledge, and to the extent possible, clamoring to claim the adjective "science" as a descriptor of their methods and outcomes.

Psychology, literally the "study of the soul" (Greek, *psyche*), provides an example of these transitions. The writings of classical and medieval intellectuals are liberally sprinkled with treatises entitled "On the Soul," indicating a keen interest in psychology. However, Freud's *Interpretation of Dreams* consciously avoids discussions about the soul. Such entities are

13. Two useful sources for this process are George M. Marsden, *The Soul of the American University: From Protestant Establishment to Established Nonbelief* (New York: Oxford University Press, 1994), and William C. Ringenberg, *The Christian College: A His-tory of Protestant Higher Education in America*, 2nd ed. (Grand Rapids: Baker Academic, 2006). For more recent developments within church-related schools, see James Tunstead Burtchaell, *The Dying of the Light: The Disengagement of Colleges and Universities from Their Christian Churches* (Grand Rapids: Eerdmans, 1998).

impervious to the scientific approach he strives to bring to the study of psychology. Likewise, the university, for obvious reasons, had much to say about education long before "education" was a label affixed to a college department. However, the pragmatic philosophy undergirding John Dewey's *Democracy and Education* helps redefine education in the instrumental direction it largely takes in today's university. Max Weber's germinal address, "Science as Vocation," expresses the notion that the academy is about the pursuit of scientific truth.[14] Thus, scholars are obligated to exclude value judgments from their task. This fact/value dichotomy undergirds Weber's *The Protestant Ethic and the Spirit of Capitalism* and exemplifies his desire to establish sociology as a descriptive science that avoids imposing moral or theological values on the social phenomena examined. As the chapter on Darwin's *Origin of Species* points out, biologists had widely embraced theistic forms of evolution prior to Darwin. However, while others were eager to engage the philosophical, moral, or theological implications of his conclusions, Darwin usually sidestepped such controversies by stating that they took him outside the boundaries of his work as a scientist. In the cases above, even when Christianity is not directly criticized, the methods and assumptions of modern scholarship effectively marginalize it. Since faith's claims are broad in scope, violate the demand for empirical testing and verification, and are prescriptive in nature, its pronouncements are—at best—relegated to the expressive arts where they can be quarantined as subjective value statements.

The Evolving University

There are several purposes behind this brief sketch of western educational history. First, the stereotypical mental picture of an ivy-covered university edifice creates an impression of timelessness for the university. However, while universities themselves often have histories that span centuries, it is important to recognize how ideas central to their educational mission have undergone significant changes over time.

14. Weber's designation of science as a "vocation" is not accidental. He intends to indicate that the "calling" of the scientist (scholar) is mutually opposed to that of the clergy, who deal exclusively with the affective (i.e., non-factual) realm. See Max Weber, "Science as Vocation," in *From Max Weber: Essays in Sociology*, trans. and eds. H. H. Gerth and C. Wright Mills (New York: Oxford University Press, 1946), 129–57.

A second goal of this overview is to situate the texts examined within this book in a temporal context. This context, in turn, sheds light on the broad diversity of ideas represented in these twelve books. Plato's world is a universe removed from that contemplated by Dewey, and their formulations of education reflect this difference. Likewise, throughout our twelve books, we find vast divergences of opinion about the goal of education, who should be educated, the proper methods for discerning truth, the means by which this truth should be disseminated, and the nature of truth itself.

While the chapters that follow will flesh out more of the specifics of the first two goals, a third aim of the historical survey requires attention. An underlying theme of our survey is that education is never theologically neutral. Its goals, disciplinary orthodoxies, and methods all embody assumptions about pivotal questions concerning truth, reality, the goal of human existence and the nature of the obstacles that hinder attainment of those goals, and the possibilities and limits of human discovery. These are precisely the questions that take us to the heart of Christian faith as well. Thus, we should note three educational shifts that often create problems for the task of integrating Christian faith and scholarship in the modern university.

First, while the unity of knowledge was assumed throughout most of Western history, knowledge has now become fragmented and siloed. We are far removed from Plato's view that all true knowledge emanates from "The Good" or the earlier Christian conviction that identifies knowledge of and unity with God as the hub around which all learning converges. Indeed, the vast majority of history's intellectuals would be shocked to discover that, in the interest of imparting specialized knowledge, little or no effort is dedicated to helping students understand what unifies the various facets of learning. In previous ages, discernment of how knowledge converged into a unified comprehension of human life was the fundamental indicator that education had indeed occurred. In the context of curricular fragmentation, however, Christian educators may find it difficult to express how faith is related to the concerns of their specific disciplines without the means to link this to the bigger picture of God as the creator and sanctifier of all.

A second problematic area results from the first. Fragmentation of knowledge ultimately leads to the fragmentation of the knower. If the educator's task is to impart career-oriented knowledge and skills, then we easily default to the fact/value dichotomy embedded in contemporary academic assumptions that exile our moral and spiritual dimensions to the private (i.e., nonacademic) sphere. While we often embrace this dichotomy, even if unconsciously, earlier educators such as Plato viewed this as a highly destructive form of education. In his analysis of *The Republic's* best-known section, the "Allegory of the Cave," Plato speaks of the "clever rogue,"[15] —one who possesses a strong intellect and solid skills (which current universities impart), but lacks moral and spiritual wisdom (which the majority of universities put in the "not our job" category). The fragmentation of the rogue makes him (or her) dangerous because knowledge and skills impart tremendous power. Without a moral and spiritual rudder, however, we have no reason to believe that power will be used for good rather than evil. While, presumably, Christian educators would find it tragic to divorce our moral/spiritual identity from the technical and intellectual expertise acquired at the university, the fact/value dichotomy entrenched within our educational assumptions imply that these concerns have no legitimate place in the classroom.[16]

Finally, bringing a Christian voice to the academy encounters significant challenges because of the decisive shift in how we understand academic success. Today, the general assumption is that an education has been a success if graduates emerge with marketable knowledge and skills. As a result, the question "Is college education worth it?" is almost inevitably answered in terms of future earning prospects. This makes it difficult to fathom that, just a few decades ago, identifying a financial motive for pursuing post-secondary education would have been viewed as damning evidence that one was entirely unfit for the university.[17] While Christian educators should not ignore preparing students for the workforce, if placement rates and salary levels are the sole measure of educational success, it is ultimately reductionistic—it dehumanizes individuals created in God's image to purveyors of professional roles. Obviously, such dehumanization is something the Christian scholar will want to avoid, but our current views

15. Plato, *The Republic*, trans. Benjamin Jowett (New York: Vintage, 1991), 519a.

16. A helpful summary about moral and spiritual formation in the classroom is available in Perry Glanzer's chapter, "Who Are We to Form Students?: The Importance of Remembering Who We Are," in *Building a Culture of Faith: University-Wide Partnerships for Spiritual Formation*, eds. Cary Balzer and Rod Reed (Abilene, TX: Abilene Christian University Press, 2012), 109–23.

17. The radical shift represented by careerism and income potential as goals of the university is evident in that, until the twentieth century, the university's education, defined as the liberal arts, stood in contrast to education in what were called the servile arts, the skills by which one earns a wage. See Josef Pieper, *Leisure: The Basis of Culture*, trans. Gerald Malsbary (South Bend, IN: St. Augustine's Press, 1998), 44–45.

of the university's mission exert tremendous pressure toward just this sort of reductionism.

The point of the observations above is not that Christians should engage in a wholesale rejection of the educational trends of the last few centuries. In fact, I think much has occurred that is positive, and I will, in short order, speak briefly about how our disciplines can deepen faith. Instead, the goal is to note that no educational structure is morally or spiritually neutral. To the extent that we fail to recognize embedded obstacles to an integration of faith and learning, we will be hindered in attempts to find a robust place for Christianity in our teaching and scholarship.

Calling a Book "Great"

As the title indicates, the aim of this book is to explore the ideas of twelve books that we have identified as "great." The designation "great" or "classic" is controversial because there are no universal criteria for inclusion or exclusion. With a minimal amount of research into "great books" lists, one quickly discovers that this designation is dependent on the sorts of goals one has in mind. The title of this book specifies one "context-dependent" screen used in determining our great books. We have chosen works that have been influential within the university. Indeed, their frequent use within the *classroom* context makes them "classics" by definition, even if this definition is infrequently used today.

We have also drawn on another nuance of the term "classic" by using longevity as a factor in our selection process. By favoring books that have stood the test of time, we have allowed history to assume some of the responsibility for our choices. This criterion inevitably leads to the unfortunate consequence that all the books included were penned by Western (with one exception) males. Although there are good reasons to believe that the future of the university will increasingly include other voices, facts—as the saying goes—are stubborn things. The fact is that the voices that have most profoundly shaped the university, and the disciplines taught within it to date, are voices of Western males.

While we have allowed longevity to guide our choices, it is a qualified definition of the term. Subjects we now refer to collectively as "sciences" were all of deep interest from the ancients to the early modern period. However, even though their subject matter has always been part of the intellectual discourse, disciplines such as biology, economics, psychology, sociology, and education have only recently (in relative terms) become separate areas of study. Our selections in these disciplines have been made with an eye toward works that were pivotal to their emergence from the broader category of "liberal arts" to become specific departments within the university structure. As a result, just as the filter of longevity leaves out many recent voices, this qualified definition of longevity also excludes many voices, namely those of classical and Christian thinkers, whose views on politics, economics, education, sociology, and other areas have had greater longevity. While one could argue that the more ancient resources often provide a more profound understanding than the contemporary choices, scholarly consensus tends to favor the more contemporary sources.

This explanation of our criteria will not make our selections any less controversial, and we freely acknowledge that others could build a powerful case that alternative texts have been more formative for our respective disciplines. Thus, we maintain a level of humility about whether we have identified the "most important" texts for interaction. At the same time, we are confident that students in these disciplines would be short-changed if they have not been exposed to the books surveyed in the following chapters.

A Two-Way Integration

The contributors of this volume come to this project with twin passions. As scholars, their passion will be evident in the careful reflection they bring to the exposition and analysis of their specific great work. A passion for their faith will be evident in their observations about how fellow believers might process the ideas within the books. The interdependence of these twin passions reminds us that, seen properly, the task of integrating learning and faith is a bi-directional process. Our faith often challenges limitations imposed by disciplinary orthodoxies and generally accepted methods. Thus, for example, reigning conceptions of nature as neutral and value-free undergo transformation when we think of our world as creation—a realm that reflects the love and intentions of God. However, from our perspective as scholars, we also recognize that disciplinary knowledge can (and should) challenge our theology. While we are committed to the trustworthiness of God's revelation, we recognize that our theology—the attempt to give expression and order to revelation—is subject to error and incompleteness. At different points in history, for example, science has corrected past theological models of cosmology. Moreover, while theology reminds us that we cannot fully understand the nature of what is wrong in our world without the concept of sin, scholarship can better help us grasp the various ways that sin becomes embedded and perpetuated.

While our contributors will engage in a bi-directional integration in which faith and scholarship mutually inform each other, this does not imply that the observations and critiques will be universally shared by other scholars. For a variety of reasons, what one Christian commentator finds problematic or laudatory in a particular text will differ significantly in the evaluation of another equally qualified and sincere Christian scholar. Similarly, the particular issues brought to the foreground for critique may be viewed by others as too secondary to highlight in the allotted space. Variables arising from the perspective of their role as scholars—when and where educated, differences in the level of concern about theoretical, methodological, or practical aspects of their discipline, research interests, and other elements—will also shape the critiques. Finally, our contributors span a broad range of Christian traditions—Orthodoxy, Roman Catholicism, and a spectrum within Protestantism—and variations within these influences will exert force on each scholar's perspectives. In short, our intent is not to provide a comprehensive or definitive Christian critique of these twelve books, but to offer a concrete example of how an informed scholar may bring Christian faith into conversation with the ideas of a germinal academic work.

As a final note, it would be unfair to the contributors to this book if I neglected to acknowledge the impossibility of the tasks they have been assigned. Each is the custodian of a book (usually a rather voluminous book at that) selected precisely because it is deep and rich in content. We have asked them to describe the circumstances in which their text arose, to summarize the contents and explain why these ideas had such enduring influence within the university, and to offer an analysis of the book through Christian eyes. Given the word limits with which our contributors have to work, this is certainly a recipe for frustration. A full-orbed engagement obviously requires a much longer treatment. Therefore, we encourage readers to take each chapter as intended. It is an intellectual appetizer designed to draw readers into an ongoing conversation between Christian faith and the academy's rich resources.

The order in which the "great works" appear in this book does not reflect value judgments about the relative importance of the works. Instead, we have listed them chronologically. Thus, if the book is read sequentially, beginning with chapter one and reading through to the end of the book, you will not simply encounter the ideas contained in these texts, but you will also catch hints of pivotal developments in the educational enterprise. At the same time, each chapter can be read separately, providing the opportunity to reflect upon a foundational work that has shaped a critical discipline within the university structure. Whether the chronological route is chosen or a more selective path is taken, we recommend a broad reading of the chapters for their beneficial insights both in their respective fields of study and in how they relate—positively and negatively—to Christianity.

CHAPTER 1: PHILOSOPHY

Plato, *Republic*

BY RICO VITZ

"The safest general characterization of the European philosophical
tradition is that it consists of a series of footnotes to Plato."
—Alfred North Whitehead, *Process and Reality*[1]

"It's all in Plato, all in Plato: bless me,
what do they teach them at these schools!"
—Professor Digory Kirke (from C.S. Lewis, *The Last Battle*[2])

Introduction

WHEN PLATO (C. 428–347 BCE) was about thirty years old, his friend and
mentor, Socrates (c. 469–399 BCE), was executed by the Athenian government. In order to convey some sense of how this must have affected Plato,
let me describe briefly the events leading up to Socrates' death. From what
we know about him from two of Plato's shorter writings, *Apology* and *Crito*,
Socrates was a humble man of modest means. His companions deeply ad-

---

1. Alfred North Whitehead, *Process and Reality*, corrected edition, eds. David Ray
Griffin and Donald W. Sherburne (New York: Free Press, 1979), 39.

2. C. S. Lewis, *The Last Battle*, The Chronicles of Narnia (New York: Harper Collins,
1984), 195.

mired him as a wise man who sought the truth not only about the quality of his own character and that of his fellow Athenians but also about the moral values of their culture. In time, influential religious and political leaders came to perceive Socrates as a threat to the social order that they worked to craft and to maintain. Consequently, they convicted him of impiety and sentenced him to death. Seeing that their friend was in grave and imminent danger, a number of Socrates' companions pleaded with him to flee the city before these leaders seized the opportunity to end his life. He remained, however, since he viewed facing death as a greater act of virtue both as a citizen of Athens and, more importantly, as one committed to "the god." Shortly after he refused his companions' pleas, the leaders of Athens killed him. Thus, by Plato's account, it came to pass that Socrates was martyred for his love of wisdom and the threat this posed to the unjust leaders of Athens and the corrupt social and political system by which they ruled.

How did Plato react? A natural response would have been for him to try to avenge the person he loved, and in a sense, this is just what he did. He did so, however, in accordance with two requests that Socrates made in his final days. The first was that if those who loved Socrates were to avenge him, then they must do so by causing the people who killed him the same kind of grief that Socrates caused those he loved. How so? If they found people who cared for money or anything else more than they cared for virtue or who thought they were somebody when they were nobody, then they should reproach them as Socrates reproached his companions. In so doing, they should strive to convince those who are corrupt to "care for the right things" and to be humble.[3] The second was that "[o]ne must obey the commands of one's city or country, *or persuade it as to the nature of justice.*"[4] This, in essence, is what Plato aimed to do in the *Republic*, namely, to avenge Socrates by persuading his fellow citizens who coveted money and honor that they ought to love wisdom and, more particularly, justice.

Insofar as those who desire money and honor more than virtue have remained ubiquitous, both throughout history and around the globe, the

---

3. Plato, *Apology*, in *Plato: Complete Works*, ed. John M. Cooper (Indianapolis: Hackett, 1997), 36 [Stephanus pagination: 41e]. It is a standard practice for scholars to cite Plato's works by referring to the "Stephanus pagination," which editors and translators usually include in the margins of their texts. In the event that you might have access to a version of Plato's works other than Cooper's, I will include references to the Stephanus pagination, as above.

4. Plato, *Crito*, in *Plato: Complete Works*, ed. John M. Cooper (Indianapolis: Hackett, 1997), 45, emphasis mine [Stephanus pagination: 51b].

central message of Plato's *Republic* has not lost its value. Moreover, since it has had such a profound impact on Western civilization, it has become a classic work with which educated people ought to be familiar.

In the hope of providing you with a reasonable introduction to this classic text, I will attempt to do three things in the course of this essay. I will begin by providing an overview of the work. I will continue by explaining the enduring significance of the text for the university itself, for philosophy, and for related disciplines. I will then conclude by explaining the enduring significance of the text for developing a greater understanding both of Christian doctrine and of the Christian way of life.

The Book

Overview

The *Republic* is a fictional dialogue between Socrates and a handful of his associates. The focus of their discussion is the nature of justice. Those whose thoughts on the topic have been formed by popular contemporary discourse might mistakenly infer that the dialogue focuses on issues of "social justice," frequently thought of as the equitable distribution of social goods. For Plato, however, an adequate discussion of justice is not narrowly confined to these issues—more precisely known as issues of *distributive justice*. Nor does it merely extend beyond these to include issues of *commutative justice*—e.g., justice in commercial interactions—and issues of *retributive justice*—e.g., justice in assigning punishments for criminals. Rather, on Plato's account, an adequate discussion of justice must include not merely the nature of a just *society* but, more fundamentally, the nature of a just *person*.[5] Because of the fundamental significance of just persons,

---

5. Regarding the fundamental emphasis on justice as a quality of persons, there is an interesting point of similarity between Plato's *Republic* and the New Testament. The Greek word that is generally translated as "justice" in the *Republic* is *dikaiosune*. This same word is frequently translated as "righteousness" in the New Testament. Cognates of *dikaiosune* are treated similarly—e.g., *dikaios*, *dikaia*, and *dikaion*—are generally translated as "just" in the *Republic* and frequently translated as "righteous" in the New Testament. For instance, when Ananias healed Saul and spoke to him about Jesus, he said, "The God of our ancestors has chosen you to know his will and to see the Righteous One [*ton dikaion*]" (Acts 22:14 NIV; see also, e.g., Matt 27:24, Acts 7:52, 1 Pet 3:18). Some have argued, in fact, that "righteousness" would be a more fitting translation of *dikaiosune* throughout Plato's works—see George Rudebusch, *Socrates* (Oxford: Wiley-Blackwell, 2009), 25–26.

without whom there could be no just society, Plato's *Republic* offers detailed arguments concerning human nature and the proper form of education, which raises up people of noble virtues who are capable of creating and sustaining a just society.

Summary

The dialogue opens in Book I with a conversation about whether a just person is actually better off than an unjust person. The discussion soon turns, however, to a more fundamental question concerning the nature of justice itself.

As they begin to clarify the nature of justice in Book II, the participants distinguish three types of goods: (1) those that are good in and of themselves, (2) those that are good both in and of themselves and because of their consequences, and (3) those that are good merely because of their consequences. Joy is an example of the first kind of good; good health, an example of the second kind; and money, an example of the third. Socrates argues that justice is a member of the second, and most noble, class since it is good both in and of itself and because of its consequences—most importantly, *eudaimonia*, or human flourishing.[6]

At this point in the dialogue, an interesting methodological shift takes place. Socrates notes that one can make a distinction between justice as a virtue of individual human beings and justice as a virtue of a human social group, like a city, or *polis*. The focus of the discussion so far has been on justice as a virtue of individual human beings. Socrates suggests, however, that it might be easier to start by identifying the nature of a just human social group and to infer from this what the nature of a just person is. The participants agree to adopt this strategy. They proceed by noting that different people have different kinds of talents—farming, shoemaking, weaving, and so forth—but that a just *polis* will need leaders, or "guardians," to coordinate the wide variety of affairs by which people use their talents to earn a living. Recognizing that this kind of leadership will require a great deal of wisdom, the participants conclude that the education of the guardians will be of prime importance for a just society.

6. The Greek term *eudaimonia* is often translated as "happiness." This is misleading, however, since Plato has in mind not the pleasant psychological *state* that the English term "happiness" usually brings to mind, but the *activity* of human flourishing that comes from living in accordance with one's true nature.

In the remainder of Book II and throughout Book III, Socrates and his companions discuss the kind of education that is necessary for the guardians so that they might establish justice in the *polis*. In particular, they emphasize the need for excellent literature that, unlike many of the tales of the Greek gods, extols things that are good, true, and beautiful. Towards the end of Book III, they make a key observation, namely, that different educational exercises will be necessary for the different *parts* of a person's soul.

Clarifying the nature of the soul as well as the principal virtue of each part is a primary goal of Book IV. Continuing to utilize the methodology adopted in Book II, the participants in the discussion begin by clarifying the various classes in a just *polis*. They identify three: (1) the guardians, (2) the soldiers, and (3) the laborers, e.g., makers of crafts, artisans, and farmers. The guardians and the soldiers work together to rule the *polis*. *Wisdom* is the principal virtue of the guardians, by which they govern the *polis*. *Courage* is the principal virtue of the soldiers, by which they guard it from dangers. *Temperance*, or self-control, is a virtue both of the guardians and of the soldiers, as well as of the laborers, who provide for the material needs of the citizens. The *polis* itself possesses the virtue of *justice* when each class of people manifests its principal virtue in using its talents to execute its duties.[7]

Having clarified the nature of a just *polis*, the participants are poised to complete the strategy they adopted in Book II, explaining the nature of a just human being. Following Socrates, they agree that the human soul itself has three principal parts. The names of these parts get translated in different ways. In an effort to avoid either using terms that seem oddly foreign or terms that are misleadingly familiar, let me refer to them as "mind," "spirit," and "desire." When the mind and the spirit are functioning properly, a person is wise and courageous. When desire is functioning properly, following the lead of mind and spirit, the person is temperate and manifests self-control in pursuit of the satisfaction of his or her material needs. A person possesses the virtue of justice when each of the parts of the soul manifests its principal virtue in harmony with the virtues of the other parts.

At the end of Book IV, Socrates begins to shift the focus of the discussion from the nature of justice to the nature of injustice, but at the beginning of Book V, his companions press him to describe in greater detail the social arrangements within a just *polis*. The participants begin by discussing

---

7. These are the "four cardinal virtues" of classical education: justice, wisdom, courage, and temperance.

the nature and role of women and come to a consensus on two principal points. The first is that women are, as a rule, physically weaker than men. The second, and more important point, is that the souls of women are of the same nature as the souls of men. Hence, just as there can be men that excel in manifesting the virtues of any given class of citizens, there can be women who excel in manifesting these virtues, including the virtues of the guardians. Therefore, a just *polis* could be governed either by a Philosopher King or by a Philosopher Queen. Hence, they conclude, among the ruling class, women must have access to the same kind of education as men.

Having noted that both men and women are capable of becoming lovers of wisdom who are capable of ruling a just polis, in Book V, Socrates and his associates turn their attention back to the nature of the just life. They recognize, however, that many people do not hold those who are truly wise in high esteem and, worse yet, that there are many charlatans who merely claim to be philosophers and, in so doing, give both philosophers and philosophy a bad name. Thus, in Book VI, they attempt to clarify the nature both of a true lover of wisdom and of wisdom itself, which the guardians would need to possess so that they could foster a just society in which men and women could flourish. True lovers of wisdom, they argue, would need not only to be sincere seekers of eternal and changeless truths but also men and women who possess virtues of character. On their account, such people would be not only intelligent truth-seekers but also, e.g., courageous, temperate, orderly, humble, and gentle. In order to clarify the nature of wisdom itself, Socrates uses the analogy of the Divided Line.

In short, the Divided Line consists of two major, and unequal, sections. The first major section is the realm of the sun—that is, of things that are accessible to the senses. This first realm consists of two parts: (1) shadows and reflections of physical objects and (2) physical objects themselves, such as plants, animals, and manufactured goods. According to Socrates, people can have images of the former and beliefs about the latter, but neither is the object or source of wisdom. The second major section is the realm of eternal truths, which lead to the Good. This second realm also consists of two parts: (1) physical objects viewed as images of the Forms, e.g., diagrams of geometric figures, and (2) the Forms themselves, e.g., Beauty and Justice. On Socrates' account, the images of the Forms are known by means of one operation of the mind, namely, "thought" (*dianoia*); the Forms themselves are known by another, namely, "understanding" (*noesis*). It is ultimately the latter, the Forms themselves, that the true philosopher seeks to know, not by means of "thought" (*dianoia*) but by means of "understanding" (*noesis*).[8]

Book VII opens with what is probably the most famous parable of education in the Western world: Plato's allegory of the cave.[9] Prisoners are chained in a cave facing a wall. Immediately behind them on the ground is a narrow passage by which they could escape and make a rough ascent out of the cave, if they could break free. From this opening, diffused sunlight enters the darkened chamber. Above the narrow passage that leads out of the cave, elevated and near the opposing wall, is a fire. Also elevated above the passage, between the prisoners and the fire, is a walkway. While they are chained, the prisoners see shadows on the wall that they are facing and, in their ignorance, take these images to be the things themselves. If they were to break free of their chains and turn around, they would be able to see those changeable beings inside of the cave, or in the realm of the sun, but they would not have access to the Forms that can be found only in the world outside of the cave, or in the realm of eternal truths, which lead to the Good. Thus, while imprisoned in the cave, the prisoners could not become wise. In order to do that, they must both be freed from the chains that bind them and escape.

Making the ascent out of the world with which people are most easily familiar and in which they frequently become much too comfortable is a long and challenging task, however. In fact, according to Socrates, it is only those older than fifty who have distinguished themselves "both in practical matters and in the sciences" who are fit for the final task in the quest for wisdom and, subsequently, for leading others to wisdom—hence the importance of a lengthy, carefully constructed, systematic process of education.[10] This process begins by helping young people move away from their mere familiarity with sensible objects, through discursive reasoning about mathematics, broadly construed, to reflective understanding of those Forms that are ingrained in people's souls.

Since the first seven books of the *Republic* are the most essential for the purpose of this essay, let me offer a very cursory summary of the final three books of the text. In Book VIII, Socrates returns to an issue he began

8. Note both the *object* and the *means* of true wisdom. These will be particularly important later in the essay.

9. In the following summary, I will try to do it justice—no pun intended—but you really must read the *Republic* itself to appreciate its beauty and depth.

10. Plato, *Republic*, in *Plato: Complete Works*, ed. John M. Cooper (Indianapolis: Hackett, 1997), 1154–55 [Stephanus pagination: 540a-c].

to raise towards the end of Book IV—namely, clarifying the nature of injustice—and describes the nature of four defective forms of government.[11] In Book IX, Socrates clarifies the role of pleasure in the lives of just people[12] and the likelihood that the just would be involved in politics as it is usually practiced.[13] The dialogue concludes, in Book X, with a discussion about the nature of good literature, an argument for the immortality of the soul, and Socrates' telling of a parable about the afterlife, the "Myth of Er."

The Republic and the University

Having summarized the content of Plato's *Republic*, I will now explain the significance of the text for the university. In the interest of brevity, I will limit my focus to three of the most prominent reasons that the work both has traditionally shaped and should continue to shape the university's mission.

Significance for the University

One reason that the *Republic* is so important is that it is a perennial reminder of the original and central purpose of the university. It might be helpful for me to explain this point by contrast. Let me highlight an example from contemporary social and political discourse, namely, the debate about whether people should go to university, and if so, why. The current dialogue about these questions goes roughly as follows.

Those who answer affirmatively frequently offer two rationales for favoring a university education. The first is that people need to go to university so that they can get well-paying and stable jobs. In support of this answer, they cite data such as the following from a 2013 report by the United States Bureau of Labor Statistics. With respect to pay, they note that

11. These are: *timocracy*, which degenerates into *oligarchy*, which degenerates into *democracy*, which degenerates into *tyranny*.

12. According to Socrates, in the lives of the just, the pleasures both of "spirit" and of "desire" follow the command of the "mind" and, more specifically, of the divinely-implanted "understanding" (*noesis*).

13. On Socrates' account, the life of a just person would include participation in the political processes of the kind of ideal republic that the participants in the dialogue are describing. It would likely not, however, include participation in the kinds of political systems one normally finds on earth, unless the just person is aided by "some divine good luck." See Plato, *Republic*, 1199 [Stephanus pagination: 592a].

the median income of people, aged twenty-five years and over, with at least a Bachelor's degree is substantially *higher* than that of those with a high school diploma—roughly $56,000 for the former and $34,000 for the latter. With respect to stability, they note that the unemployment rate of people twenty-five years and over with at least a Bachelor's degree is substantially *lower* than that of those with a high school diploma—roughly 4 percent for the former and 8 percent for the latter.[14]

The second rationale is that people need to go to university so that they can become better citizens, that is, people who are more adept at processing information related to contemporary political discourse. In support of this answer, they note, for instance, that university students are supposed to become acquainted with a broad range of ideas so that they are able to understand a wide variety of perspectives. Similarly, they point out that such students are supposed to develop their critical thinking skills so that they are able to gather and to assess information more astutely.

Those who are skeptical of these rationales frequently raise two objections. The first is that the rapidly rising costs of today's administratively top-heavy universities—and, consequently, the debt with which university students are saddled—simply do not outweigh the benefits. As evidence for their point, skeptics call attention to the fact that roughly two-thirds of university students graduate with debt totaling over $32,000, or nearly three-quarters of the average starting salary of those who are fortunate enough to get a job.[15] Moreover, they might note, only about half of students who enter a university will complete the requirements to earn a Bachelor's degree within six years, and many will never finish.[16]

14. See the United States Department of Labor, Bureau of Labor Statistics' recent data on "Earnings and Unemployment Rates by Educational Attainment," which is accessible at *http://www.bls.gov/emp/ep_chart_001.htm* (accessed August 18, 2013).

15. Regarding the percentage of university students who graduate with debt, see the Project on Student Debt's recent report, "Student Debt and the Class of 2011," which is accessible at *http://projectonstudentdebt.org/files/pub/classof2011.pdf* (accessed August 18, 2013). Regarding the amount of university graduates' debt, see Fidelity Investments second "Cost-Conscious College Graduates Study," which is accessible at *http://www.fidelity.com/inside-fidelity/individual-investing/college-grads-surprised-by-student-debt-level-exceeds-35000* (accessed August 18, 2013). Regarding the average starting salaries of university graduates, see the National Association of Colleges and Employers' 2013 *Salary Survey*. The Executive Summary of the survey is available at *http://www.naceweb.org/uploadedFiles/NACEWeb/Research/Salary_Survey/Reports/salary-survey-april-2013-executive-summary.pdf* (accessed August 18, 2013).

16. For example, see the data provided by the National Information Center for Higher Education Policymaking and Analysis, which is accessible at http://www.higheredinfo.

The second objection is that a university degree is not a necessary condition for being a good citizen. As evidence for this point, skeptics could call attention to many members of the so-called "Greatest Generation," who did not have the opportunity to finish high school, let alone attend university. Alternatively, they could call attention to many of the people who serve either on local police forces or in branches of the military.

With which side would Plato stand? The answer is: Neither. According to Plato's principles, this contemporary debate wildly misrepresents the essential purpose of education. The most glaring error is the characterization of education *principally* as a means by which one accumulates monetary benefits, rather than as a means by which one cultivates virtue. But, one might object, each side in the debate believes that a major purpose of the university is to create good citizens, and that is the purpose of education on Plato's account. Is it not? It certainly might seem like Plato's view—at least at first glance—but in this case, the appearance is deceiving. Notice that even if people become more adept at assessing information related to contemporary political discourse or if they obtain positions in civil service professions, it does not follow that they will become virtuous people who work to foster a just society. In fact, as any casual observer of the nightly news can attest, being intellectually clever or a member of a civil service profession may merely empower a person to be more effectively *unjust*.[17] In essence, being a "good" citizen, in the contemporary sense, does not require being a "wise" citizen, in the Platonic sense. So, on Plato's account, neither side in the contemporary debate properly values the cultivation of a love of wisdom by which a truly just society could be developed and sustained.

Thus, one reason that Plato's *Republic* is important for the university is that it serves as a reminder of the university's original and core mission, namely, to inspire each student to love "the Good" and to equip each to take the next step in his or her journey toward the acquisition of wisdom. To the extent that any particular university executes this mission properly, it empowers its students to become truly virtuous people who live well and strive to foster a just society.

---

org/dbrowser/index.php? submeasure=27&year=2009&level=nation&mode=graph&state=0 (accessed August, 18 2013).

17. Cf. Plato, *Republic*, 1136 [Stephanus pagination: 518b-519a].

Significance for the Discipline of Philosophy

A second reason that the *Republic* is so important is because of the depth of its influence in philosophy and the breadth of its influence among philosophers. Let me sketch, just briefly, its impact in each.

The *Republic* is a classic work not merely in philosophy *per se* but in each of the discipline's five most important subfields, namely, (1) *metaphysics*, which studies the nature of fundamental reality, (2) *epistemology*, which studies the nature of knowledge, (3) *ethics*, which studies not merely what people ought to do but, more importantly, what kind of character people ought to acquire, (4) *aesthetics*, which studies the nature of beauty, and obviously (5) *political theory*, which studies the nature of just societies. In the *Republic* alone, Plato develops seminal positions in every one of these areas.

The text is significant, however, not only for the depth of its influence in philosophy, but also for the large number of eminent philosophers and philosopher-theologians that it influenced. For ease of presentation, I will simply focus on two "lines" of Plato's intellectual descendants.

The first—let us call it the "Platonic line"—consists of philosophers and philosopher-theologians who were sympathetic to Plato's philosophical program and attempted to appropriate and to adapt its essential principles for their own purposes. One particularly noteworthy figure in this line is Philo of Alexandria (c. 20 BCE–50 CE), a Hellenized Jew who attempted to synthesize Judaism and the philosophical insights of Plato, to whom he referred as "the greatest of all" and "the most holy."[18] Philo's philosophically-informed conception of Judaism influenced a number of ancient Christian writers—such as Justin Martyr (c. 110–165) and Clement of Alexandria (c. 153–217)—and, possibly, some of the New Testament authors—such as John the Theologian (c. 10–100), the Apostle Paul (c. 5–67), and the author of the letter to the Hebrews. Another particularly noteworthy figure in this line is Plotinus (c. 204–270), the founder of Neoplatonism, whose work had a significant influence on two giants of first-millennium Christian philosophical theology: Augustine (354–430) and Pseudo-Dionysius the Areopagite (fl. late 5th/early 6th centuries).[19]

18. Daniel R. Schwartz, "Philo, His Family, and His Times," in *The Cambridge Companion to Philo*, ed. Adam Kamesar (Cambridge: Cambridge: 2009), 30.

19. For present purposes, I am focusing on some of the most familiar and easily identifiable influences of Plato within the Platonic line. The fact of the matter, however, is that the ideas and terms of Plato's work composed much of—so to speak—the conceptual air that early Christians breathed. If one looks closely, one can see these ideas and terms

The second—let us call it the "Aristotelian line"—consists of philosophers and philosopher-theologians who were sympathetic to the work of Plato's greatest pupil, Aristotle (384–322 BCE), and attempted to appropriate and to adapt the essential principles of his philosophical system. Although Aristotle's work played some role in the development of Neoplatonism, it was largely neglected in the Western philosophical world for hundreds of years. It came to particular prominence, however, with the late medieval development of Scholasticism—first among Islamic philosophers like Avicenna (980–1037) and Averroes (1126–1198), then among Jewish philosophers like Maimonides (1135–1204), and finally among Christian philosophers such as Albert the Great (c. 1200–1280) and his most famous student, Thomas Aquinas (c. 1225–1274). Aquinas is widely regarded as the most important philosopher-theologian in Western Christianity because of his attempt to synthesize Christian teachings with the works of influential figures both in the Platonic line—such as Augustine and Pseudo-Dionysius—and in the Aristotelian line—such as Aristotle and Averroes.

The philosophers who succeeded the Scholastics, from the modern period through the twentieth century, were all affected by the influences of the Platonic and the Aristotelian lines of Plato's intellectual descendants. In fact, Plato's influence in philosophy has been so profound that it motivated Whitehead's famous quip that the entire European philosophical tradition is, essentially, "a series of footnotes to Plato."[20]

Significance for Related Disciplines

A third reason that *The Republic* is so important is because of the scope of its influence beyond the discipline of philosophy alone. To illustrate this point, let me simply highlight three examples from the book you are currently reading. First, Plato's metaphysics and epistemology influenced the theology of Augustine, as noted above.[21] Second, his conception of the soul influenced the psychology of Sigmund Freud (1856–1939), who referred

---

being appropriated for uniquely Christian purposes by major Christian intellectual figures of the first millennium; e.g., Athanasius of Alexandria (c. 297–373), Basil the Great (329–379), Gregory of Nyssa (c. 335–395), and Gregory the Theologian (c. 329–389), who labored to refute heresies and, in so doing, helped to develop the Nicene Creed, i.e., the early Christian creed that remains the standard expression of faith in traditional Christian worship to this day.

20. Whitehead, *Process and Reality*, 39.

21. For example, see Books VI and VII of the *Republic*.

to him as "the divine Plato."[22] Third, his account of education influenced the educational theory of John Dewey (1859–1952), who regarded Plato's account as one of the three major "epochs" of educational philosophy that preceded his own work on the topic.[23]

These are merely the influences of Plato's work on some of the other authors represented in this volume. If we wanted to do so, however, we could demonstrate the exceptionally vast influence of his seminal texts, most notably the *Republic*, on a wide variety of other disciplines. In short, it is difficult to understate the historic influence of Plato's work, in general, and of the *Republic*, in particular, for the various disciplines within a university.

The Republic and Christianity

Having explained some of the reasons why Plato's *Republic* is significant for the university, I will now explain some of the significance of the text for Christians. In the interest of brevity, as in the previous section, I will limit my comments to two particularly salient reasons.

22. Regarding Plato's tripartite conception of the soul, see Books IV, VIII, and IX of the *Republic*. To the extent that Plato influenced Freud, it seems to have been more with respect to Freud's *defense of his conception of sexuality* rather than with respect to his *creation of psychoanalytic theory itself*—see "Three Essays on the Theory of Sexuality," in *The Standard Edition of the Complete Psychological Works of Sigmund Freud*, ed. James Strachey, vol. VII (London: The Hogarth Press, 1953), 134, 136; "Beyond the Pleasure Principle," in *The Standard Edition of the Complete Psychological Works of Sigmund Freud*, ed. James Strachey, vol. XVIII (London: The Hogarth Press, 1955), 57–58; "Group Psychology and the Analysis of the Ego," in *The Standard Edition of the Complete Psychological Works of Sigmund Freud*, ed. James Strachey, vol. XVIII (London: The Hogarth Press, 1955), 91; "An Autobiographical Study," in *The Standard Edition of the Complete Psychological Works of Sigmund Freud*, ed. James Strachey, vol. XX (London: The Hogarth Press, 1959), 24. See also Letter 101 (March 1, 1899), in *The Origins of Psychoanalysis: Letters to Wilhelm Fliess, Drafts and Notes: 1887–1902*, eds. Marie Bonaparte, Anna Freud, and Ernst Kris (New York: Basic Books, 1954), 270–72. Freud's reference to "the divine Plato" occurs in the preface to the fourth edition of his "Three Essays on the Theory of Sexuality."

23. Regarding Plato's account of education, see Books II, III, V, and X of the *Republic*. To help put in perspective just how significant Dewey regarded Plato's influence, the other two "epochs" that he identified were the Enlightenment epoch of the eighteenth century and the "institutional idealistic" epoch of the nineteenth century. See John Dewey, *Democracy and Education: An Introduction to the Philosophy of Education* (New York: Free Press, 1944), 88–99.

Significance for Christian Doctrine

One reason that the *Republic* is important for Christians is that a proper understanding of the central elements of Plato's philosophical program, as presented in the *Republic*, is essential for understanding the historical formulation of Christian doctrine. In light of the previous section, there are two reasonably obvious ways in which this is the case.

The first is that an understanding of the central elements of Plato's philosophy is essential for understanding the works of Plotinus, which is necessary for understanding the works of Augustine, who is one of the most influential figures in the Western Christian tradition—that is, among Roman Catholics and Protestants. The second is that an understanding of the central elements of Plato's works is essential for understanding the work of Aristotle, which—in conjunction with an understanding of the works of Augustine—is essential for an adequate understanding of the work of Aquinas, who is another of the most influential figures in the Western Christian tradition—especially among Roman Catholics.

There is, however, a second and deeper way in which an understanding of the central elements of Plato's philosophical program, as presented in the *Republic*, are crucial for understanding essential aspects of the central core of the ancient Christian faith.[24] The ancient Christian approach to philosophy was neither to regard it too lowly, as Tertullian (c. 160–225) did, nor to value it too highly, as Origen (c. 185–254) seems to have done in some of his writings. Rather, ancient Christians appropriated philosophical—and especially, Platonic—ideas, in their own unique ways, to help articulate and to defend orthodox Christian doctrine. Perhaps the greatest example of this is the way in which Christians like Athanasius, Basil, Gregory of Nyssa, and Gregory the Theologian appropriated certain philosophical concepts to articulate and to defend the doctrines of the Trinity, the Incarnation, and the Hypostatic Union. A

Let me pause, here, to emphasize the significance of the last paragraph. The doctrines of the Trinity, the Incarnation, and the Hypostatic Union, as

---

24. I am using the phrase "ancient Christian faith" to refer to the faith of the church of the first millennium, which existed prior to both (1) the schism between Rome and the eastern sees of Antioch, Alexandria, Jerusalem, and Constantinople, and (2) the subsequent breaking away from Rome by Reformers in Canterbury, Wittenberg, and Geneva. Thus, I am using the phrase to refer to the essential but substantive core of sacred tradition that is shared not only by Roman Catholics and Protestants but also by Orthodox Christians.

they were formulated and refined in the seven Ecumenical Councils of the ancient Christian Church, constitute a major portion of the essential core of the ancient profession of the Christian faith.[25] In more common language, these three doctrines constitute a major portion of the heart of what C. S. Lewis (1898–1963) called "mere Christianity."[26] A person can, obviously, understand these doctrines well enough to profess the Christian faith without having read Plato's *Republic*. (No, Grandma and Grandpa did not need to be Plato scholars to be Christians.) We Christians are called, however, to love God with our whole mind (see, e.g., Matt 22:34–40; Mark 12:28–31; cf. Deut 6:4–5). Consequently, those of us who have the ability and the means to do so should strive to develop a greater understanding of the faith of the ancient Christian church, not only so that we might "stand fast and hold the traditions which [we] were taught, whether by word or our epistle" (2 Thess 2:15, NKJV) but also so that we might, more effectively, teach these things to the generations of Christians who will follow us (cf. Deut 6:7). Since the ancient Christian tradition did not develop in a cultural vacuum, we have to develop an understanding of the cultural context in which our tradition developed. This means, at least in part, that we have to develop a richer understanding of some of the philosophical ideas that influenced the ancient

25. The following, admittedly all too brief, historical summary might help put the context of these doctrines in clearer perspective. The first two councils (Nicea, 325; Constantinople, 381) took place even before the church began to settle the issue of the New Testament canon, i.e., the official list of books that compose the New Testament. At these councils, in response to heresies like Arianism and Macedonianism, the church developed the "Nicene Creed," which formally articulates the doctrine of the Trinity, including the divinity both of Jesus Christ and of the Holy Spirit. At the third council (Ephesus, 431), in response to the heresy of Nestorianism, the church defined Christ as the Incarnate Word and his mother, Mary, as "Theotokos," i.e., "God bearer," or "Mother of God"—as opposed to merely "Christotokos," i.e., "Christ bearer," or "Mother of Christ." (The controversy about how to refer to Jesus's mother is deeply Christological: The former titles identify her as the mother of one person who is both God and human; the latter titles identify her merely as the mother of a human being.) At the fourth (Chalcedon, 451), in response to the heresy of Monophysitism, the church defined the Hypostatic Union of Christ, i.e., the union of two natures, God and man, in one person, Christ. At the fifth (Constantinople II, 553), in response to the lingering effects of Nestorianism and Monophysitism, the church reaffirmed the understanding of Christ, as developed in the previous councils. At the sixth (Constantinople III, 680), in response to the heresy of Monothelitism, the church reaffirmed the true humanity of Christ. At the seventh (Nicea II, 787), in response to the iconoclastic heresy, the church reaffirmed the propriety of the traditional use of icons in Christian worship.

26. C. S. Lewis, *Mere Christianity*, rev. ed. (New York: Macmillan, 1952).

Christian church. Chief among these are the ideas of Plato, especially those in his magnum opus, the *Republic*.

Significance for the Christian Way of Life

A second reason that the *Republic* is important for Christians is that an understanding of Plato's psychology—specifically, his conception of the soul—is helpful for understanding the Christian way of life. Given the common disconnect between contemporary pop Christianity and the faith and practice of the ancient Christian Church, the preceding claim might sound a bit puzzling. Why would Plato's psychology matter for understanding the Christian way of life? The answer becomes clear when one considers the ancient Christian understanding of how one attempts to cultivate a pure heart.

On the traditional account, Christians are called not merely to use their minds to think *about* God. Rather, they are called to strive to "see" God. This traditional allusion to having a vision of God refers not to an operation of the "eye of the body" but to an operation of the "eye of the heart," i.e., the mind (*nous*). All people are invited to "come and see," but by and large most people, including most Christians, fail to see God. Why? Because most of us are, to one extent or another, spiritually blind. It is only the "pure of heart" who are capable of seeing God (Matt 5:8), and most of us are not even remotely close to attaining such purity. In fact, unlike the Christians of the early church, many—perhaps most—contemporary Christians are not even actively seeking purity of heart. Please do not misunderstand; I am not denying that most contemporary Christians might *prefer* a pure heart or that they might *hope* for a pure heart, but to prefer or to hope for such a heart is quite different from *actively seeking* to develop one, as was the ancient Christian practice.

How, on the traditional Christian account, does one actively seek purity of heart? Ancient Christian writers described this condition in terms familiar to their listeners, which means that they described it in Platonic terms. In the familiar psychological language of their day, to have a "pure heart" is to have something like what Plato called a "just soul." More specifically, on their account, to have a "pure heart" is to be a person in whom (1) one's *mind* (*nous*) is actively and continually seeking God in prayer, (2) one's *spirit* is disposed to love God and neighbor and to care for God's creation, and (3) one's *desires* for food, money, honor, sex, and so forth are properly regulated. A person who lacks purity of heart, on the ancient Christian account, lacks harmony in his or her soul. Being fundamentally at war with himself or with herself, such a person tends to be preoccupied with satisfying his or her own sensual desires (cf. Romans 7:21–23). As a result, such a person is properly disposed neither to love God and neighbor nor to care for God's creation. For that reason, he or she remains spiritually blind, unable to see God clearly.[27] To be healed, by God's grace, and to attain this (*noetic*) vision requires (1) *fasting* for the purpose of taming one's desires, (2) *almsgiving* for the purpose of training one's heart to love, and (3) contemplative *prayer* for the purpose of seeking, and ultimately seeing, God.[28] These practices, instituted by God and commanded by Christ in the Gospels, are the means by which one actively seeks to attain purity of heart—or, in Paul's words, to "work out [one's] salvation with fear and trembling" (Phil 2:12).

To sum up, without an accurate understanding of Plato's conception of the soul, contemporary Christians are likely not to understand the terminology that ancient Christians used to describe purity of heart. Consequently, they will likely not be equipped to understand the classic writings on Christian discipleship and spiritual formation that shape the traditional practices of the Christian life. Moreover, contemporary Christians will likely have an impoverished understanding both of the nature of traditional Christian practices like fasting, almsgiving, and contemplative prayer, and of the way to use these practices in the pursuit of purity of heart.

That's all well and good, you might think, but why should I care? Here is why. When people do not understand the reasons for certain practices,

27. Notice that I said "*overly* preoccupied." The traditional Christian goal is not to achieve a kind of gnostic "freedom" from one's body. Rather, it is to order one's bodily appetites in accordance with God's design.

28. Notice that the traditional Christian way of life focuses on *contemplative* prayer, rather than on the boisterous prayers of praise and repetitive prayers of petition that may constitute the whole of contemporary Christian worship. For a contemporary introduction to contemplative prayer, see Thomas Merton, *Contemplative Prayer* (New York: Doubleday, 1969); and Igumen Chariton, comp., *The Art of Prayer*, trans. E. Kadloubovsky and E. M. Palmer, ed. Timothy Ware (London: Faber and Faber, 1966). For an ancient and classic introduction, see Evagrios the Solitary, "On Prayer," in *The Philokalia*, trans. and ed. G. E. H. Palmer, Philip Sherrard, and Kallistos Ware (London: Faber and Faber, 1979), 55–71; and Benedicta Ward, trans., *The Sayings of the Desert Fathers* (Kalamazoo, MI: Cistercian Publications, 1975). Those who find the idea of "completative prayer" foreign or uninviting might benefit by starting with a book like Dennis Okholm's *Monk Habits for Everyday People: Benedictine Spirituality for Protestants* (Grand Rapids: Brazos, 2007), especially Chapter 3: "Learning to Listen," 38–45.

they either never try them or they try them briefly and abandon them soon thereafter. Sadly, this all too frequently describes the relationship between contemporary Christians and traditional Christian practices like fasting, almsgiving, and contemplative prayer. As a result, many—perhaps most— contemporary Christians fail to make any noticeable progress in the process of *theosis*, or sanctification.

In the hope of driving the point home, let me present it in more personal terms. Lacking purity of heart, many of us naturally fail to recognize God's concerns, like our call to love *this particular* neighbor and our call to care for *this particular* aspect of God's creation. Moreover, having failed to seek God's grace by making fasting an essential part of our way of life, many of us do not tame our self-oriented desires. Thus, we often lack other-regarding desires for those divine concerns that we do happen to recognize. Similarly, having failed to seek God's grace by making the practice of almsgiving an essential part of our way of life, many of us lack the kind of profound disposition to empathize with others that is so characteristic of the One we call our Lord.[29] Consequently, we often lack the motivation to act on those God-pleasing, other-regarding desires that we do have. Finally, having failed to seek God's grace by making contemplative prayer an essential part of our way of life, many of us fail to enter into intimate communion not only with God but with our neighbors and, ultimately, with all of God's creation. In short, rather than growing in the likeness of Christ, many of us remain all too much in the greedy and vainglorious image of those who love money and honor. As a result, we remain rather indistinguishable from the rest of the unjust people who are ill-suited to help foster a just society, let alone to inspire others to follow Christ.

One way to help correct this problem is for us to reclaim the practical piety of that great "cloud of witnesses" constituted by our early Christian brothers and sisters (cf. Heb 12:1). To do that, however, we will have to acquire a better understanding of the ancient Christian faith and the historical context in which it was formulated. Since that context was imbued with the language of Plato's philosophy, we would do well to acquaint ourselves with some of its central concepts, as presented in the *Republic*.

---

29. Concerning the relationships among perspective taking, empathy, valuing the welfare of others, and prosocial behavior, see especially the works of Daniel Batson and of Martin Hoffman.

Conclusion

Let me conclude by summarizing what I have said above. When he was about thirty years old, Plato witnessed the execution of his friend and mentor by the unjust leaders of Athens and the corrupt social and political system by which they ruled. His response was, in part, to attempt to avenge his friend's death in the noble manner that his friend requested, namely, by attempting to persuade his fellow citizens that they ought to love wisdom and justice more than money and honor. One of the clearest and most influential aspects of that attempt was his development of the *Republic*, in which he offered detailed arguments concerning human nature and the proper form of education, by which people could nurture the kind of virtues that are necessary for creating and sustaining a just society.

As I hope to have shown, this great work has exerted a significant influence both on the foundation of the university and on the formulation of ancient Christian faith and practice. Hence, it is an important source for understanding both the history of education and the history of Christianity. More importantly, as long as there remain religious and political leaders who love money and honor more than wisdom and justice, it will likely remain an important touchstone for discussions about character and culture.[30]

30. I would like to thank David Bradshaw, Paul Carelli, and Dan Speak for their helpful comments on earlier versions of this chapter.

CHAPTER 2: THEOLOGY

Augustine, *Confessions*

BY DON THORSEN

Introduction

IN THE OPENING OF his *Confessions*, Augustine begins with prayer, and confesses praise to God. But the *Confessions* represents more than a devotional book. It contains the profound writings of a man who laid bare his innermost self before God and before anyone who perchance reads his confessions of sin as well as praise.

The *Confessions* also contains foundational Christian theology about the nature of God, creation, humanity, sin, evil, redemption, and virtuous living. Augustine talks about how God created the world, how people desire to praise God, and how their hearts—representing the depth of who they are—remain restless until they rest in God. He says, "You stir man to take pleasure in praising you, because you have made us for yourself, and our heart is restless until it rests in you."[1] For centuries, Christians thought about their relationship with God in terms of the fulfillment of their deepest desire, and Augustine presents a persuasive exemplar for why everyone ought to turn to God, their creator and redeemer.

---

1. Augustine, *Confessions*, trans. Henry Chadwick, Oxford World's Classics (New York: Oxford University Press, 2008), 1.1 (3). Because the *Confessions* has been published in so many translations and versions, Augustine's book and section numbers are cited first, and then the page numbers from Chadwick's translation are cited in parentheses.

After the authors of scripture, Augustine is arguably the most important theological contributor to the development of Christianity. Among his
many writings, nothing became more influential than Augustine's book
entitled the *Confessions*. The *Confessions* represents a startlingly intimate
self-examination of a person's life, confessing shameful sins and intellectual
blunders that would humiliate the ordinary person, even by contemporary
standards of tell-all memoirs. Given the context of when Augustine wrote
the *Confessions* at the end of the fourth century, his honesty challenged
readers to examine their lives, assess themselves critically, and turn to God.
As modeled in his book, theological reflection is best done in the context of
prayerful, worshipful relationship with God.

Augustine was born in 354 in the African city of Thagaste (now Souk
Ahras, Algeria) to a pagan father Patricius and Christian mother Monica.
Augustine was an excellent student, but became distracted due to a long-
term affair with a young woman in Carthage, who gave birth to their son
Adeodatus. In order to further his education and professional life as a professor of rhetoric, Augustine eventually moved to Rome and later to Milan.
He was attended by Monica, Adeodatus, and Adeodatus' mother, who lived
as a concubine with Augustine for fifteen years. Augustine and the mother
of Adeodatus, whose name was never identified, eventually separated, presumably to aid Augustine in his professional ambitions.

After experiencing various stages of intellectual and spiritual turmoil,
recorded in the *Confessions*, Augustine converted to Christianity in 386,
and was baptized by the eminent Ambrose, Bishop of Milan. Soon thereafter, Augustine decided to return home. On the journey, Monica passed
away, and Adeodatus died one year after returning to northern Africa. Augustine settled in the city of Hippo Regius (now Annaba, Algeria), where
he was ordained a priest in 391. Augustine quickly rose to prominence in
the church and was appointed Bishop of Hippo in 395, an office in which
he continued until his death in 430.

Augustine was a prolific writer throughout his life, and as the newly
appointed Bishop he undoubtedly faced multiple reasons that prompted
the writing of the *Confessions*, which was completed between 397–400.
Generally, the *Confessions* introduced readers to the new Bishop of Hippo,
and it includes intimate insight into his life as well as his beliefs. As such,
his writings served as a role model to his parishioners, both for conversion
and for the Christian life. Although others had written autobiographies,

Augustine's writings astonished people with his depth of personal and theological reflection.

The *Confessions* may have also served as a kind of apologetic for why he rose so quickly to the bishopric of Hippo. After all, Augustine was remembered by people in northern Africa, when he had lived more like a pagan than a Christian. No doubt, questions about Augustine's Christian character were fueled by the lingering Donatist controversy, wherein Christians who had wavered in their outward testimony to Christianity due to persecutions were considered traitors to the faith. Within this context, Augustine wrote the *Confessions*, which not only won over his contemporaries, but continues to influence people, both Christian and non-Christian.

Summary of the Book

Although the *Confessions* consists of thirteen books, it substantively divides into two parts. The first part (Books 1–10) contains a spiritual autobiography, characterized by honest self-assessment and confession of sins committed, sins forgiven, and insight into Christian living. The second part (Books 11–13) contains an abstract of Augustine's theological worldview, which undergirded his understanding of Christianity and, in view of that, answered some of the most fundamental questions about God, creation, people, sin, evil, redemption, time, and eternity. The profundity of Augustine's theology, however, does not occur only in the latter half of his book. He interweaves autobiography and theology throughout his *Confessions*.

Spiritual Autobiography

Book 1: Augustine begins his book by confessing the greatness and goodness of God, and the sinful immorality of people. He personally identifies with the depth of moral depravity, and talks about it from the time of people's infancy. Augustine describes himself as an ordinary, albeit intelligent child. But even in his youth, Augustine is troubled with the growing awareness of pride, sin, and people's inexorable tendency toward evil.

Book 2: As he matured, Augustine became sexually promiscuous. He sees his lust as sin, but such concupiscence is understandable to him, due to the way that people satisfy their desires through sensual indulgence. What perplexes Augustine the most was a theft he committed with friends, involving the pilfering of pears from a neighbor's house. The theft was not in itself loathsome, but Augustine interpreted it as an unmitigated act of rebellion against God. He laments: "I loved my fall, not the object for which I had fallen but my fall itself. My depraved soul leaped down from your firmament to ruin."[2]

Book 3: While studying law in Carthage, Augustine reads Cicero's *Hortensius*. Augustine becomes inspired both by the quality of Latin rhetoric and by the promotion of philosophy, which means the "love of wisdom." A resultant openness to truth, wherever it led him, seems to set up the intellectual pilgrimage that Augustine goes on to describe in the *Confessions*. At the same time, Augustine was put off by the incoherence and immorality contained in a literal reading of Christian scripture. To him, the Manichaean philosophy provided a more persuasive dualistic view of the world, despite having a materialistic view of God, who is finite. Eventually, the myths of Manichaeism dissatisfied Augustine's rational inclinations, and he progressively turned to Platonic philosophy since it emphasized spiritual truths in addition to physical truths. According to Augustine, what inhibited people in their spiritual understanding were three kinds of sin: pride (and power), lust, and curiosity that led to inordinate pursuit of satisfaction from material things in this world rather than from God.

Book 4: Augustine gives evidence of the growing influence of Platonic or, perhaps better, Neo-Platonic ideas related to the transcendent superiority of spiritual, immaterial existence. He considers the material world to have existence separate from God, and thus is worthy of study in and of itself. For example, Augustine dabbled briefly with the study of astrology, but rejected its fatalistic tendencies. He is wary of knowledge about the material world, since Augustine considers evil to have originated there.

Book 5: After moving to Rome and then Milan, Augustine came under the preaching influence of Ambrose, Bishop of Milan. Augustine was impressed with Ambrose's figurative (or symbolic) interpretation of scripture, influenced by Neo-Platonic philosophy. A figurative interpretation of Genesis, for example, helped Augustine overcome the intellectual and moral hurdles that had prevented him from affirming the doctrinal beliefs of the Catholic Church—the authorized religion of the Roman Empire.

Books 6–7: After reading more about Platonism and how God should be understood spiritually rather than materially, Augustine was increasingly drawn to the scripturally based beliefs of Christianity. He says, "In reading the Platonic books I found . . . the gold which you willed your

2. Ibid., 2.9 (29).

people to take from Egypt, since the gold was yours, wherever it was."[3] Like the Hebrews' experience of receiving gold given to them by Egyptians at the time of the Exodus, Augustine believed that Platonism aids Christians in developing a more credible theological worldview. But Platonism alone was unable to aid in understanding such pivotal Christian truths as those pertaining to the incarnation of Jesus. Be that as it may, according to Augustine, "in all the Platonic books God and his Word keep slipping in."[4]

Book 8: This chapter represents the pivotal point in the autobiographical part of the *Confessions* because it describes the conversion of Augustine. He had come to accept Catholic Christianity intellectually, but Augustine had difficulty accepting it personally and morally. Augustine had dismissed his concubine in an effort to rejuvenate his ethical life, but he only took up with another lover. After contemplating such biblical stories as the prodigal son, Augustine retires to his garden where he struggles with various biblical, philosophical, and moral quandaries. To be sure, he is of a divided mind, a divided will. Mysteriously, Augustine hears a child-like voice that says repeatedly, "Pick it up, read it; pick it up, read it."[5] In response, he picks up a copy of the Christian scriptures and in time reads Romans 13:13-14: "let us live honorably as in the day, not in reveling and drunkenness, not in debauchery and licentiousness, not in quarreling and jealousy. Instead, put on the Lord Jesus Christ, and make no provision for the flesh, to gratify its desires" (NRSV). These words prompt a turning point for Augustine—a conversion. He says: "I neither wished nor needed to read further. At once, with the last words of this sentence, it was as if a light of relief from anxiety flooded into my heart. All the shadows of doubt were dispelled."[6]

Book 9: In the last book of the autobiographical part of the *Confessions*, Augustine decides to return to northern Africa, where he would serve God in ministry. His mother Monica had rejoiced in the conversion and baptism of her son, but she died on the return trip. Before death, Augustine and Monica together shared a glimpse of heaven, and she no longer feared death. Augustine ends his autobiography with prayer and a reminder of hope in the eternal Jerusalem.

3. Ibid., 7.14, 15 (121, 123).
4. Ibid., 8.3 (135).
5. Ibid., 8.29 (152).
6. Ibid., 8.29 (153).

Christian Worldview

In the final four chapters of the *Confessions*, Augustine begins to articulate the theological worldview that undergirds his spiritual journey. Augustine does not elucidate every Christian belief and value in depth. In many instances, he develops his theology further in later publications. But the *Confessions* provides an incisive prolegomenon to his theological worldview.

Book 10: Augustine begins with a kind of Christian anthropology that explains how and why he endeavored to write his confessions. People experience sense perceptions and their mind (or rationality) makes memory possible. In particular, Augustine examines human memory, since it retains some awareness of God. Similar to Platonic notions of ascent from the material to the immaterial, and from the human to God, Augustine believes that people retain some memory of happiness in relationship with God. However, because people focus on the finite world instead of the infinite God, they sin by succumbing to temptations of pride (and power), lust, and curiosity about that which is other than God. According to Augustine, only Jesus Christ can finally mediate between people and God, and graciously redeem them from sin and judgment.

Book 11: Augustine continues to talk about the theological worldview that undergirds his confessions by evaluating the nature of creation and of time, and their relationship to how people possess memory of the past as well as of God. According to Augustine, God created the material world and also time. Since God is eternal, the limitations of past, present, and future apply only to people. So, what precisely is time? Augustine talks about it terms of being a "distension" (or extension) of the mind. He says, "But of what is it a distension? I do not know, but it would be a surprise if it is not that of the mind itself."[7]

Books 12: Augustine contemplates creation and the truthfulness of scripture. He believes that Genesis 1 advocates creation "out of nothing" (Latin, *ex nihilo*). Augustine says, "all things were made not of the very substance of God but out of nothing, because they are not being itself, as God is, and a certain mutability is inherent in all things."[8] Matter did not emanate from God as some Platonists believed; God created the world as being distinct from God, good, and purposeful. In interpreting Genesis 1, Augustine thinks that there exist multiple meanings in scriptural texts. For

7. Ibid., 11.33 (240).
8. Ibid., 12.25 (258).

example, the creation account may be interpreted literally as a historical text, but alternative literal interpretations may include spiritual or figurative (or symbolic, allegorical) meanings that are more profound. Augustine prayerfully asks God, "As long as each interpreter is endeavouring to find in the holy scripture the meaning of the author who wrote it, what evil is it if an exegesis he gives is one shown to be true by you, light of all sincere souls, even if the author whom he is reading did not have that idea and, though he had grasped a truth, had not discerned that seen by the interpreter?"[9] A scriptural interpreter may thus discover a deeper and more profound meaning in the scriptural text, regardless of whether the authors knew about it.

Book 13: Augustine maintains that the book of Genesis alludes to the trinitarian nature of God, and about how the creation narrative is a figurative reference to the Christian church and God's relationship to it. Of course, he was not the first exegete to discount a literal, historical interpretation of the creation narrative. Origen, for example, thought that a figurative interpretation of Genesis 1–2 made the most logical and spiritual sense. According to Augustine, the creation narrative in Genesis 1:2, 26 refers to the Holy Spirit of God present at creation, just as scripture elsewhere talks about Jesus Christ as co-creator. Furthermore, Genesis 1 descriptions of the firmament, sea, land, fruit, fish, and birds are thought to refer figuratively to scripture, unbelievers and believers, good works, and sacraments.[10] Even references to the creation of people in the image of God are to be interpreted spiritually as references to salvation, faith seeking understanding, and the joy of knowledge of God.[11] These spiritual, transcendent interpretations require the gracious guidance of the Holy Spirit, and they supersede physical, mundane interpretations of scripture. Augustine concludes the *Confessions* with multiple prayers, and these final words to God: "What man can enable the human mind to understand this? . . . Only you can be asked, only you can be begged, only on your door can we knock (Matt 7:7–8). Yes indeed, that is how it is received, how it is found, how the door is opened."[12]

---

9. Ibid., 12.27 (259–60).
10. For example, see ibid., 13.24–25 (294–97).
11. For example, see ibid., 13.34 (303–4).
12. Ibid., 13.53 (304–5).

Importance of Book for the University

Perhaps one of the most significant intellectual influences of Augustine is his synthesis of scripture and Platonic philosophy. He was not the first Christian to do this; others such as Clement of Alexandria and Origen had written similar syntheses. But Augustine was the most influential proponent in seeing how Platonic dualism can be understood as complementary to Christian belief in God who, on the one hand, is sovereign, immaterial (spiritual), independent, infinite, and eternal. On the other hand, the world is material (physical)—created by God—and is real, good, and purposeful, despite being contingent upon God, finite, and subject to time. The world reflects the perfect, universal forms (or ideas) described by Plato, though Augustine locates the perfect, universal forms upon which material existence is based in the mind of God. As such, the plenitude of the world should be valued, studied, and utilized in benevolent ways.

Augustine's theology, also known as Augustinianism, employs philosophical arguments reminiscent of Plato and Neo-Platonists, such as Plotinus, in metaphysically grounding scriptural teachings. Throughout the *Confessions*, Augustine refers to the influence of Platonism, directly and indirectly, through references to specific authors and concepts that contribute to the intellectual verification of theology. Augustine's synthesis influenced Christianity and Western civilization for centuries, only waning under the rise of Thomism in the thirteenth century, when Thomas Aquinas synthesized scripture and Aristotelian philosophy. A resurgence of Augustinianism occurred during the sixteenth century Reformation, when Martin Luther and John Calvin appealed to Augustine's theology in founding Protestantism in Continental Europe.

In addition to the prominence of Augustine's theological accomplishments, the autobiographical genre he uses in writing the *Confessions* had longstanding influence upon Western thought and literature. Readers throughout the centuries have been amazed by the introspection, vulnerability, and character development exhibited by Augustine. To some measure, Augustine wrote the *Confessions* in order to convert people to Christianity. Short of conversion, however, he also inspired readers to self-reflect and then record those reflections, confessing that which is vital to life, even if explicitly religious confessions are not made. A prominent example of such confessionalism was undertaken by Jean-Jacques Rousseau, who wrote his own *Confessions* in the eighteenth century. In recognizable contrast to Augustine, Rousseau emphasized a humanistic approach to admitted confessions, exemplifying an alternative Enlightenment worldview.

In his autobiography, Augustine talks about his education and occupation as a professor of rhetoric. He was a good student and learned a great deal about scripture; Augustine also learned a great deal about classical literature and education. In the *Confessions*, he mentions Aristotle, Cicero, Virgil, Horace, and Ovid as well as Platonists. After all, Augustine credits Cicero for inspiring him to seek truth, wherever it may be found. However, he is wary of the lack of morality and religious concern found in Roman writings. Augustine attributes much of the moral laxity among his fellow Romans to the lack of nurturing virtue in education. From his perspective, it is not enough to communicate knowledge and critical thinking to students; they also need to be educated with concern for character development and virtuous living. The *Confessions* represented a powerful role model for promoting education that nurtures the character as well as intellect of students, starting from childhood instruction and continuing all the way through their higher education.

Augustine's *Confessions* impacted medieval learning, first in the ecclesiastical centers of learning and then in universities, even beyond the medieval era. A key to this influence had to do with his arrangement of learning so that it all points to God as an act of worship. Although Augustine promoted Christianity, he did not suggest that his conversion provided new content to what he had known before. But it does place the content in a new context that allows for proper understanding of the place and goal of learning. Augustine's earlier professional ambition and use of education as a means of status provides a nice example of the transformation. In short, his critical understanding of education helps to explain why Christian theology was viewed as the "Queen of the Sciences" for centuries within universities.

Augustine greatly influenced Western civilization, in general, and Europe in particular. However, we should not neglect the fact that he was African, and the intellectual contributions of Africa (and Asia, for that matter) are often neglected or ignored by so-called Western civilization. Nonetheless, Augustine was born in northern Africa, and he lived, ministered, and wrote there almost his entire life, save for a few years in Italy. This fact is often lost upon the Eurocentrism or Western privilege of so-called civilization found among those who live in the Northern Atlantic part of the world. But Western civilization—which is a term used in this volume,

for the lack of a better way to talk about the location of our higher education—did not come from individuals who lived only in European or other
Western contexts.

Importance of the Book for Christians

Of the many ways that Augustine influenced Christianity, perhaps the most
significant was his emphasis upon the sovereignty of God, and the implications of God's sovereignty upon relations with people. God is sovereign
both over creation of the world and the redemption of people. Augustine
criticized philosophers, such as the Manicheans, for disbelief in "the supreme, sole and true God . . . incorruptible, immune from injury, and
unchangeable."[13] His view of God thus mirrored Platonic ideas about God
as supreme, sovereign, and unchangeable—the theistic view that Augustine
considered foundational in scripture. In praise to the glory and majesty of
God, Augustine said:

> Who then are you, my God? What, I ask, but God who is Lord . . .
> Most high, utterly good, utterly powerful, most omnipotent, most
> merciful and most just, deeply hidden yet most intimately present,
> perfection of both beauty and strength, stable and incomprehen-
> sible, immutable and yet changing all things, never new, never
> old, making everything new and "leading" the proud "to be old
> without their knowledge."[14]

Augustine's *Confessions* did much to promote the importance of scripture,
including its primacy as a religious authority and its truthfulness. People
today take for granted the canon of scripture, but no universally accepted
standard or measure (that is, canon) of sacred writings had been determined by Christians or the church when Augustine was born. In fact, the
first conciliar affirmation of the scriptural canon did not occur until the
Synod of Hippo in 393, not long before Augustine became Bishop. Since
scripture as a single, recognizable religious authority was still novel to
many Christians, he did much to promote it, as the *Confessions* contains
scriptural references on almost every page of the book.

13. Ibid., 7.1 (111). Albert Outler translates Augustine here as referring to "the sovereign and only true God"; see *Augustine: Confessions and Enchiridion*, vol. 7, trans. and
ed. Albert C. Outler, The Library of Christian Classics, eds. John Baillie, John T. McNeill,
and Henry P. van Dusen, 26 vols. (Philadelphia: Westminster, 1960), 134.

14. Augustine, *Confessions* 1.4 (4–5).

With regard to Christian cosmology, Augustine disagreed with Platonic views about the eternality of the world. If God is sovereign, then the world had to be created "out of nothing," or what later was described by Christians as the doctrine of *creatio ex nihilo* (Latin). Augustine said: "That is why you made heaven and earth out of nothing, a great thing and a little thing, since you, both omnipotent and good, make all things good, a great heaven and a little earth. You were, the rest was nothing."[15] As such, the world is both real and good because God created it. People may learn about the world and should use empirical investigations to their benefit. Such learning may also extend to scientific investigation, and Christians during the Scientific Revolution in the seventeenth and eighteenth centuries appealed to patristic authors such as Augustine in support of their explorations and experimentation.

Although Augustine believed that God created the world out of nothing, he did not have a simplistic understanding of creation or of biblical interpretation. Augustine believed that scripture may have multiple levels of meaning. There may be a literal interpretation of a scriptural text, but there may also be spiritual or figurative interpretations that exist and provide transcendent meaning. With regard to creation, Augustine considered the spiritual meaning of the creation narratives in the book of Genesis to be the most important. Along with previous biblical interpreters, such as Origen, a literal interpretation of Genesis 1–2, for example, understood historically, was not logically coherent. However, a literal interpretation understood spiritually revealed transcendent theological insight about Christian beliefs and practices.[16]

The doctrine of the Trinity became one of the central topics of debate during the fourth century. Basically, formulation of the doctrine represented a shorthand reference to Christian belief in one God, who scripture reveals in three distinct personages: Father, Son, and Holy Spirit. The term *Trinity* was coined by Tertullian during the third century, and the substance of the doctrine appears throughout the Nicene Creed—the first ecumenical Christian creed in the fourth century. Although the word *Trinity* did not explicitly appear until later creeds, the doctrine became and continues to be one of the defining beliefs of Christianity. Augustine talks about the Trinity in the *Confessions*, and he helped to articulate as well as propagate

15. Ibid., 12.7 (249).

16. See *On Christian Doctrine*, which Augustine wrote for the sake of interpreting and teaching scripture.

the doctrine among Christians. In trying to communicate the mystery of the Trinity, Augustine uses an anthropological (or psychological) analogy in order to make sense of the biblical doctrine. Just as people consist of "being, knowing, willing," they reflect God's Trinitarian nature; Augustine says, "contemplate how inseparable in life they are: one life, one mind, and one essence, yet ultimately there is distinction, for they are inseparable, yet distinct."[17] Of course, human analogies are finite in nature, and they cannot exhaustively describe God who is infinite.

A prominent theme throughout the *Confessions* is the reality and pervasiveness of human sin. In particular, Augustine conceived of sin in his own life as rooted in pride. He spoke of his sin in the following way: "I had become deafened by the clanking chain of my mortal condition, the penalty of my pride."[18] In the *Confessions*, he also talks about Christian belief in inherited sin, that is, "the chain of original sin by which 'in Adam we die' (1 Cor 15:22)."[19] Between the sin people inherit and their own individual sins, all are thought to be utterly incapable of righteous living or of meriting redemption from God. On the contrary, only God can save people from their sin, and it is God who must elect those who will receive eternal life.

As Augustine reflected upon the *Confessions* in later life, he said: "Moreover, in those same books, concerning my account of my conversion when God turned me to that faith I was laying waste with a very wretched and wild verbal assault . . . I certainly declared there that God by his grace turns men's wills to the true faith when they are not only averse to it, but actually adverse."[20] Often in the *Confessions*, Augustine shares his belief about how God's providential plan for his salvation was slowly revealed. He was not always aware of God's plan, but in hindsight—from the perspective of his writing of the *Confessions*—Augustine became cognizant and appreciative of how the sovereign God works efficaciously in all people's lives. He says: "we have seen in your Word, in your unique Son, 'heaven and earth,' the head and body of the Church (Col 1:18), in a predestination which is before all time . . . But then you began to carry out your predestined plan

17. Augustine, *Confessions* 13.279 (279). See also Augustine's extended treatment of Trinitarian issues in his book *On the Trinity*.

18. Augustine, *Confessions*, 2.2 (24).

19. Ibid., 3.9 (82).

20. Augustine, *On the Gift of Perseverance*, 20.53, in *Augustine: Confessions and Enchiridion*, vol. 7, trans. and ed. Albert C. Outler, The Library of Christian Classics, eds. John Baillie, John T. McNeill, and Henry P. van Dusen, 26 vols. (Philadelphia: Westminster, 1960), 25.

in time so as to reveal hidden secrets and to bring order to our disordered chaos."[21]

If God predestined and created all that exists, then how does Augustine account for evil? The so-called problem of evil plagued people—Christian and non-Christian—long before the time of Augustine. But he offered a widely believed solution to the problem: Evil does not exist; it is nothing. When people devote themselves to that which is less than God, they sin because their choices are evil, that is, they base their lives upon physical, material realities rather than upon God and spiritual, immaterial realities. Such choices do not constitute reality per se, though their effects are dreadful. Augustine says: "For you [God] evil does not exist at all, and not only for you but for your created universe, because there is nothing outside it which could break in and destroy the order which you have imposed upon it."[22] Thus, Augustine provided an apologetic for how God may be seen as omnipotent and good, despite the effects of evil.[23]

Although Augustine was arguably the most influential theologian in church history, his beliefs were not universally accepted. One of the more noteworthy examples has to do with the extent of people's sinfulness and the degree to which they are (or are not) involved in their redemption. Augustine is known for his condemnation of Pelagius, who Augustine accused of the heresy of promoting works-righteousness. However, in his censure of Pelagianism, Augustine downplayed the role people play in salvation. Other Christians such as Caesarius of Arles and later Thomas Aquinas argued that God preveniently gives grace to people so that, despite inherited sin, they genuinely have responsibility for ongoing sins, and they are also accountable to respond in faith to God's gracious offering of the gift of salvation. This alternative to Augustinianism is best thought of as being semi-Augustinian, rather than Pelagian (or semi-Pelagian); God enables people to exercise sufficient freedom to accept or reject God's gracious overtures with regard to conversion and the Christian life. Semi-Augustinian views became dominant among Roman Catholic and Orthodox Christians, and later Protestant adherents included Anglicans, Arminians, Wesleyans, and others. In fact, with regard to salvation, semi-Augustinianism surpassed Augustinianism in the ancient church just as it does today. It was the Continental Protestants, such as Luther and Calvin, who appealed to Augustine

21. Augustine, *Confessions,* 13.34 (303).

22. Ibid., 7.13 (125).

23. For more apologetics, see *The City of God against the Pagans* by Augustine.

in arguing for the total depravity of people along with the unconditionality and irresistibility of God's predestined election of people to salvation.

Three years before his death, Augustine wrote the *Retractions* (427), which contained commentary on the more than one hundred writings circulated during his lifetime. There he reflects: "My *Confessions*, in thirteen books, praise the righteous and good God as they speak either of my evil or good, and they are meant to excite men's minds and affections toward him. At least as far as I am concerned, this is what they did for me when they were being written and they still do this when read."[24] Augustine acknowledged the widespread influence of the *Confessions*: "Which of my shorter works has been more widely known or given greater pleasure than the . . . books of my *Confessions*? And, although I published them long before the Pelagian heresy had even begun to be, it is plain that in them I said to my God, again and again, 'Give what thou commandest and command what thou wilt.'"[25]

Conclusion

Augustine was a prodigious theological, philosophical, and literary figure throughout Western civilization as well as Christianity. Despite the fact that he wrote primarily as a Christian theologian, the *Confessions* and other writings by him continue to be read, studied, and applied in universities, regardless of whether they are Christian or non-Christian institutions of higher education. In order to trace the intellectual development of Western civilization, it is indispensable to consider Augustine's theological and literary contributions.

24. Augustine, *Retractions,* 2.6, in *Augustine: Confessions and Enchiridion*, vol. 7, trans. and ed. Albert C. Outler, The Library of Christian Classics, eds. John Baillie, John T. McNeill, and Henry P. van Dusen, 26 vols. (Philadelphia: Westminster, 1960), 24.

25. Augustine, *On the Gift of Perseverance,* 20.53 (24–25).

CHAPTER 3: DRAMA

Shakespeare, *Hamlet*

BY DAVID D. ESSELSTROM

Introduction

Any work of art emerges from three stories, three distinct but connected histories. The events and forces leading up to the undertaking of the work comprise the first story. The second story stretches from the first brush stroke on the canvas or the first chisel blow to the stone, from the first note etched on the musical staff or the first word scribbled on the blank page, to that moment when the writer, composer, painter, or sculptor—fearful that continuing would but mar the emerging form rather than reveal it further—steps away saying, "There is no more to be done." How the world responds to the work from appreciation of the patron or the applause of that first crowd to the support of readers and audiences and the ruminations of critics over the centuries—this ongoing response is the third story.

William Shakespeare's *The Tragedy of Hamlet, Prince of Denmark,* when examined through these three related but different narratives, blossoms as a work richly contributing to our understanding and appreciation of humankind, art, nature, and God.[1] The work is important to the university because of its impact. Of all of Shakespeare's plays, *Hamlet* is one of

---

1. William Shakespeare, *The Tragedy of Hamlet, Prince of Denmark,* in *The Riverside Shakespeare,* 2nd ed., ed. G. Blakemore Evans and J. J. M. Tobin (New York: Houghton Mifflin, 1997), 1189–1245. Subsequent references to the play are provided parenthetically.

the most often performed and the one over which more ink has been shed than any other. The work is important to Christians of a scholarly bent because it illustrates the rising tensions and concerns erupting from the splitting of Christendom into, at first, openly oppositional camps. *Hamlet* also illustrates and explores the growing self-awareness/conscienceness that augments the post-Reformation existential experience of Christians and non-Christians both, but most distinctly the thoughts and reflections of scholars, Christian and secular alike. *Hamlet* is important to all Christians, whether they be scholars or no, because it grapples with the interplay of humankind and providence, asking and examining key questions about how we live with each other and how we live in time.

The first and third stories are the longer since, for *Hamlet,* the first covers not only Shakespeare's life before his writing of the play but also the time in which he lived and the influences on that time, in other words, all of human history to that point. The third story includes all the social and critical discussions from Shakespeare's time to our own, covering and comprising our understanding and interpretation of *Hamlet* since the play's initial performance. Do we have time to examine fully all three stories? Not here, not now. But we can examine a few thematic lines that anchor the stories to our common understanding.

Let us look first at Shakespeare's time. William Shakespeare was born on, or near, April 23, 1564, the date scholars agree is probably his birthday. The truth is that we have insufficient evidence to claim a certain date. We do have a baptismal record from Holy Trinity Church for a "William Shakespeare" of Stratford-upon-Avon, dated April 26, 1564. We surmise, reasonably, that he was born a few days before the date on the baptismal record.

The date, however, is significant. Shakespeare was born into an England in turmoil. Elizabeth I ascended to the throne on November 17, 1558, five and a half years before Shakespeare's birth. Her ascent was not without controversy and bloodshed. Elizabeth, the daughter of Henry VIII and Anne Boleyn, was declared illegitimate shortly after she was born and her mother executed. Through an intricate series of intrigues and betrayals that put today's soap operas on notice, Elizabeth claimed the throne. Claiming and keeping are two different things. In 1570, the Pope declared Elizabeth unfit for rule and released her subjects from their obligation to obey her. In 1588, Spain launched the Spanish Armada to punish England for real and supposed wrongs, to claim Spain's irrefutable dominion of the seas, and to conquer, if possible, England itself. The fourteen-year-old William

Shakespeare more than likely did not take part in the defeat of the Spanish Armada, a naval victory that altered the course of English and world history, but he would certainly have been aware of it.

Shakespeare's world was mired in religious friction contributing to, and affected by, the political turmoil. On October 17, 1521, Pope Leo X declared England's Henry the Eighth, father of Elizabeth I, "Defender of the Faith" for his writing *Defense of the Seven Sacraments,* which called into question the theology of Martin Luther. Though the Pope later rescinded the title after Henry severed England from the Catholic Church, the British Parliament bestowed the title on Henry and all succeeding monarchs as head of the Church of England.

The Protestant Reformation itself springs from, and illustrates, an intellectual and artistic upheaval that began a few centuries earlier. The Renaissance demonstrates the power of ideas to transform people and cultures. It begins at the boot of Italy as a result, in part, of the confluence of forces brought together, first in the eleventh century, to regain Christian Europe's access to, or control of, the sacred places noted in the Bible and situated in the Middle East. We call these efforts the Crusades. By the end of the thirteenth century, after nearly ten tries to retake the Holy Land, these attempts at conquest ceased in acknowledged failure. However, irrefutable and inexorable change had already ignited in Europe. Fortunes were lost and fortunes were made during the Crusades, but the commerce—troops, ships, supplies, loot—that passed through the boot of Italy sparked an intellectual and artistic upheaval that made its way throughout Italy and into the rest of the Europe.

In each geographical region, the genius of the Renaissance manifests itself differently. In Italy in the fourteenth century, the Renaissance flowers as the visual arts: painting, sculpture, and architecture. In England in the fifteenth and sixteenth centuries, the intellectual and artistic ferment of the Renaissance energizes and transforms the verbal arts. Chaucer writes *The Canterbury Tales* in Middle English at the end of the fourteenth century. Less than 200 years later, thanks, in part, to the spread of the printing press, Early Modern English stabilizes the conventions of spelling and usage. In 1589, George Puttenham's *The Art of English Poesie* appears and lists 120 different tropes and figures (schemes). Most modern English handbooks collapse tropes and figures into "figurative language," identifying five to twenty different tropes, such as metaphor, simile, hyperbole, onomatopoeia, and synecdoche. Shakespeare studied, and mastered, a richer, more varied

English language than is currently encountered by our K-12 students. He knew the difference between a *Zeugma* and a *Chiasmus*.

Shakespeare's early life gives little hint of his talents nor does it suggest what compelled him to move from Stratford-upon-Avon to London. We know he was the third child of John Shakespeare and Mary Arden. His father was a "glover" or leather merchant who prospered through the selling of farm products and wool. His mother was the daughter of a wealthy farm owner. Specific records of Shakespeare's early education are scant or non-existent, but since his father held various civic positions in town, it is safe to say that Shakespeare most likely attended school and did indeed there learn to read and write.

We know Shakespeare married Anne Hathaway on November 28, 1582. Susanna, their first child, was born on May 26, 1583. Twins Judith and Hamnett came along two years later. Then the paper trail goes cold for seven years and picks up again with Shakespeare in London, making a name for himself in the theatre. We know this because he has detractors. Robert Greene, writing in a volume called, in part, *Greenes Groats-Worth of Witte* mentions a playwright who is most probably Shakespeare. He says, "[F]or there is an up-start Crow, beautified with our feathers, that with his Tygers hart wrapt in a Players hyde, supposes he is as well able to bombast out a blanke verse as the best of you: and being an absolute Johannes fac totum, is in his owne conceit the onely Shake-scene in a countrey."[2] The "you" to whom Greene addresses this complaint are fellow playwrights such as Thomas Kyd and Christopher Marlowe. Greene's work appears posthumously in 1592.

Much of scholarship covering Shakespeare's life centers on his writing, on the plays and poems. Trying to lift biographical information from such sources is always problematic. This is doubly true in Shakespeare's case. With the plays, for example, we know that he was writing them to be performed to audiences from the groundlings, who stood the whole performance in front of the stage, to the moneyed aristocrats seated in rustic luxury in the surrounding balconies and boxes. He was not writing to please the palates of academicians or plague the patience of high school students ages hence. We know that he wrote the plays not for posterity, as he did his poems, but for profit. Since he was writing for profit and since copyright protection was not available, he did not publish his work and thereby made it easier

---

2. Robert Greene, quoted in Stephen Greenblatt, *Will in the World* (New York: Norton, 2004), 213.

for others to use. We know that he himself borrowed heavily from others. For example, although the plot device driving *Romeo and Juliet* is quite old, the specific source for Shakespeare is most likely the poem *The Tragical History of Romeus and Juliet* (1562) by Arthur Brooke. Shakespeare's *Hamlet* is drawn, most likely, from a thirteenth-century work by Saxo Grammaticus, *Deeds of the Danes*. The prince in that work is named "Amleth." Shakespeare moves one letter to get "Hamlet." Some scholars speculate that Thomas Kyd may have written an earlier play, an "Ur-Hamlet," from the same material and that this play is the direct source of Shakespeare's.[3]

Along with the borrowing of source material, we know that Shakespeare wrote, most frequently, with his company in mind. He was part owner of the Globe Theatre and of the company, Lord Chamberlain's Men, later the King's Men after the accession of James I in 1603. Shakespeare's plays, then, were written, no doubt, with the occasional collaboration of members of that company and other fellow writers. Scholars believe we have access to his penmanship since we have a few "foul pages," scraps of paper with lines written in Shakespeare's own hand. It was perhaps from these scraps but certainly from the prompt books of the company that the first folio of his plays was printed in 1623. This was not the first appearance of his plays in print but the earlier quartos were no doubt purloined and are, without doubt, of dubious merit.[4]

Hamlet was probably first performed in 1600–01 at the Globe Theatre in London. The theatre was built in 1599 and burned after a performance of *Henry VIII* in 1613. Shakespeare died in 1616.

By way of introduction, I have attempted to tell, though briefly, the first and second histories of *Hamlet*.

Synopsis: The Tragedy of Hamlet, Prince of Denmark

As with any good play, *Hamlet* contains several plot lines. The main dramatic thread concerns the young prince, Hamlet, whose father—also named Hamlet—has died shortly before the opening of the play. Hamlet's

---

3. Amanda Mabillard, *Shakespeare's Sources for Hamlet*, Shakespeare Online, August 20, 2000, *http://www.shakespeare-online.com/sources/hamletsources.html* (accessed June 18, 2013).

4. See Lucas Erne, *Shakespeare as Literary Dramatist* (Cambridge: University Press, 2003).

mourning is complicated by the rushed marriage of his widowed mother to Hamlet's uncle Claudius, his dead father's brother.

The play gets underway when a ghost, looking much like Hamlet's father dressed for combat, treads the battlements of Elsinore Castle, startling guards and Hamlet's friend and school-mate, Horatio. Hamlet is brought in to confront the ghost. He does so, and the ghost tells Hamlet that his brother, young Hamlet's uncle, murdered the father.

Thus Shakespeare steps into a very popular genre, the revenge play. Our hero is given his mission—avenge the death of his father. Now we follow him as he overcomes obstacles to achieve success and wreak his revenge.

But Shakespeare complicates things from the get-go. The initial obstacle Hamlet faces is two-fold. First, how is he to be assured the ghost is telling the truth? Perhaps the ghost is leading young Hamlet to his own doom. Second, if the ghost is telling the truth and Claudius did kill his father, then Hamlet himself may be in danger. He is a threat to Claudius, and, therefore, Claudius will be watching him carefully.

Hamlet then has two objectives. The first is to find a way to get corroborating evidence of his father's murder. The word of the ghost is insufficient. The second is to work to allay the king's suspicions. This Hamlet plans to do by letting his melancholy, already observed by all, drift into apparent madness. He makes Horatio and the guards swear an oath of silence. They are not to give any sign that they know Hamlet, however odd he may act, is only pretending.

Another plot thread concerns Laertes, Ophelia, and Polonius. Laertes, the brother of Ophelia, is returning to Paris. He warns Ophelia not to take Hamlet's advances seriously. Polonius, the father, seconds this advice. In fact, he tells Ophelia to stay away from young Hamlet.

Polonius, adviser to Claudius, offers the king and queen, Gertrude, a hint as to the source of Hamlet's acting oddly. He has been rebuffed by his daughter. The king, Claudius, has his own ideas about the causes of Hamlet's erratic behavior. He has sent for two of Hamlet's childhood friends, Rosencrantz and Guildenstern, to act as spies.

Claudius and Polonius listen while Hamlet talks with Ophelia. Polonius thinks Hamlet's odd behavior with his daughter is evidence that her forced rejection of him is the source of his instability. Claudius is unconvinced.

Hamlet, meeting Rosencrantz and Guildenstern, knows that these two boyhood friends have been brought to Elsinore by Claudius to spy on him. They confess as much, but say that his uncle and mother only want to help Hamlet. They also tell Hamlet about the arrival of traveling players to Elsinore.

Hamlet, who has been brooding over his lack of progress in finding corroborating evidence that will justify action and perhaps move him toward it, sees in the arrival of the players an opportunity. He will have the players present a play, for which he has written a small speech, that mimics the murder of old Hamlet by Claudius. The players begin to perform, "The Murder of Gonzago," and Claudius starts, calls for light, and storms off. Hamlet and Horatio take this as sufficient corroborating evidence. The ghost is telling the truth.

Hamlet refrains from killing Claudius at the first opportunity. Claudius is on his knees, apparently in prayer. We, the audience, hear Claudius murmur that he did, indeed, kill his brother and feels bad for doing so, but not bad enough to confess his crime and relinquish that which he has gained through his sinful deed.

In his mother's chamber, Hamlet berates her for falling for Claudius over her noble first husband, old Hamlet. He senses someone is listening to them behind a curtain. He stabs through the curtain, thinking the eavesdropper is Claudius, only to discover the bleeding and dying Polonius.

Claudius, realizing his life is in danger since Hamlet certainly was hoping to kill him rather than Polonius, concocts a plan to send Hamlet to England on a mission of state. Rosencrantz and Guildenstern, carrying a letter from Claudius to the king of England, are to accompany Hamlet to make sure the mission is successful. The mission, according to the letter, is for young Hamlet to be murdered as soon as their ship docks in England.

In grief over the death of her father, Ophelia falls into real, not feigned, madness and drowns after tumbling into a river. Laertes returns, enraged at the death and hasty burial of his father, only to hear of the death of his sister. Claudius tells him it is all the fault of Hamlet.

Hamlet himself returns to Denmark with news that Rosencrantz and Guildenstern continue for England on a slightly altered mission. Hamlet has forged a letter saying the two spies should be put to death.

Hamlet and Laertes confront each other at the burial of Ophelia. Hamlet says that he did indeed love her. Laertes thirsts for revenge. Claudius enlists Laertes aid in a plot to kill Hamlet with a poison-tipped sword.

Later, Hamlet is invited to fencing match involving Hamlet and Laertes. It is sport. They are playing for "hits" and not to the death. Horatio warns Hamlet against it. But Hamlet says he will do it since he now believes in providence. In the match itself, Laertes has the poison-tipped blade. Claudius also puts poison in a goblet of wine. Hamlet and Laertes fight. After a few thrusts and parries on the part of the swordsmen, Gertrude unwittingly reaches for the poisoned wine. Claudius tries to stop her. She drinks.

Laertes stabs Hamlet. They grapple and switch swords. Hamlet stabs Laertes with the poisoned sword. Gertrude swoons, saying she has been poisoned. Laertes falls and confesses all to Hamlet before dying. Hamlet rushes the king, forces the rest of the wine down his throat and stabs him with the tainted sword. Claudius dies. Hamlet, dying, urges Horatio to continue living to tell his story.

Christian Worldview

An interesting portion of the third story is, of course, the continuing popularity of Shakespeare's work. His plays continue to be produced around the world. Films continue to be made of his works or based on his works. Versions of *Hamlet* over the last hundred years or so range from Sarah Bernhardt playing the title role on stage in 1899 to Sir Laurence Olivier's film version in 1948. Then comes Mel Gibson's take of the role in 1990, followed by Kenneth Branagh's faithful adaption of the entire text of the play in a film released in 1996. Hamlet has long been the role to which every serious actor aspires and every comic actor sees as a rich challenge. Shakespeare's works continue to be studied in high school and university classrooms. Critics use his plays as a benchmark against which other dramatists and all other writers are measured.

Shakespeare, as we see in the play *Hamlet,* is pulled in many different directions. The character Hamlet has been compared to Martin Luther. After all, Hamlet and Horatio study at Wittenberg, environs familiar to Luther and Melanchthon.[5] Hamlet is also seen as a progenitor of modern existential hero facing the despair of evident meaninglessness. The famous "To be

---

5. For example, see John O'Meara, *Otherworldly Hamlet: Four Essays* (Montreal: Guernica Editions, 1991).

or not to be" soliloquy in the first scene of the third act is understood, by some, as a heartfelt and authentic cry of nihilistic agony.[6]

However, we can tease out a few elements of worldview evident in this play that illustrate and underscore the tension between apparent oppositional Christian perspectives. First, there is the understanding that the afterlife is in some way tied to this one, that what we do matters. It is interesting to see how the works versus faith controversy is addressed in the play. Certainly, the ghost of old Hamlet voices the works perspective. He is in purgatory paying for, or working off, the sins that he committed while alive but for which he did not seek forgiveness soon enough. In the first confrontation between Hamlet and his father's apparition in the first act, the ghost of Old Hamlet says:

> I am thy father's spirit,
> Doom'd for a certain term to walk the night, And for the day
> confin'd to fast in fires,
> Till the foul crimes done in my days of nature
> Are burnt and purg'd away. But that I am forbid
> To tell the secrets of my prison house,
> I could a tale unfold whose lightest word
> Would harrow up thy soul, freeze thy young blood,
> Make thy two eyes, like stars, start from their spheres,
> Thy knotted and combined locks to part,
> And each particular hair to stand on end
> Like quills upon the fretful porcupine.
> But this eternal blazon must not be
> To ears of flesh and blood. List, list, O, list! (1.5.7–22)

But this quasi-Catholic or high church view does not match the one seemingly adopted by Hamlet at the end of the play, a view that seems to be almost Lutheran in its acceptance, seemingly, of providence. Laertes challenges him to a fencing match, a bout for points according to the hits or touches made by the opponents and not a fight to the death. Horatio, Hamlet's friend who knows all that has happened and knows, too, that Claudius remains bent on the destruction of his nephew, thinks the match is a set up. Hamlet feels—suspects—this as well.

Horatio then cautions that Hamlet should forego the match if he has even the slightest hesitation or misgiving. Hamlet's reply is telling:

6. See Harold Bloom, *Bloom's Modern Critical Views: William Shakespeare* (New York: Infobase, 2010).

> Not a whit, we defy augury: there's a special providence in the fall
> of a sparrow. If it be now, 'tis not to come; if it be not to come, it
> will be now; if it be not now, yet it will come: the readiness is all:
> since no man knows aught of what he leaves, what is't to leave
> betimes? Let be. (5.2.220–224)

Also of interest is another conflicting note found in the famous "To be or not to be" soliloquy where Hamlet asks, "For who would bare the whips and scorns of time/ . . . When he himself might his quietus make/ With a bare bobkin" (3.1.69–75). This scene comes shortly after he has met the traveling players and has listened to, and been moved by, a recitation on the death of Priam. Hamlet wonders not just about death but about our fear of death. He argues, here, that the source of the fear is ignorance. Hamlet says, "But that the dread of something after death/ The undiscover'd country from whose bourn/ No traveler returns, puzzles the will" (3.1.77–79). But, of course, if the ghost is to be trusted about the information on the murder of old Hamlet, it can probably be trusted on its report about the conditions of the afterlife, at least that part of it spent in purgatory.

Which perspective Shakespeare supports or advocates cannot be determined nor is it necessary that we do so. Shakespeare is working between the two. Were we cynical, we would argue that he is milking each view for its dramatic potential. A ghost could be an emissary from Hell and is, therefore, a demon leading one to destruction. This possibility is crucial to the forward action of the play. Or a ghost might be some apparition sent by benign or beneficent elements to urge caution or action. Hamlet's acceptance of his fate, whatever may come, could spring from an acceptance of God's ordained plan or merely the high spirits one has from surviving several close calls. That these plot elements are effective belabors the point; these two views do, indeed, have dramatic potential. Shakespeare recognizes that this is the case because the very tension this opposition presents is the tension experienced, and navigated, by his audience. Most people in England at the time were not merely Catholic *or* Protestant but rather Catholic *and* Protestant.

Many scholars see this time as the beginning of the modern consciousness and find in the split dividing Christendom the first glimpse into the yawning chasm of meaninglessness that is the existential condition of modern—and postmodern—humankind. Where can one stop, and why should one stop, once one begins to question authority? Or more germane, where can one begin the quest for certitude after having questioned all authority and found it—all of it—wanting?

Here we find ourselves in the middle of the field on which the Christian scholar meets secular seeker. Dante's fretful wanderings in the "dark wood"[7] fuel Descartes's quest for the grounds of certainty.[8] Shakespeare picked his way through this pockmarked terrain before us. We fool ourselves if we think the path any clearer to us than it was to him. Christian scholars too often tilt at the windmills of unbelief rather than wrestle the angels of doubt and uncertainty.

Importance to the University

Shakespeare's works, especially his *Hamlet,* have a continuing and sustaining impact on the university for two solid reasons: one, Shakespeare shows what can be done with words, and, two, Shakespeare's words offer seemingly infinite opportunity for interpretation and reinterpretation. On such mulch the university thrives.

The first reason is easy to explain and unpack. No one else has matched Shakespeare and his use of the language. If we take a look at Shakespeare's development from the early to the later plays, we see a sensitivity that switches from playing with language to investigating character. So not only does Shakespeare use language more nimbly than all other writers, but he also uses it in the service of penetrating and revealing character, enriching not only our understanding and appreciation of literature but also of life itself. He does so without didacticism. He is such a good wizard that we forget he is behind the curtain. His illusion becomes our reality.

The second reason is easier to illustrate than explain. I, the writer of this essay, am by practice and inclination a rhetorician. I look at texts from the perspective of rhetorical theory. I am also a creative writer and student of creative writing. I add this wrinkle to my inquiry. Therefore, in responding to *Hamlet,* I begin by asking two questions: What is Shakespeare doing in the writing of the play? I am not asking what he means by the play, or

7. Dante Alighieri, *The Divine Comedy,* trans. John Ciardi (New York: New American Library, 1970).

8. See Rene Descartes, *A Discourse on the Method of Correctly Conducting One's Reason and Seeking Truth in the Sciences,* trans. Ian Maclean (New York: Oxford University Press, 2006).

what we should take to be the meaning of it, but rather what he is doing. And what are the characters doing in the play? I might, eventually, get to issues of meaning, but first I want to deal with the doing.

This perspective allows me—forces me, some would say—to look in *Hamlet* for particular through lines, elements that propel or pull the dramatist as he or she discovers and reveals the story. For Hamlet that through line is his situation. As the play opens, he cannot quite make sense of the unexpected death of his father and the hasty marriage of his mother. He is lost, emotionally. The ghost appears and apparently solves his problem. The ghost fills him in on the true story of the death of his father; not bad luck or bad fortune but rather a bad person, his own brother, put an end to him. But for Hamlet, and for Shakespeare the dramatist, this introduces a new problem. Can Hamlet trust the word of the ghost? He needs corroborating evidence. This quest, in my estimation, carries Hamlet through much of the play. This quest opens up other issues for Hamlet as he realizes that his actions will bring about reactions that most probably will result in his own death. This quandary, the price of action, is his preoccupation and not suicide or anachronistic meaninglessness, as some would argue. Although this quandary does open up these philosophical issues for Christian and secular scholar alike, my purpose is, first, to see how questions drive or hinder action, for Hamlet and for the rest of us.

As I see it, two distinct sections to the story in *Hamlet* rest on either side of what I affectionately call the plot's black hole. I have written many a play, and I, too, have fallen into the first draft quagmire where I separate the action and have to follow two story threads and then can't see a way to weave the two narrative strands back together again, logically and reasonably. This is what happens to Shakespeare.

Here is where it happens. In Act IV, Scene 2, Rosencrantz and Guildenstern are to take Hamlet to England, ostensibly for his own safety, but in actuality to be put to death by order of Claudius. Then in Act IV, Scene 6, sailors hand Horatio a letter from Hamlet saying that he, Hamlet, is back in Denmark. Some interesting things happen to Hamlet between these scenes.

First, Hamlet—we learn from the letter and later dialogue between Hamlet and Horatio—on the ship for England becomes suspicious of the motives his two supposed friends. He breaks into their luggage and finds the sealed letter from Claudius. He breaks the seal and reads the letter commanding that the king of England kill Hamlet the moment the ship docks.

Hamlet destroys the letter, writes another, and then agonizes for a moment over the broken seal. Then Hamlet remembers that he, too, wears the royal signet ring and can re-seal the letter as good as new. He slips the letter back in their luggage so that Rosencrantz and Guildenstern will be none the wiser.

Thereby, Shakespeare weasels his way out of the problem. Of course, Hamlet is still on board a ship bound for England with Rosencrantz and Guildenstern. That is a problem. What is a writer to do? Something outrageous. What about pirates? That works. Hamlet's ship is set upon by pirates, and all on board fight to repel the attackers. In this battle, Hamlet does the swashbuckling thing and swings to the deck of the pirate ship to bring the fight to his enemy. Of course, at that moment, the two vessels pull apart. Rosencrantz and Guildenstern are bound for England, carrying their own death warrant, and Hamlet, sword in hand, watches as the gap between him and his boyhood friends grows wider, waves and wind fueling the separation. At the same time as the ship for England pulls away from the pirate vessel, Hamlet tenses, his fully armed foes surrounding him. Shakespeare, inventive writer that he is, once again reaches into his hat for something outrageous. Rather than ram their cutlasses through Hamlet's body and toss his corpse into the sea, the pirates—reasonable businessmen—agree, for a price, to sail Hamlet back to Denmark and deposit him on the shore.

Do I point this out to make the argument that Shakespeare is an inept playwright? No. However, Leo Tolstoy thought so and makes the argument in *Tolstoy on Shakespeare* (1906). Tolstoy and Chekhov were friends, and although Tolstoy loved Antonin Chekhov's short stories, he thought his plays were worse than those of Shakespeare.

Scholars examine the differences that drive the character of Hamlet as we discover him on one side and then the other of this "black hole." These are the intellectual stands and quibbles that drive and sustain the university. Shakespeare arouses passions. And the tapestry of his work is so rich and varied that insights into the heights and depths that contour life can be found there or claims can be made that singularly odd shapes—that may, or may not, be there—appear in the warp and woof of the weave. We argue over all these things. That is what we scholars do.

Conclusion, or Why a Christian Should Care

All art diverts us. Good art opens us. It also frustrates us. Shakespeare, over the centuries, has been a staple of the stage in English, and even non-English, speaking countries. The very longevity and timeliness of his artistry and vision establish and sustain his place in the university.

Why does a Christian need to be opened by theatrical art? First, art opens us because the work of art itself, *Hamlet* in this instance, is an accessible record of the human imagination wrestling with ideas, exploring forms, and tracing the contours of relationships. Reading or watching *Hamlet* does not merely entertain us but rather offers us the possibility of closely observing the mind intently at work on the business of living. We should, in most instances, come away from art not merely diverted for a time, or amused for an instant or two, but changed, enriched by possibilities that should augment our own experience of living. Scripture tells us that such a rich experience of life is open to us. Therefore, we need to be open to it.

Then we have the problem of frustration. Art frustrates us precisely because it is open. We ask the poet what a poem means. The poet points to the poem itself and tells us the poem is the best and only expression of its meaning. We cannot pin art down. One work is not synonymous with another. No work of art can be captured in a paraphrase or synopsis. Even my summary of the story of *Hamlet* is but a dim and distant reflection of the work itself. And even with this, I may be claiming too much for my efforts.

This very frustration, however, is the purpose of art. Art makes us think about the questions without forcefully and unequivocally supplying answers. In thinking about the questions—how I live with others, with myself, with the physical world, with the spiritual realm—we wrestle with who we think we are and who we are becoming. Narrative art—plays are examples—forces, or enables us, to experience the passage of time and to follow the results of actions without suffering the consequences of either. As with the lessons from our own lives, we do not have to learn anything from art, or from our lives, unless we make the conscious decision to do so.

I argue that it is precisely such a choice that we are advised, if not commanded, to make.

CHAPTER 4: LITERATURE

Cervantes, *Don Quixote*

BY ANDREA IVANOV-CRAIG

Introduction

WE HAVE ALL HEARD of him, or perhaps, seen him: the gaunt, somewhat tall, bearded figure in the horribly ramshackle armor atop an emaciated horse, his rubicund sidekick astride a donkey trailing behind. With the word "quixotic," he has made his contribution to our English language lexicon despite his native Spanish heritage: now we have him to thank when we think of anything whimsical, impractical, and slightly crazy. "Tilting at windmills," we may say. Where did this character come from, and what does he continue to represent? The great twentieth-century literary critic Lionel Trilling wrote: "It can be said that all prose fiction is a variation on the theme of *Don Quixote*. Cervantes sets for the novel the problem of appearance and reality."[1]

The Ingenious Hidalgo of La Mancha Don Quixote is the story of a poor country gentleman who, instead of just reading about knights in shining armor, decides to become one. Because of its formal innovations, *Don Quixote* is commonly regarded as the first modern novel in Western literature. It is important to Christians because it dramatizes the struggle of a man of faith in a hostile environment, and because it critiques the inability

---

1. Lionel Trilling, *The Liberal Imagination* (New York: Dryden Press, 1948), 209.

to discern properly the relationships between fiction and history, appearance and reality, symbol and truth. It is important to everyone because it is a downright hilarious book. This man names his horse, "Superhack," or "Hack before all Hacks" (*Rocinante*), makes a helmet with a cardboard visor, and assaults puppets failing to save a puppet princess.

Don Quixote comes to us from the pen of Miguel de Cervantes Saavedra. Born in 1547 in Alcalá de Henares, Cervantes descended from lower gentry as the son of a poor surgeon. He was educated by Jesuits in Cordoba and by the humanist teacher, Juan Lopez de Hoyos, in Madrid. Serving in the Spanish Legion during the 1571 battle of Lepanto, Cervantes lost the use of his left hand. While still in service, he and his brother were taken hostage by pirates in 1575 and served as slaves in Algiers. His brother was ransomed before he was, and Cervantes tried to escape several times before he was finally ransomed in 1580. He began to write plays upon his return, and in 1585, published *La Galatea*, a pastoral novel. His marriage to Catalina de Salazar in 1584 and his fathering of an illegitimate daughter led him to seek more stable employment. Cervantes secured a position in arms requisition for the Spanish Armada. Unfortunately, it led to his imprisonment for "irregularities" in the books; more specifically, he was accused of fraud and the appropriation of church property. Cervantes is said to have conceived of Part I of *Don Quixote* while in prison in Seville. Its publication in 1605 made him an overnight sensation. Part II of *Don Quixote* was published just a year before his death in 1616, and just a year after the unfortunate spurious Part II was published by Avellenada. Cervantes died on April 22, separated only a few days from the death of William Shakespeare.[2]

Contextually, *Don Quixote* emanates from Early Modern Spain and the Baroque period, but Cervantes lived also during the end of the Renaissance and the *Siglo' D'Oro* or Golden Age. Critics commonly refer to the *"desengaño"* (disillusionment) reflected in the novel, particularly in Part II.[3] *Don Quixote* is partly a product also of Cervantes' critique of the Roman

2. The information in this biographical sketch is a composite of generally known dates and events listed in Roberto González Echevarría, "Introduction to Cervantes," *Don Quixote*, trans. John Rutherford (New York: Penguin, 2000), vii–xxii; "Chronology," in Cervantes, *Don Quixote*, trans. Rutherford, xxxv–xxxvii; and Harold Bloom, introduction to *Don Quixote*, trans. Edith Grossman (New York: HarperCollins, 2003), xxi–xxxv.

3. Otis Green, *The Castilian Mind in Literature from El Cid to Calderón*, vol. 4 of *Spain and the Western Tradition* (Madison: University of Wisconsin Press, 1966), 43–77; Robert Bayliss, "What *Don Quixote* Means (Today)," *Comparative Literature Studies* 43, no. 4 (2006) 382–97.

Catholic Church in the wake of the Spanish Inquisition. The primary subject for satire, however, relates to the complaints against books of chivalry, and the local priest who condemns many of the books in Quixote's library, who is really the spokesman for Cervantes' literary aesthetic.

With the idealization of Dulcinea, Cervantes takes on Catholic concepts of *eros* as analogous to the relation of the soul to God. The novel also reflects the four humors theory as adapted by Juan Huarte de San Juan, a sixteenth-century psychologist. Don Quixote, "The Ingenious Hidalgo of La Mancha," suffers from an excess of the choleric humor, or "excessive heat of the brain."[4] Most ostensibly, *Don Quixote* is a parody of older genres of literature: pastoral romance, picaresque novel, and chivalric romance, or books of chivalry. Pastorals involved nobles venturing out into the woods and fields, pretending to be shepherds and shepherdesses, and becoming entangled in hopeless love triangles; the picaresque novel was an autobiographical tale about a low-born, usually urban, anti-hero who lived by his wits and his stomach; but it is the books of chivalry, particularly *Amadis de Gaul*, that Quixote most cites.[5] So it is that in the Prologue to Part I, we have the character of the author's friend, reminding the author that his "only concern" with this book is to "destroy the authority and influence that books of chivalry enjoy in the world."[6]

Summary

Don Quixote is the story of a "hidalgo," the lowest rung of gentleman on the sixteenth-century Spanish social ladder. He sells off his land to buy books about knights on noble quests, dedicating their lives to the honor and glory of their feudal lords, their virtuous ladies, and their Sovereign Lord, often in the only guise through which he was known—the Holy Roman

4. Juan Huarte de San Juan, *Examen de ingenios para las ciencias* (1575), quoted in Green, *Spain and the Western Tradition*, 4:260. Sancho Panza, who has a sanguine nature, can afford to lose a little blood with the 3,300 lashes he is sentenced in order to "disenchant" Dulcinea.

5. Garci Rodgríguez de Montalvo, *Amadis de Gaula* (1508).

6. Cervantes, *Don Quixote*, trans. John Rutherford (New York: Penguin, 2000). Other evidence in the novel suggests that Cervantes' critique of the books of chivalry was not all because of his dislike for the genre itself, but rather that so many individual examples were written poorly and without verisimilitude; see Part I, ch. 6 and Part II, ch. 47. All future references to this translation will be cited as follows: "Cervantes, *Don Quixote*, trans. Rutherford."

Catholic Church. In short, Don Quixote spends too much time reading these fantasies, becomes mad, and thinking himself a knight, goes off in search of adventures. Despite the efforts of his niece, housekeeper, the local priest, and barber to keep him at home, Don Quixote goes out three separate times over the course of Part I (1605) and Part II (1615). After his first solitary sally, he picks up Sancho Panza, arguably Western literature's first comic sidekick, whom he enthralls with promises of the governorship of an island. He has already pinpointed a local farmer's daughter, Aldonza Lorenzo, whom he once loved from afar, as the lady Dulcinea del Toboso, the inspiration for his knight errantry. The second sally makes up the rest of Part I, during which Don Quixote repeatedly mistakes people, objects, and animals for creations out of his books of chivalry. The most famous of these mistakes includes attacking a windmill because he believes it is a giant *only disguised* as a windmill, and his release of the chained criminals (galley slaves) because he thought them unfairly imprisoned. With the help of Dorotea and Cardenio, Lucinda and Don Fernando—four noble characters whose own subplot is itself one of Cervantes' interpolated tales—Sancho and Don Quixote are brought home through a ruse of the priest and barber.

Part II begins with Don Quixote's convalescence, during which he discovers that all of his previous adventures (Part I) have been published as a book. The first few chapters relate this news, and introduce the character of Sanson Carrasco, a minor university graduate, who gives him a review of the book; these chapters also showcase the continued efforts of the locals to test out his wits. They are powerless to stop him from venturing out again. The third and final sally includes several key episodes. First, the enchantment of Dulcinea, during which the (idealized) lovely princess is supposedly turned into a common peasant girl (a fabrication Sancho makes to cover his tracks). Second, during the descent into the Cave of the Montesinos, Don Quixote is lowered into an underground cavern, sleeps, and then claims to have had a three-day adventure in the crystal castle of ancient Montesinos. His telling Sancho that he saw Dulcinea as the coarse peasant girl, and that her girlfriend asked him for money, makes Sancho doubt Don Quixote's veracity as well as sanity. Last, Don Quixote is hosted by the corrupt Duke and Duchess, who having read about Don Quixote, treat him as a real knight and convince Sancho that he must disenchant Dulcinea.

The structure of the novel, though episodic, holds together because of the rise and decline of Don Quixote. This is measured first in terms of his ascendancy and defeat by those who wish to have him regain his sanity and end his quest. Early in Part II, he encounters the "Knight of the Wood," who challenges him to a jousting match. Through comic mishap, Don Quixote wins, and the Knight of the Wood, whom we learn is really Sanson Carrasco, stomps off in disgruntled defeat, vowing revenge. He gets it. Late in part II, Carrasco meets Don Quixote while he is being entertained by yet another nobleman, but this time Carrasco goes as the "Knight of the Mirrors," and he wins the match. Don Quixote must go home and give up knight errantry for a year. This loss leads to his trip home, and his vow to take up the idyllic life of a shepherd after the manner of the pastoral novels; a wonderful irony, this hope keeps him and Sancho going for a while. His character's development is secondly measured by the gradual release of his delusions. Though he shows moments of lucidity throughout the novel, he seems clearer-minded but more depressed in the latter half of Part II. When he returns home, he becomes ill, renounces chivalry, reclaims his true identity as "Alonso the Good," and promptly dies of a fever.

Importance to the University

For centuries, *Don Quixote's* formal innovations and thematic concerns have kept the novel alive in the world of letters as well as in the popular imagination. Formally, Cervantes introduced the use of multiple (ironic) narrators, as well as invented an overall "novelistic formula . . . based on the opposition between an illusion-haunted hero and prosaic social reality."[7] Thematically and generally speaking, *Don Quixote* is a book about reading books, living life, and the difference between the two.

It is no coincidence that the presentation of the illusion of reality, verisimilitude, undergirds the very conditions of the modern novel. The major debate over the interpretation of this novel also involves themes of appearance versus reality. Does Don Quixote refract reality through the lens of fantasy to his credit or discredit? Is he an inspirational dreamer, or is he an object lesson in the destructive effects of reading too many bad novels? Before 1800, the novel was read as primarily comic and Don Quixote as a laughable fool. After that, however, Don Quixote became less of a ridiculous figure and more of a sublime and tragic one. In the late 1960s, critics such as Anthony Close claimed the transition to a sublime and tragic figure

---

7. Anthony Close, *The Romantic Approach to Don Quixote* (New York: Cambridge University Press, 1977), 2.

was largely because of the German Romantic interest in the novel,[8] which celebrated a hero who created fantasy worlds, a book which synthesized disparate genres, and the use of a Romantic irony, a "dual awareness of polarities not reconcilable."[9] These "hard" critics, as they became known, argue that *Don Quixote* is first and foremost a parody of books of chivalry—and by extension, of their unsophisticated readers whose poor aesthetic taste aside, cannot tell the difference between reality and fantasy. For instance, Anthony Close calls "misguided" the "idealization of the hero," the "denial of the novel's satiric purpose," the "belief that the novel is symbolical," and interpretations "which reflect the sensibility of [our] modern era."[10]

The "soft" critics, on the other hand, are those who argue, in line with post-Romantic ideology, that Don Quixote is a satire of provincial and backward thinking society, especially when it reaches the excesses of moral and religious censorship. Against the behavior and thinking of Quixote's supposedly "purer" higher-ups, his silly adventures become a noble and imaginative quest to change the nature of society and, by extension, reality. Those who encounter him change with him and are, for the most part, edified in some way. The Spanish critics of the late nineteenth and early to mid-twentieth century fall into this camp. For instance, Américo Castro writes, "The major theme of *Don Quixote* is the interdependence, the 'interrealization' of what lies beyond man's experience and the process of incorporating that into his existence."[11] Ortega Y Gasset's *Meditation on Don Quixote* was famous for its equation of *Don Quixote* as a resource of symbolic resonance as he contemplated the question: "What is Spain?"[12]

We have much to learn from both schools, and from those who have moved beyond the debate to a kind of synthesis. Lionel Trilling said that Cervantes starts off with a narrator who has a survivalist mentality: only those things which keep you fed, housed, and clothed ultimately matter.

8. Close, *Romantic Approach*, 35–36. See also P. E. Russell, "*Don Quixote* as a Funny Book," *Modern Language Review* 64, no. 2 (1969) 312–26.

9. Evelyn Meyer, "The German Romantic Tradition: (Mis) Reading *Don Quixote*," in *Cross-Disciplinary Essays on "Don Quixote*," ed. James A. Grabowska and Kimberly E. Contag (New York: Edwin Mellen, 2007), 7–18, 11.

10. Close, *Romantic Approach*, 1.

11. Américo Castro, "The Incarnation of Dulcinea," trans. Zenia Sacks Da Silva, in *Cervantes Across the Centuries*, ed. Angel Flores and M.J. Bernadete (New York: Dryden, 1948), 136–78, 139.

12. Julián Marías, introduction to *Meditations on Don Quixote* by José Ortega Y Gasset (New York: Norton, 1963), 11–26.

"But Cervantes changes horses midstream," writes Trilling.[13] Reality, in the wake of Quixote's glorious crusades, becomes chock-full of potential—people become avatars of possibility. Reality resides more in Quixote's vision: "the real reality is rather the wildly conceiving, the madly fantasying mind of the Don."[14] Thus characters, such as the noble Dorotea, meet Quixote and Quixote's naysayers and agree to help bring him home by pretending to be a princess in distress. By going along with Don Quixote—both figuratively and literally—circumstances occur that happily sort out her real distress and allow her to be reunited with her lover.[15] Conversely, there is nothing admirable about Don Quixote repeatedly attacking innocent people and animals because he thinks they are enemies of some kind. In addition, there are far too many references to the absurdities of chivalric romances to mistake Cervantes' complaint: lack of verisimilitude. The joke may be on us if we elevate an old fool who confuses bad fantasy with historical fact. Perhaps the best approach is a hybrid one. In *Eros and Empire*, Henry Higuera writes that "the ideal treatment" would "show in detail how the work deals with the great questions of human fate *through being* such a funny book."[16]

The formal innovations that lead many to call *Don Quixote* the first modern novel involve Cervantes's experimentation with narration and verisimilitude. "Whose Quixote is it?" is first a question about who is telling this story. Cervantes introduces multiple narrators, most namely, the Arab Historian, Cid Hamete Benengeli, whose manuscript recounting Don Quixote's adventures the current narrator (presumably, the author of the Prologue) discovers while he is shopping at a marketplace. Benengeli is with us for the rest of the novel, Part II included, but not without the caveat that Arabs are "all liars."[17] Cervantes' effort to parody chivalric romance's supposed reliance on "historical" sources also includes desultory remarks on the duties of historians, that they should be "truthful and unprejudiced,"[18] precisely what the current narrator is not. Quixote's other invisible partners include the reputed enchanter who mysteriously follows the Don and Sancho around unbeknownst to anyone—especially the reader—and therefore enables all of Don Quixote's adventures in Part I to appear as a book in Part

13. Trilling, *The Liberal Imagination*, 208.

14. Ibid., 208–9.

15. Cervantes, *Don Quixote*, trans. Rutherford, Part I, chapter 36.

16. Henry Higuera, *Eros and Empire* (London: Rowman & Littlefield, 1995), 9.

17. Cervantes, *Don Quixote*, trans. Rutherford, 76.

18. Ibid.

II. Such an innovation goes beyond satire to a breach of verisimilitude in order to implicate the reader in the very traps that plague the novel's characters.[19] Through the use of such devices as a lying narrator, Cervantes is teaching us how to read a realistic novel. E. C. Riley writes that he "discovered through prose fiction that art is a kind of illusion in which the reader joins, as in a game, with complete consciousness of its unreality, and that the more powerful the appearance of reality is, the greater the illusion."[20]

"Whose Quixote is it?" is secondly an allusion to the number of interpretations the novel has had, and the astonishing ways it has been reappropriated by different constituencies in each era. Miguel Unamuno wrote, "Each generation adds something" to the Don Quixote who lives and exists "with a life and existence perhaps more intense and effective than if he had lived and existed in the ordinary manner."[21] However, it is difficult not to agree with Anthony Close in seeing that the predominance of "readings" in the last 200 years have been romantic, whether they are done by scientists, politicians, or filmmakers. Robert Bayliss lists multiple examples of such enlistment, including the European Space Agency's development of a 2005 project called "Don Quijote," consisting of an asteroid-targeting pair of unmanned spacecraft, "Sancho" and "Hidalgo."[22] Another example includes the 2005 action "Operation Dulcinea" by Venezuelan President Hugo Chavez. Seeing that the people needed inspiration in light of their current troubles, he authorized the distribution of one million free copies of the novel as a reminder that Don Quixote was a champion of justice.[23] Mainstream filmmakers have also adapted the basic storyline of the deluded individual who ends up doing good. Terry Gilliam's *The Fisher King*

19. John Allen explains this phenomenon in "Levels of Fiction," in *The Norton Critical Edition of "Don Quixote"* by Miguel de Cervantes, trans. John Ormsby, ed. Joseph R. Jones and Kenneth Douglas (New York: Norton, 1981), 919–27; first published in *Don Quixote: Hero or Fool? Part I*, University of Florida Monographs: Humanities No. 29 (Gainesville: University of Florida Press, 1971).

20. E. C. Riley, "Novel and Romance in *Don Quixote*," in *Norton Critical Edition of "Don Quixote,"* 914–19, 918; first published in *Suma Cervantina*, ed. J. B. Avalle-Arce and E. C. Riley (London: Tamesis, 1973), 310–22.

21. Miguel de Unamuno, "On the Reading and Interpretation of *Don Quixote*," in *Norton Critical Edition of "Don Quixote,"* 974–79, 975; first published in *Selected Works of Miguel de Unamuno*, trans. Anthony Kerrigan, Bollingen Series, LXXXV (Princeton: Princeton University Press, 1967).

22. Bayliss, "What *Don Quixote* Means (Today)," 383.

23. Ibid., 384–86.

(1991)[24] features Robin Williams as a mentally ill homeless man in search of a grail, and more recently, *The King of California* (2007)[25] stars Michael Douglas as a recently released mental patient with a dream to find a treasure under a suburban Costco. In short, *Don Quixote* is in the common domain, figuratively speaking. Bayliss cites the Prologue author's comment that invites readers to "say anything you desire about this history" and interprets it to be an open call for all manners of readings.[26]

As with all great books, but particularly one as iconic as *Don Quixote*, the issue is not just theoretical or hopelessly subjective but ethical: what constitutes fair and responsible interpretation? Putting aside the problem of determining Cervantes' "true" intentions for the novel, it is unlikely his "open call" was meant to be a serious free-for-all. This fact is clearly suggested because, within his lifetime, he excoriated one "Alonso Fernández de Avellaneda" for publishing an apocryphal sequel to the 1605 *Don Quixote* in 1614.[27] Given the novel's critical and interpretative history, it is not that no one correct interpretation exists; it is more that we need to look at the difference between responsible readings and convenient reductions. E. C. Riley's gloss on this situation is helpful: "somehow the comic parody of an older myth has generated an authentic new myth. To see how that happens we have to read the book after all."[28]

Importance to Christians

Don Quixote is important to Christians because it a story not only about the difference between appearance and reality, but also about the relationships between reality and truth. More specifically, the novel constructs themes of faith in the unseen, the madness of the cross, and our place as created beings in the cosmic and social orders.

24. *The Fisher King*, directed by Terry Gilliam (1991, TriStar Pictures).

25. *King of California*, directed by Mike Cahill (2007, Millenium Films).

26. Bayliss, "What *Don Quixote* Means (Today)," 389.

27. Alonso Fernández de Avellaneda, *Segundo Tomo del Ingenioso Hidalgo Don Quijote de la Mancha* (Tarragona, 1614). Avellaneda is the pen name of an unknown Spanish writer. Called "El Quijote apócrifo" (the spurious Quixote), this novel is discussed in several sources in Cervantes scholarship. See *Columbia Electronic Encyclopedia*, 6th ed., s.v. "Alonso Fernández de Avellaneda," and Edward H. Friedman, "Fame and Misfortune: The Cost of Success in Don Quijote," *Bulletin of Hispanic Studies* 82, no. 5 (2005) 649–69.

28. E. C. Riley, "From Text to Icon," *Cervantes Bulletin of the Cervantes Society of America*, 8, special issue (1988) 109–15, 115.

In John 20:29, Jesus tells Thomas, "Blessed are those who have not seen and yet have come to believe."[29] The echo of this verse sounds when we hear Don Quixote admonish some traveling merchants who will not swear to Dulcinea's beauty. "If I were to let you see her," Don Quixote tells the merchants, "what merit would there be in confessing so manifest a truth? The whole point is that, without seeing her, you must believe, confess, affirm, swear and uphold it."[30] A similarly faith-related allusion occurs later in the book when Don Quixote swears his loyalty to Dulcinea, for "In me she does battle and conquers, and in her I live and breathe and have my being."[31] The paraphrases of Acts 17:28 and Galatians 2:20 are unmistakable. Moreover, as Higuera points out, "Dulcinea is not only a woman acting as a protreptic toward God but in her more divine aspect, is herself, God. Cervantes is portraying and analyzing not only the relation between a hero and a woman, but also the relation between the soul and God."[32] This analogy is familiar terrain for Christians for its reference to the Song of Songs and the church as the bride of Jesus Christ.

Much scholarly ink has been spilled on the topic of Don Quixote's love for Dulcinea, but Higuera's summary of Anthony Close's argument is one of the best indications of the topic's complexity. In short, Don Quixote knows Dulcinea is not really a princess "because he never forgets that she is also Aldonza."[33] God in man, as much man as God, Jesus is the divine Incarnation. Don Quixote never truly confuses Dulcinea with God, although much of the language he uses to address her (or the idea of her) certainly may suggest this: Don Quixote "rais[es] his eyes to heaven, and fixing his thought, as it seemed on his lady Dulcinea, he said 'Assist me, dear lady, in this first affront.'"[34] From the very beginning, Don Quixote fabricates his addresses to her from books of chivalry, but Sancho does not know this. In Part I, Chapter 25, Don Quixote finally has to explain to Sancho that he barely knows the real Dulcinea, an illiterate farm girl, but that "for what I want of Dulcinea del Toboso, she is as good as the most exalted princess in

---

29. *The New Interpreters Study Bible*, NRSV (1989) (Nashville: Abingdon, 2003). All future references to the Bible come from this edition.

30. Cervantes, *Don Quixote*, trans. Rutherford, 46.

31. Ibid., 276.

32. Higuera, *Eros and Empire*, 30.

33. Ibid., 25.

34. *Don Quixote*, trans. Rutherford, 38–39.

the world."[35] In other words, she is a symbol, and Don Quixote knows this. At least in this instance, Don Quixote understands the difference between literal and figurative reality, symbol and truth. Once this fact is established, readers can measure other uses of scripture and theological reference in the novel to determine differences between Don Quixote's mission and that of Christianity.[36]

Don Quixote is also important to Christians because, as Foucault tells us, "the madness of the cross" theme was foremost on the theological radar of the sixteenth century.[37] In 1 Corinthians 1:18, Paul states, "The message about the cross is foolishness to those who are perishing, but to us who are being saved it is the power of God." At least one contemporary commentary tells us that "the ancient Greek word that Paul uses . . . more accurately denotes madness or senselessness." [38] In some ways, we can read Don Quixote as a "fool for Christ," even if only by analogy. His persecution is similar to what we might expect if we promote a belief system that significant sectors of the society still consider absurd and silly. However, even if chivalry is dead, Christianity is not. Perhaps this is the problem: the ridiculousness of Don Quixote and his outrageous antics were surprising and shocking enough to get the attention of worldly citizens of the Spanish Golden Age, while the practice of Christianity has been so well institutionalized in our own that it cannot raise a stir. Foucault writes:

> The great theme of the madness of the cross . . . began to disappear in the seventeenth century . . . Or rather, it continued . . . It no longer demanded that human reason relinquish its pride and its certainties to lose itself in the great unreason of sacrifice. . . . [After the world converted to Christianity] Christians themselves then considered Christian unreason as peripheral to reason, now seen as being identical to the wisdom of God made man.[39]

35. Ibid., 216.

36. Henry Higuera provides a complex analysis of not only references to Dulcinea but also to natural law theology and concepts of a just war. Unfortunately, there is not space to do justice to his argument, and the reader should know that he argues that "Cervantes thinks that the Bible has vitally important things to teach us about the world," but that "the Bible is not of decisively higher rank, as a source of truth, than Don Quixote itself." See Eros and Empire, 187.

37. Michel Foucault, History of Madness, trans. Jonathan Murphy and Jean Khalfa, ed. Jean Khalfa (London: Routledge, 2006), 30.

38. Rowland Croucher and others, "The Madness of the Cross," John Mark Ministries, no pages, online: http:// www.jmm.org.au/articles/9396.htm (accessed June 1, 2013).

39. Foucault, History of Madness, 152.

The brutal impact of Christ on the Cross was normalized, and the barber and priest attempt to do just that to Don Quixote. At least some of the time, Don Quixote's behavior does remind us of how shocking and risky sacrifice should be. The cultural and institutional mainstreaming of Christianity in the United States has taken the edge off the Christian "madness of the cross" theme, and its consequences have produced at least one effect not wholly unlike that caused by the Catholic faith in seventeenth-century Spain: orthodoxy leading to complacency. Don Quixote does some unequivocally foolish and even stupid acts; we have to be careful not to take the Romantic reading too far in evaluating our own practice of "shocking" Christianity. However, Don Quixote's lunacy does bear a slight resemblance to Christ's "lunacy" in that Quixote risks life and limb (however ineffectively) to succor those (he perceives are) in need.

Don Quixote is finally important to Christians because it portrays human conflict in both worldly and divinely created orders. The theme is introduced early in the novel when the housekeeper asks Don Quixote, "Wouldn't it be better to stay peacefully in your house and not wander around the world searching for bread that's made from something better than wheat?"[40] Implied but not forgotten in his mission to bring back knight errantry is a more subtle class conflict. First of all, Alonso Quixano takes a title of nobility, one to which, even as poor country gentlemen, he is not entitled. The antics of the Duke and Duchess in Part II, the highest nobility in the novel, soon remind us of how far out of line the "Don" has wandered. Having heard about Quixote's adventures through the published version of Part I, the Duke and Duchess lure Don Quixote and Sancho into elaborately-staged pranks through which they are repeatedly humiliated.[41]

It is clear also that Don Quixote and Sancho have transgressed their places in the cosmic order. Immediately before he meets the Duke and the Duchess, Don Quixote mistakes millers and fishermen for captors, destroys a boat, and nearly drowns. Don Quixote and Sancho slink off in resignation: "and dismissing the pair as madmen, they went away, the millers to their mills and the fisherman to their huts. As for Don Quixote and Sancho, they went back to their animals, and to being animals."[42] The rhetoric of the passage suggests that everyone returns to his or her rightful station, except for Don Quixote, who returns to "being" an "animal," or in some

40. Cervantes, *Don Quixote*, trans. Grossman, 55.
41. Cervantes, *Don Quixote*, trans. Rutherford, Part II, chapters 30–35.
42. Ibid.

translations, his "beast-like existence."[43] The passage thus invokes the idea of the Great Chain of Being, a grand organizational scheme whose concepts were "part of the intellectual furniture of every educated Spanish writer and reader."[44] Adopted from Aristotle, Christian thinkers used this concept to explain how God arranged each created being, from and highest archangel to the smallest stone. To wish for a superior position was arrogance, but to relinquish oneself to an inferior one was not only degrading but demoralizing. This teaching pervades the work of Spanish devotional writers contemporary to Cervantes, who write that in this series established by God "none usurps the position of its neighbor."[45] As Ian Johnston notes, "For human beings the central moral purpose of life was to acknowledge one's position on the scale," and this position had accompanying privileges and responsibilities.[46]

In Cervantes' time, the link between social and divine orders was strong. In *Don Quixote* class rank carries moral obligations, just as created rank does in God's Great Chain of Being. Cervantes describes another guest hosted by the Duke and the Duchess, "one of those grave churchmen who rule noblemen's houses: one of those who, not having been born noble themselves, never manage to teach those who are noble how to live up to their rank."[47] This comment lambasts the unethical conduct of the Duke and Duchess, reasserts *noblesse oblige*, and criticizes corrupt clergy. Taken as a whole, this episode returns us to Paul's statements in 1 Corinthians 1:18 and 26–27, that God's system is beyond earthly wisdom; he does indeed use the "despised" to bring low the "high" or esteemed. The Duke and the Duchess' cruelty render them despicable and Quixote a light by comparison; yet, that does not mean that Quixote can change his social station in life as easily as do the knights in Quixote's books of chivalry, where "there are some [who] were and no longer are, and others [who] are what they once were not."[48] Cervantes' reading of the Bible, his knowledge of Catholic theology, and his life in imperial Spain puts him far off from

43. Cervantes, *Don Quixote*, trans. J.M. Cohen (New York: Penguin, 1950), 661.

44. Green, *Spain and the Western Tradition*, 2:15.

45. Fray Luis de Leon (d. 1591) in *De los nobres de Cristo*, quoted in Green, *Spain and the Western Tradition*, 2:15.

46. Ian Johnston, "Ancient and Modern Science: Some Observations," hellenica. world.com, *http://www.mlahanas.de/Greeks/Evolution.htm* (accessed June, 23 2013).

47. Cervantes, *Don Quixote*, trans. Rutherford, 696.

48. Ibid.

our post-Romantic perspective. The housekeeper's conservative advice, although stultifying, is also on the question of motive. What do we hope to gain by climbing the social ladder or by achieving worldly fame and honor?

Conclusion

Don Quixote is a book about reading books, living life, and the difference between the two. Its contribution to Western civilization cannot be overestimated, since Cervantes' interest in developing a realist narrative that remedies some of the faults of previous fictional genres lead to the first of modern novels. Formally, this novel introduced ironic narration through the use of multiple narrators, one of which is known for his "tendency" to lie. Thematically, *Don Quixote* asks us to decide if its protagonist is truly mad, noble, or both, and it asks us to think seriously about the overlapping and dividing lines between fiction, history, truth, and reality. Cervantes' life experiences and other writings suggest that he was an orthodox Catholic who nevertheless critiqued the Church's errors, as well as Christianity's great truths: the vitality of Christ's sacrifice on the cross, the difference between faith in the unseen and faith in a fantasy, and finally, the difference between equality of the soul and equality of worldly position. Lest our admiration for our impossible fool and dreamer grow too great, we have to remember that Cervantes allowed Don Quixote to die in the end, returning him to sanity and the bosom of the Catholic Church. On the other hand, although Don Quixote dies, Cervantes did not succeed in killing him off. As successive generations of readers have shown, Cervantes ironic techniques opened the gateway to new readings, making the question of "Whose Quixote is it?" an invitation to consider a host of ethical issues on interpretation, truth, and having the final word.

CHAPTER 5: PHYSICS

Francis Bacon, *Novum Organon*

BY LESLIE WICKMAN

Introduction

FRANCIS BACON WAS BORN in London in 1561, the fifth son of Sir Nicolas Bacon, Queen Elizabeth I's Keeper of the Great Seal. His family was well connected in Elizabethan society. Bacon was educated at Trinity College, Cambridge, and later completed his study of law at the Honourable Society of Gray's Inn. He served the British Parliament from 1584 to 1617, and was knighted by King James I in 1603. Bacon acted as solicitor general, attorney general, Privy Councilor, Lord Keeper of the Great Seal (following in his father's footsteps), and ultimately Lord Chancellor. In 1621, after becoming Viscount St. Alban, his political career disintegrated when he was impeached by Parliament for accepting bribes. With his political career behind him, Bacon was able to dedicate more time to his various writing projects. Many of his works were published while still in office, but he became even more productive after his departure from public life. Bacon died in 1626, allegedly after an experiment with freezing a chicken to preserve its meat left him with a deadly respiratory ailment.

Bacon's avant-garde work on science, *Novum Organon (New Instrument): True Suggestions for the Interpretation of Nature,* was so named as a response to Aristotle's collection of works of logic, which were dubbed the *"Organon"* by ancient commentators, particularly Aristotle's followers, the

Peripatetics. Bacon's *Novum Organon* was originally intended to be part of a larger collection of six books entitled *Instauratio Magna* (The Great Instauration, or The Great Renewal, 1653) that was never finished. *Novum Organon* itself appears to be incomplete, as within it the author proposes a list of topics to be addressed to which he never returns. *Novum Organon* was first published in 1620, at a time when a great deal of revolutionary observational astronomy was being done by the likes of Tycho Brahe, Johannes Kepler, and Galileo Galilei. In fact Galileo's *Sidereal Messenger* was published just a decade earlier (in 1610), announcing a surfeit of empirical evidence for a heliocentric solar system to a public still overwhelmingly adhering to the geocentric Aristotelian worldview. The recently past medieval period left the Aristotelian Scholastics striving to make Aristotle's philosophy relevant to their day.

The ancient Greek Aristotelians believed that the variety of phenomena observed in nature followed rational patterns as opposed to randomly occurring behaviors, and thus nature could be understood. The Aristotelians used logic to deduce various theorems about nature from their "First Principles" (things held as obviously true and beyond question), such as the following:

- Everything goes around the earth; therefore the earth must be at the center of the cosmos.

- The heavens are the divine realm; so the heavens must be perfect and the earth imperfect.

- The sphere is the perfect shape; therefore celestial objects must be perfect spheres.

This Aristotelian worldview prevailed for nearly two millennia, from about 340 BCE until at least 1600 CE. During the Scientific Revolution of the Renaissance, empirical observations of nature increasingly revealed the fallacies of the Aristotelian methods. While deductive reasoning was very applicable to philosophy and mathematics, it did not work as well for natural science. As Bacon writes, "The art of logic . . . has tended more to confirm errors, than to disclose truth."[1]

Francis Bacon wrote this pivotal tome as a rejection of the longstanding Aristotelian approach to natural philosophy (the precursor to natural

1. Francis Bacon, *Novum Organum*, ed. Joseph Devey, Forgotten Books (New York: Collier, 1901), Preface, 7.

science) as proceeding logically from First Principles. Bacon insisted instead that truth must be discovered; that meant the natural world could only be understood properly through the inductive tools of observation and experimentation, as opposed to logical deductions from First Principles by way of the revered practice of philosophy passed down from the ancient Greeks. Bacon's opening statement in the preface to his book states, "They who have presumed to dogmatize on nature, as on some well investigated subject, either from self-conceit or arrogance, and in the professional style, have inflicted the greatest injury on philosophy and learning."[2]

It is important to note that Bacon was not the only intellectual of his day (or even earlier) who was concerned about the growing conflict between logically deduced theorems and empirical observations. Others credited as early developers of the Scientific Method for their emphasis on the importance of observation, experimentation, measurements, and mathematical analysis include Roger Bacon (1214–1294; very early advocate of the scientific method), Galileo Galilei (1564–1642; provided observational evidence for the heliocentric model), Robert Hooke (1635–1703; used the scientific method to make significant contributions in cell biology, astrophysics, telecommunications, and transportation), and Isaac Newton (1642–1727; used the scientific method to make significant contributions in mechanics, gravity, optics, and calculus).

Summary of Book

Novum Organon, loosely translated, means "New Method" (or more precisely, "New Instrument"), and that is what Bacon is proposing for the scientific enterprise in his book: a new instrument or method for interpreting nature. As the ancients have debated the extreme positions of absolute knowledge (First Principles) and absolute doubt (World as unknowable), Bacon is attempting to carve a middle path that encourages a bottom-up approach that values the senses, empirical data, and critical thinking.

In the Preface, Bacon notes that logic and reason alone do not yield results that correlate with empirical observations. He then makes clear that he is attempting to split the pursuit of science apart from philosophy and its love affair with deductive logic, stating that the two disciplines (in Bacon's parlance, "tribes" or "kindred families") can assist each other. However, in the process he refers to those who choose "anticipation of the mind" (i.e.,

2. Ibid., Preface, 5.

philosophy, useful for cultivation of the sciences) over "interpretation of nature" (i.e., science, useful for discovery) as perhaps being motivated "on account of their haste or from motives arising from their ordinary life, or because they are unable from weakness of mind to comprehend and embrace the other (which must necessarily be the case with by far the greater number)."[3] So it is hard to imagine that he was finding many followers, financial backers, or potential collaborators among the philosophers of his day.

In Book 1 of *Novum Organon*, Bacon mounts a rather caustic critique of Aristotelian philosophy as applied to the study of nature, or natural philosophy. He argues quite forcefully that Aristotle's widespread popularity and far-reaching influence put scientific progress on hold for nearly 2,000 years. He harshly criticizes the Aristotelian use of the syllogism for winning arguments rather than seeking the truth.

Bacon presents a long list of "Aphorisms" summarizing the limitations of the human mind, the futility of continually philosophizing about nature for gaining greater understanding of it, and the madness of trying to deduce truths about nature from traditionally held principles or the depths of the human psyche. He states his own version of the old adage that cautions us against insanely trying the same things over and over again while expecting different results. Drawing from the failures of the past, Bacon explains the need for this "new method," which calls for a new breed of scientists to investigate nature through observation and experimentation. As he states in Book 1, Aphorism 11, "As the present sciences are useless for the discovery of effects, so the present system of logic is useless for the discovery of the sciences."[4] Bacon goes on to condemn the abuse of logic as science in his day, but for the sake of emphasis probably takes his argument a bit too far in claiming, "The syllogism is not applied to the principles of the sciences, and is of no avail in intermediate axioms, as being very unequal to the (subtlety) of nature."[5] Syllogism is an organized approach to reasoning that can be applied to either inductive or deductive processes, and is quite necessary in order to "ascend" (to use Bacon's verbiage) from specific, repeatable scientific data to more generalized theories.

Bacon introduces his discussion of the "idols" that prevent the human mind from seeing nature accurately with these words: "There is no small

3. Ibid., Preface, 9.
4. Ibid., Book 1, Aphorism 11, 12.
5. Ibid., Book 1, Aphorism 13, 13.

difference between the idols of the human mind and the ideas of the Divine mind—that is to say, between certain idle dogmas and the real stamp and impression of created objects, as they are found in nature."[6] He goes on to discuss four types of idols of the mind: Idols of the Tribe, the Den, the Market, and the Theater. Briefly, Idols of the Tribe are common to the entire human race, skewing the perception of nature as viewed from our space-time and sensory capacity limited anthropocentric perspective. Idols of the Den are even more parochial, as each individual person has his or her own blinders that prevent him or her from perceiving nature clearly, be they educational, prejudicial, dispositional, or otherwise. Here Bacon quotes Heraclitus: "men search for knowledge in lesser worlds, and not in the greater or common world."[7] Idols of the Market arise from confusing interactions between people, mainly due to lack of clarity in communication. As Bacon writes, "there arises from a bad and unapt formation of words a wonderful obstruction to the mind."[8] Finally, Idols of the Theater are the "fictitious and theatrical worlds" created in human minds by "various dogmas of peculiar systems of philosophy." All of these idols must be discarded in order for the senses to perceive clearly and for the mind to interpret nature properly.

Bacon goes on to assert that the human mind—left to its innate inclinations—seeks order, simplicity, and connections with what is already familiar. These tendencies or anticipations make us seek to reinforce first impressions and early conclusions, rather than to think critically about them. As Bacon writes, "man always believes more readily that which he prefers . . . his feelings imbue and corrupt his understanding in innumerable and sometimes imperceptible ways."[9] Therefore, the practice of the new method is somewhat counterintuitive, but its disciplined practice enables humans to overcome the innate shortcomings of their comprehension. We naturally seek logically to deduce new theorems from long-held beliefs; we look for connections and affirmations of what we think we already know. Moreover, our senses are flawed and deceive us.

Conversely, the new method uses observation and experimentation to gather and evaluate new data, and in this process the ability to disprove a hypothesis or theory is more powerful than the ability to prove anything. If

6. Ibid., Book 1, Aphorism 23, 16.
7. Ibid., Book 1, Aphorism 42, 21.
8. Ibid., Book 1, Aphorism 43, 21.
9. Ibid., Book 1, Aphorism 49, 26.

experimental results are inconsistent with the hypothesis, then the hypothesis is disproven. However, if experimental results are consistent with the hypothesis, then the new findings merely strengthen the hypothesis, adding to the body of evidence supporting it, but never absolutely proving it.

Ironically, Bacon reveals his own bias toward the familiar when he categorizes "the planetary orbits" as an example of "names of things which have no existence,"[10] even though Copernicus and especially Kepler had already done a decent job of describing the planetary orbits of the solar system in a way that correlated well with empirical observations. This simply goes to show how powerful is the influence of the idols of the tribe, even on a person whose passion is to overcome them. Nonetheless, Bacon clearly believes that his new method can be a great leveler of art, skill, and intellect. His proposal ensures that whoever practices the method properly will achieve good results, thus eradicating the shortcomings and failures of individuals' as well as humanity's mental processes.

Bacon is well-versed in contemporary experimental activities, as evidenced by his comments on Gilbert's writing on magnetism, Galileo's theory of tides, and the newly developed microscope. While holding the pursuit of knowledge above all, he lauds the place and power of discoveries in the hierarchy of human actions, especially as they lead to inventions that give humanity increasing power over the universe of things. Bacon cites three contemporary examples that he believed had the greatest influence on the modern world and the affairs of humankind: the printing press (in the areas of communication and literature), gunpowder (in the area of warfare), and the nautical compass (in the area of navigation and exploration). He shows great faith that such new inventions will not be misused: "Only let mankind regain their rights over nature, assigned to them by the gift of God, and obtain that power, whose exercise will be governed by right reason and true religion."[11]

The takeaway for Book 1 is a wholesale rejection of the philosophical tradition as applied to science, including Plato, Aristotle, the Skeptics, and the Scholastics. This refutation clears the way for Bacon's "new method" for the interpretation of nature, which holds out great hope for the future of science.

In Book 2 of *Novum Organon*, Bacon expounds on his new method in some detail, starting with a discussion of forms (causes, or natural laws)

10. Ibid., Book 1, Aphorism 60, 32.
11. Ibid., Book 1, Aphorism 129, 106.

and natures (basic physical properties of objects, or effects), and the power to transform or "superinduce" objects or substances.[12] The operations of science are 1) the identification of the relevant form (cause or law) of a thing; and 2) the transformation of an object. Transformation of an object depends on what he refers to as latent structure (physical-chemical properties) and latent process (such as biological growth), both of which are by definition hidden or obscure and difficult to understand.

Bacon then attempts to demonstrate his method of discovering the form or law of a nature or effect such as heat. One quickly realizes that, in this exercise, Bacon's method is essentially reductionist in that he attempts to simplify each thing into its component parts, characteristics, and circumstances of occurrence. The concept portrayed involves an attempt to assemble a comprehensive list of instances in which the nature (e.g., of heat) is found, such as the sun's rays, animal dung, and so on, constructing a "table of existence and presence."[13] Then he lists counter-examples or divergences: instances in which the nature (e.g., of heat) is not found in the same items previously listed (such as the sun's rays reflected in the earth's polar regions, or animal dung that has gone cold), thereby constructing a "table of deviation or of absence in proximity."[14] Bacon goes on to construct yet a third list, a "table of the degrees or comparative instances,"[15] listing instances in which the specific nature varies either by degree, or by complete absence. Once these three extensive tables of evidence (or "tables of first review"[16]) are constructed, the Baconian scientist begins his or her analysis, which begins with the process of eliminative induction, or exclusion of nonsensical and contradictory instances that are not consistent with the definition of a form or cause. For example, if the specific nature or effect under investigation is completely absent in a particular instance, then that nature is thus shown not to be caused by the specific form in question. After this initial process of threshing the data to reject exclusions and eliminate errors and inconsistencies, the "liberty of understanding, or commencement of interpretation, or the first vintage"[17] commences, and

12. Ibid., Book 2, Aphorism 1, 108.
13. Ibid., Book 2, Aphorism 11, 123.
14. Ibid., Book 2, Aphorism 12, 123.
15. Ibid., Book 2, Aphorism 13, 136.
16. Ibid., Book 2, Aphorism 21, 159.
17. Ibid., Book 2, Aphorism 20, 152.

the scientist is free to glean whatever affirmative lessons can be learned from the remaining data.

Bacon then addresses the next refining step in his method: that of consideration of prerogative, or privileged, instances. Prerogative instances are occurrences of a specific nature or effect that are especially indicative of a specific form or cause. Bacon assembles the following industrious list of twenty-seven categories of prerogative instances: "solitary . . . migrating . . . conspicuous . . . clandestine . . . constitutive . . . similar . . . singular . . . deviating . . . bordering . . . power . . . accompanying and hostile . . . subjunctive . . . alliance . . . cross . . . divorce . . . gate . . . citing . . . road . . . supplementary . . . lancing . . . rod . . . course . . . doses of nature . . . wrestling . . . suggesting . . . generally useful . . . and magical instances."[18]

Each category is useful in different ways, but all assist the human faculties to clarify or identify more quickly a nature's form or cause, either by pointing the intellect toward the correct conclusion or by prescribing a program of experimentation, investigation, or analysis to be followed, which eventually leads to some conclusion for that research question. These prerogative instances are expedient tools intended to give logical support to the process of induction.

In contrast to the deductive syllogism, which proceeds from the general principle to the specific case, Bacon's inductive method is an attempt to lay out all the evidence for each specific case to be evaluated. Then, through intellectual analysis of instances, one could identify causes and proceed to more general axioms.

Book 2 leaves us with unanswered questions about what additional "supports and corrections to induction"[19] are needed, how exactly axioms are generated by the process, and how (or who) Bacon expects to complete the vast survey of natural history that he considers necessary in order to make his method of interpreting nature viable. His major contributions on forms and natures, or causes and effects, can be summarized as follows: Since causes produce effects, if we do not like the effects and if we know the causes, then by altering the causes we can change the effects. Finally, Bacon wraps up the *Novum Organon* by implying that some of what was lost in humankind's dominion over nature in the biblical "fall" of creation can be, at least, partially restored through science.

18. Ibid., Book 2, Aphorism 52, 288.
19. Ibid., Book 2, Aphorism 52, 289.

Importance of Book

The reaction of Bacon's contemporaries to *Novum Organon* was mixed. The politicians of the day (including King James I, whose pleasure and support Bacon yearned to garner) were less than impressed. However, the scientists and philosophers of the Royal Society of London, founded in 1660, showed their reverence for Bacon by adopting him as their unofficial patron saint. Robert Hooke and other prominent scientists who came after Bacon showed their respect by following his method with their own investigations.

While today's scientific method bears little resemblance to the actual steps employed by Bacon, his criticism and rejection of Aristotelian philosophy (with its reliance on First Principles and the deductive syllogism) helped transform natural philosophy into natural science. His work helped to break the stalemate of progress in understanding nature that had lasted for the preceding two millennia. To be sure, certain elements of Bacon's method, such as experimentation and observation, as well as induction as a process for moving from an accumulation of evidence for a specific case to higher levels of general explanatory power, are key elements of today's scientific method. For these we owe Sir Francis Bacon a debt of gratitude.

Scientists of today make observations, formulate hypothetical explanations, make predictions, do experiments, and create models or theories to answer questions, in the iterative process called the scientific method. (This process is illustrated in Figure 1.) The goal is to obtain a compelling explanation describing observed phenomena, which makes accurate predictions and leads to a better understanding of the universe. The scientific enterprise tries to understand the wide variety of nature's effects as resulting from the action of a relatively small number of basic causes, acting in a seemingly infinite variety of combinations. In other words, scientists use the scientific method to try to simplify our understanding of the world and the way things work. The revolutionary idea behind the scientific method is that simple truths about nature are really the goal of science as opposed to an unattainable starting point. As such, inductive reasoning is well suited to achieving this end. The inductive process is more or less the deductive process in reverse: we start with many observations of and experiments with nature, and move toward a few robust explanations of how things work.

OBSERVE -> HYPOTHESIZE -> PREDICT -> TEST ->

CHECK RESULTS -> MODIFY AS REQUIRED -> REPEAT

Figure 1: Diagram of the Scientific Method

It is essential to keep in mind that the scientific method by its very structure and processes is only capable of disproving, rather than proving theories. As Bacon wrote, "in establishing any true axiom, the negative instance is the most powerful."[20] This induction-based method is structured to question whether experimental results are consistent with hypotheses and theories. If the test results are not consistent, then the hypothesis or theory is disproven; if the test results are consistent, then current evidence shows support for that particular hypothesis or theory. Indeed, the scientific enterprise seeks the best explanation possible given the existing evidence, realizing that new evidence could be discovered at any time that would overturn the best theories of today. Bacon fully understood these implications: "Our method, though difficult in its operation, is easily explained. It consists in determining the degrees of certainty."[21] A more recent quote from the late Nobel prize-winning physicist and father of quantum electrodynamics Richard Feynman echoes Bacon: "Scientific knowledge is a body of statements of varying degrees of certainty—some most unsure, some nearly sure, but none absolutely certain."[22]

These statements apply across the board to all scientific endeavors, but Bacon's statement seems almost prophetic when we consider the discoveries of quantum theory more than three hundred years after it was published. Reflecting on the then nascent theory, and exemplifying the comfortable deterministic outlook of modernity (often identified with belief in God), Albert Einstein wrote in a 1926 letter to Max Born, "I, at any rate, am convinced that *He* [God] does not throw dice."[23]

Science author and geologist Steven Schafersman has this to say about the scientific method:

20. Ibid., Book 1, Aphorism 46, 24.

21. Ibid., Preface, 6.

22. Richard P. Feynman, quoted by Melville Y. Stewart, *Science and Religion in Dialog* (West Sussex, UK: Wiley-Blackwell, 2010), 261.

23. Albert Einstein, quoted by Morris Kline, *Mathematics and the Search for Knowledge* (New York: Oxford University Press, 1985), 242.

The scientific method has proven to be the most reliable and successful method of thinking in human history, and it is quite possible to use scientific thinking in other human endeavors. For this reason, critical thinking—the application of scientific thinking to all areas of study and topics of investigation . . . is being encouraged as a universal ideal . . . The important point is this: critical thinking is perhaps the most important skill a student can learn in school . . . since if you master its skills, you know how to think successfully and reach reliable conclusions, and such ability will prove valuable in any human endeavor . . . including the humanities, social sciences, commerce, law, journalism, and government, as well as in scholarly and scientific pursuits. Since critical thinking and scientific thinking are . . . the same thing, only applied for different purposes, it is therefore reasonable to believe that if one learns scientific thinking . . . one learns, at the same time, the most important skill a student can possess—critical thinking. This, to my mind, is perhaps the foremost reason for college students to study science, no matter what one's eventual major, interest, or profession."[24]

Importance of the Book for Christians

From the very beginning of the scientific enterprise until the present day, many prominent scientists believed that science was a tool for discovering truth in the physical, created world. Francis Bacon confirms the basis for this in his quote from King Solomon in Proverbs 25:2, "It is the glory of God to conceal a thing, but the glory of a king to search it out."[25]

The following group of great thinkers who were instrumental in the development of the scientific method were all devoted believers:

- Roger Bacon, Franciscan friar (1214–1294; very early advocate of the scientific method)

- Francis Bacon, professing Christian (1561–1626; England's "father of modern science")

- Galileo Galilei, devout Catholic (1564–1642; provided observational evidence for the heliocentric model)

---

24. Steven D. Schafersman, *An Introduction to Science: Scientific Thinking and the Scientific Method* (1994), http://www.geo.sunysb.edu/esp/files/scientific-method.html (accessed June 27, 3013).

25. Bacon, *Novum Organum*, Book 1, Aphorism 129, 105.

- Robert Hooke, son of a minister/curate (1635–1703; used the scientific method to make significant contributions in cell biology, astrophysics, telecommunications, and transportation)

- Isaac Newton, student of theology (1642–1727; used the scientific method to make significant contributions in mechanics, gravity, optics, and calculus)

Furthermore, Christian apologist Michael Covington makes these points:

- Modern science arose in Christianized Western Europe.

- Jews, Christians, and Muslims believe in a Creator who made an orderly, rational, understandable universe and gave us permission to investigate and utilize it, thereby legitimizing science and technology.

- Conversely, animists believe that rocks, trees, etc. (things we think of as inanimate objects) have souls, and that we should not tamper with nature for fear of offending the spirits.

- Most Hindus and Buddhists generally believe that the physical world is an illusion or distraction that we should try to transcend or get free of.

- Atheists cannot even explain why it is possible for us to understand the universe.[26]

As Bacon and others have argued, we humans do not know very much about God's creation intuitively or by what seems obvious, as shown by the demise of Aristotle's First Principles. This theme is echoed in various passages of scripture (Isa 55:9; 1 Cor 13:12).

The Judeo-Christian tradition promotes belief in a God who created an orderly, rational, knowable cosmos, who invites his creatures to investigate his creation, because this will reveal knowledge not only of nature, but also of who he is. This same theme is also seen in various passages of scripture (Ps 19:1–2, 34:8, 97:6; Rom 1:19–20; 1 Thess 5:21).

Therefore the scientific method can help us as we seek truth. But can the scientific method help us pursue truth in disciplines other than the natural sciences? Are some topics beyond the scope of scientific investigation? Some would argue that science and spirit are mutually exclusive realms, because spiritual matters cannot be detected or tested by natural,

26. Michael A. Covington, *Christianity and Science, 1: Scientific Method* (1999), http://www.covingtoninnovations.com/tough/tough3.html (accessed June 27, 3013).

empirical means, while others would disagree. When it comes to matters of science and spirit, or theology, the search for order and meaning typically manifests itself in different ways. Science is concerned with discovering and understanding natural phenomena; the domain of science is natural order. Science seeks to know how things are, not so much why they are that way, nor how they should be. On the other hand, theology is concerned with the source, purpose, and meaning of everything; the domain of theology is nature's purpose.

Therefore, science and theology each have their place and should serve to complement rather than contradict each other. A lack of understanding about either science or theology can make people think they must choose one or the other, but a deeper, more complete understanding of each enables us to embrace them both without contradiction. If we start with the notion that truth exists about both God and nature, then those absolute truths cannot logically contradict each other. The more we correctly understand about each discipline, the better understanding we have of the whole picture. Our paths as individuals and as a society to truth about God and truth about nature are iterative: we might take two steps forward and one step back as we continue our investigations. This is in keeping with the scientific method, which, when practiced properly, holds knowledge tentatively, recognizing that new evidence might be discovered at any time that would make previous theories, or even laws, invalid.

A relevant example of the scientific method in action in Bacon's era begins with the Aristotelian view of the sun moving around the earth. Copernicus postulated, and later Galileo made observations with his telescope producing evidence that, in fact, the earth revolves around the sun, not the other way around as previously held as an obvious truth, or First Principle. This scientific revision was possible because of newly acquired empirical evidence, and it enabled humanity to view traditionally held ideas from a larger frame of reference. A similar thought revolution or paradigm shift occurred in moving from Newtonian Physics to Relativity Theory. Without going into the details, suffice it to say that scientific concepts like gravity, time, and space itself, which scientists and lay people alike thought were fairly well understood, all were turned upside down in the process.

In the same way, no one can honestly claim to have God or Christianity completely figured out. Certainly Jesus' life and teachings presented a paradigm shift to the theology of his time and culture, and we are still striving to understand the full implications of that shift.

As 1 Corinthians 13:12 says, "For now we see through a glass, darkly; but then face to face: now I know in part; but then shall I know even as also I am known" (KJV). While Paul's words in this passage were meant to apply to our knowledge and understanding of God, they also serve as a metaphor for our knowledge and understanding of his creation as well. The verse reminds us that our access to truth is tempered in this life by incomplete knowledge, limited understanding, and less than perfect interpretation of the data. This should lead us to practice our disciplines with healthy amounts of modesty, humility, and even skepticism. It seems that Bacon would agree, as he writes in Book 1 of *Novum Organon*, "The lame . . . in the path outstrip the swift who wander from it, and it is clear that the very skill and swiftness of him who runs not in the right direction must increase his aberration. Our method of discovering the sciences is such as to leave little to the acuteness and strength of wit, and indeed rather to level wit and intellect."[27]

Charles Darwin held the following opinion, which relates to this discussion: "In scientific investigation, it is permitted to invent any hypotheses and if it explains various large and independent classes of facts, it rises to the ranks of well grounded theory."[28] Consider the following two statements —one from 2003, the other from the third century:

1. "Science concerns itself with ideas about the world that can be tested, at least in principle. To be tested here means to be put into practice and seen to work... So can there be a science of spirit? I believe there can. We simply need to devise testable hypotheses about the nature of spirit ... Spirit, because of its high complexity, has the ability to control matter. If we find complex and measurable material structures behaving in ways that cannot be explained by the properties of matter, we may postulate that spirit is at work."[29]

2. "If upon entering some home you saw that everything there was well-tended, neat, and decorative, you would believe that some master was in charge of it, and that he himself was superior to those good things. So too in the home of this world, when you see providence, order, and law in the heavens and on earth, believe there is a Lord and Author of

27. Bacon, *Novum Organum*, Book 1, Aphorism 61, 34.

28. Darwin, *The Variation of Animals and Plants under Domestication,* vol. 1 (Baltimore: Johns Hopkins University Press, 1998), 25.

29. Jeffrey Nichols, *Scientific Method* (2003), http://www.naturaltheology.net (accessed December 9, 2003).

the universe, more beautiful than the stars themselves and the various parts of the whole world."[30]

To put this in another way, as we make our observations of nature, if we perceive order and complexity that exceed the normal operation of the laws of nature, then we can hypothesize that there is something more—something extraordinary or supernatural—at work. So perhaps the scientific method can be used as a tool to organize our thought processes and inform us in matters of spirit as we seek out truth in various disciplines. At the very least, the scientific method may be seen a tool for discovering God's creativity and wisdom in nature's wonders.

As Bacon writes: "For man, by the fall, lost at once his state of innocence, and his empire over creation, both of which can be partially recovered even in this life, the first by religion and faith, the second by the arts and sciences. For creation did not become entirely and utterly rebellious by the curse, but in consequence of Divine decree, 'in the sweat of thy brow shalt thou eat bread,' she is compelled by our labors (not assuredly by our disputes or magical ceremonies), at length, to afford mankind in some degree his bread, that is to say, to supply man's daily wants."[31]

---

30. Minucius Felix, *Faith of the Early Fathers: Volume I, Pre-Nicene and Nicene Eras*, ed. W.A. Jurgens (Collegeville, MN: The Order of St. Benedict, 1970), 109.

31. Bacon, *Novum Organum*, Book 2, Aphorism 52, 290.

CHAPTER 6: POLITICS

John Locke, *Second Treatise of Government*

BY JENNIFER E. WALSH

Introduction

THE SECOND TREATISE: *An Essay Concerning the True Original, Extent, and End of Civil Government* (1690) by Englishman John Locke (1632–1704) is a philosophical discourse on the nature of government that was birthed after a time of great religious and political turmoil. While Locke was still a youth, the English Civil War between Parliamentarians and Royalists, waged over the limits of government power, culminated in the public execution of King Charles I.

The successive republican government under the newly established Commonwealth of England, led by Puritan Oliver Cromwell, lasted only eleven years. The death of Cromwell in 1658 and the increasing discontentedness of the people under popular rule led to the Restoration of the monarchy under Charles's son, King Charles II. The new king, who had been previously exiled in France, was sympathetic toward Catholics, exacerbating tensions with Protestants that had lingered since the Church of England separated from the Vatican a century earlier. During his rule, Charles II tried to enact a royal decree to extend religious and political freedom toward Catholics, but this policy was blocked by Protestants in Parliament. In return, Parliament introduced legislation to exclude Catholics from political office. Specifically, Protestant opponents of the king wanted to preclude

Charles's Catholic brother and presumed heir to the throne, James, from becoming king.

To prevent these Exclusion bills from passing, Charles dissolved Parliament on three different occasions, and upon his death in 1685, James succeeded in becoming king—James II. His reign, however, was brief. When James's son by his second wife, who was also Catholic, was born in 1688, anti-Catholic opponents drove him out of the country in a "Glorious Revolution." Parliament then extended an invitation to William of Orange, husband of James's Protestant daughter, Mary, to assume the throne.

Locke was a young scholar at Oxford during the era of Commonwealth rule, but by the time he began his position as a faculty fellow, the monarchy had been restored with the ascension of Charles II. In his early writings, Locke espoused traditionalist views on politics and religion, arguing, for example, that kings were all-powerful and had the authority to curtail any religious practices that deviated from the traditional Protestant Christian faith. However, three life experiences contributed to Locke's reconsideration of this position. First, like all Oxford students, Locke had to choose between three courses of study: theology, law, or medicine. He chose medicine and focused his academic energies on the field of botany. Through his scientific education, Locke developed a keen appreciation for the natural laws evident in creation. Moreover, his training in scientific observation taught him to be attentive to patterns and to use reason to explain experiences and events. Over time, this training prompted him to make detailed notes regarding his observations about moral and philosophical matters, which informed his thoughts on natural law, human nature, and, eventually, the natural limits on power.

Second, his decision to study medicine gave him the opportunity to recommend a successful lifesaving course of treatment for a prominent English politician, Sir Anthony Ashley Cooper, who later became the first Earl of Shaftesbury. Shaftesbury's gratitude prompted him to seek Locke's consultation on other matters, and Locke eventually left his academic position at Oxford to become Shaftesbury's personal secretary. During the reign of Charles II, Shaftesbury held a position of political leadership as Lord Chancellor, Speaker of the House of Lords, which provided Locke with the opportunity to observe government operations from the perspective of a political insider.[1]

1. Alan Ryan, *On Politics: A History of Political Thought from Herodotus to the Present* (New York: Liveright, 2012), 453–96.

Third, Locke traveled to France in the late 1670s, and while he was there he observed the successful co-existence of Protestants and Catholics in civil society. This led him to reject his previously rigid views on political control of religion in favor of a more expansive view of religious liberty. In his *Letter Concerning Toleration* (1689), Locke later explained that the government could not—and should not—attempt to legislate religion because it had no natural authority over religious faith and thus could not legitimately coerce subjects to espouse one belief over another. Rather, the natural separation between political government and religious institutions meant that for matters of spiritual conscience, people ought to be left alone. While decidedly Protestant in his own thinking, Locke argued that employing coercive means against Catholics in order to compel disavowal or conversion was both ineffective and unjust.

Locke's evolved views on the limits of government are reflected in his political masterpiece, *Two Treatises of Government*. Published in 1690, it was initially believed that Locke wrote this volume in response to the Glorious Revolution of 1688; however, scholars today assert that many sections of his discourse were written years earlier. Book One, or the *First Treatise*, was a lengthy and pointed rebuttal to arguments raised in a 1679 posthumous printing of a volume by Sir Robert Filmer promoting the divine right of kings. Manuscript evidence suggests that Locke had already penned much of what we know now as Book Two, or the *Second Treatise*, by 1679–1680, and had revised and expanded the *Second Treatise* in 1683. A third "middle section" of the volume was destroyed when political tensions resulted in Locke's expulsion from Oxford in 1685 and the execution of Locke's colleagues for treasonous writings, but the two surviving books were edited once again in 1689 and published later that same year.[2]

Copies of Locke's essays were regularly imported by the American colonists in the years leading up to the Revolution, and the *Second Treatise* steadily gained in popularity as tensions with the British monarchy began to rise.[3] He was highly influential among the American founders, including

2. Locke directly acknowledges this missing section in his preface to the volume: "Reader, Thou hast here the Beginning and End of a Discourse concerning Government; what Fate has otherwise disposed of the Papers that should have filled up in the middle, and were more than all the rest, 'tis not worth while to tell thee." See John Locke and Peter Laslett, *Two Treatises of Government* (Cambridge: Cambridge University Press, 1988), 137.

3. Locke's successful refutation of Filmer meant that, by the time of the American Revolution, this first book of the volume was largely ignored. This continues into the

Thomas Jefferson and John Adams, and some of the most oft-quoted and inspirational passages of the Declaration of Independence were influenced directly by Locke's ideas in this volume.

Summary of Locke's Second Treatise of Government

The State of Nature, Civil Society, and the Origin of Government

In the *Second Treatise*, Locke introduces and develops the premise that government is a human institution designed to remedy the inconveniences that arise from complex human interactions.[4] Civil society is formed through a voluntary social contract, and the government that results is neither divine in origin nor is it superior to those whom it governs. Moreover, the power of government is not absolute. Instead, the responsibility of government is limited to securing the common good by protecting and preserving property—that is, "lives, liberties, and estates"—from domestic threats and foreign injury.[5]

Locke reasons that in a society without formal government—a condition he refers to as the "state of nature"—people are born into the human race perfectly free "to order their actions and dispose of their possessions, and persons as they think fit," and perfectly equal, "wherein all the power and jurisdiction is reciprocal, no one having more than another."[6] But, in contrast to Thomas Hobbes, who described the state of nature as violent and war-like, Locke asserts that peaceful co-existence is possible because natural law governs human behavior. Locke maintains that God created nature with a system of laws for our good; these laws not only advance our self-preservation, but they also include a right and duty to respect and protect the rights of others. Furthermore, these laws are knowable by all

present day, with many reprints of Locke containing only the more generally applicable *Second Treatise*.

4. Although many reprints of *Two Treatises of Government* are still in circulation, the version edited by Peter Laslett is considered to be among the most definitive. It is reprinted from an early copy of the manuscript donated to Christ's College, Cambridge, in 1764, and is considered to be the most accurate of versions in print today. All quoted passages are identified by Book number (the *Second Treatise* is Book II), section number, and line number. Passages have been amended to account for modern spelling and capitalization usage, but everything else is consistent with the 1764 version.

5. Locke, *Two Treastises,* II, §123, 16. Locke defines the term "property" in a way that describes our proprietary interests in life, liberty, and personal property.

6. Ibid., II, §4, 4–8.

because God created people with the ability to reason so that they might understand "that being all equal and independent, no one ought to harm another in his life, health, liberty, or possessions."[7] Humanity's inherent freedom is not an invitation to licentiousness, however, for people are still bound by the restraints of natural law. However, people were created for the purpose of doing God's will for his good pleasure; therefore, a person has the freedom "to dispose, and order, as he lists, his person, actions, possessions, and his whole property within the allowance of those laws under which he is; and therein not to be subject to the arbitrary will of another, but freely follow his own."[8]

Crime can occur in the state of nature. However, in a world without formal government or common earthly judge, each person is authorized to impose punishment on the offender in order to right the wrong that has been done. No person has jurisdictional authority over another, and thus, in the state of nature, anyone may execute judgment in order to exact retribution or to deter future transgressions. Only those limitations inherent in natural law, such as requiring punishments to be proportional to offenses, apply. The law of proportionality is suspended, however, when threats against the life of innocent people put an aggressor into a "state of war" with victims. In this situation, the people being threatened have a fundamental obligation to use lethal force to preserve themselves and to keep themselves safe, even if no harm has yet been inflicted. Furthermore, the right of self-preservation also applies when someone tries to exert absolute power over another without that person's consent. While this might seem a less egregious offense, Locke maintains that any person who would intentionally deprive others of their liberty would also be likely to take their lives if given the opportunity.[9]

Concern for survival also leads Locke to develop a comprehensive view of property that includes an explicit right to appropriate natural resources for self-preservation. Drawing upon the biblical principle of reaping and sowing, Locke's view of property includes the right to use "the labor of [one's] body, and the work of [one's] hands" so as to fulfill the command of God to work given to humankind in scripture.[10] Thus, when people use the gifts that God has given to them, they are entitled to the fruit of their

7. Ibid., II, §7, 7–10.
8. Ibid., II, §57, 24–28.
9. Ibid., II, §18.
10. Ibid., II, §27, 3–4.

labor. For example, farmers who expend labor to cultivate the land may consider the resulting produce their property, since they combined their efforts with the resources given by God to benefit themselves and others. Others need not worry about farmers taking too much for themselves, for the hoarding of goods is limited by the natural law of spoilage; excess food rots before it can be consumed and thus deters people from harvesting more than what they can use. However, the invention of money limited the usefulness of these natural laws. Labor is now valuable because it results in a gain of money, which, unlike other commodities, may be hoarded as it does not rot or spoil. Consequently, some people will use their labor to stockpile an excess of money, land, and non-perishable goods resulting in inequities between those who possess more and those who possess less. While Locke does not think this is inherently problematic as people have the right to use their property, e.g., labor, as they see fit, the protection of property rights becomes more challenging as land and other resources become scarcer.

Although people could live indefinitely in the state of nature under the laws of nature provided by God, Locke proposes that people are likely to voluntarily come together to form a civil society in order to protect better life, liberty, and property against transgressors and enemies. When they do so, the social contract requires participants to divest themselves of their natural rights to be their own legislative and executive authorities and to transfer that power over to a common judge, "which . . . is the [legislature], or magistrates appointed by it."[11] While this common judge may be a king or other royal ruler, Locke rejects the idea that civil society could appoint an absolute monarch. The defining characteristic of a civil society is voluntary and mutual submission to an earthly judge; therefore, if a sovereign power were to reign with absolute authority, he or she would be above the law, not under it. For Locke, this is a *non sequitur*, for "no [one] in civil society can be exempted from the law of it."[12]

Limits on Government

Locke posits that identifying the limits placed on governmental power begins by first acknowledging the limits placed on paternal power. Children are born as free creatures with rational capacities, but offspring are

11. Ibid., II, §89, 16.
12. Ibid., II, §94, 32.

not considered fully free and equal until rational capacities have developed. While in their infancy, they are placed under the authority of mother and father, who are charged by God to care for, educate, and supervise them until they reach the age of majority. Parental authority, which Locke asserts is equally shared between men and women, is naturally limited to those temporal things that relate to the child's education and moral training; it does not extend to areas beyond parental control, nor does it extend into adulthood. Mothers, for example, do not have the power to enact "standing rules, which shall be of perpetual obligation," nor can they "[e]nforce the observation of them with capital punishments."[13] Similarly, fathers do not have authority over the life or property of their adult offspring, for at some point the "father's empire then ceases, and he can from thence forwards no more dispose of the liberty of his son, than that of any other man."[14] Piety toward mother and father extends into adulthood, but the "honor and respect [owed to the parent] . . . puts no scepter into the father's hand, no sovereign power of commanding. He has no dominion over his sons' property or actions, nor any right, that his will should prescribe to his sons in all things."[15]

Just as parental authority is limited over children born free, governmental authority is similarly constrained over adults who voluntarily enter into civil society. First, the government must abide by that "fundamental natural law, which is . . . the preservation of the society, and (as far as will consist with the public good) of every person in it."[16] Accordingly, government must use its power at home or abroad not to serve its own ends, but to secure effectively the "peace, safety, and public good of the people."[17] It must also apply only "established, settled, known law, received and allowed by common consent to be the standard of right and wrong."[18] Laws may not be arbitrarily imposed, and all laws—including laws of taxation—must be enacted by majority consent. Second, the government must identify an impartial judge who has the authority to settle disputes under established law. Without this, people might be inclined to be too harsh or too lenient on transgressors. Third, it must be able to enforce and execute sentences on

13. Ibid., II, §65, 19–23.
14. Ibid., II, §65, 33–35.
15. Ibid., II, §69, 14–21.
16. Ibid., II, §134, 6–8.
17. Ibid., II, §131, 21.
18. Ibid., II, §124, 5–7.

those who transgress. Otherwise, victims may try to remedy injustices on their own. Finally, laws enacted by the consent of the governed may supplement the laws of nature, but they cannot contradict this "eternal rule of all men," for natural law was instituted by God for the good of all people.[19]

Abuses of Government

According to Locke, a good government acts only on the consent of its people, seeks to protect life, liberty, and property, and enacts laws to secure the protection and common good of the community; bad government does the exact opposite. Governments that are imposed on the people by unlawful conquest, violence, or force lack legitimacy and can never be considered just. Moreover, Locke argues that descendants of those who were initially conquered have a right to free themselves from ongoing tyranny, for "no government can have a right to obedience from a people who have not freely consented to it."[20]

In domestic settings, governments can act unjustly when leaders take power that rightfully belongs to another (usurpation) or when they take more power than what is allowed under law (tyranny). The latter is particularly problematic, for "where law ends, tyranny begins . . . [especially] if the law be transgressed to another's harm."[21] When this occurs, the community "perpetually retains a supreme power of saving themselves from the attempts and designs of any body, even of their legislators, whenever they shall be so foolish, or so wicked, as to lay and carry on designs against the liberties and properties of the subject."[22] Consequently, civil society has a duty to remove or disband a government that is doing harm and replace it.

Locke acknowledges that people will be hesitant to cast off a flawed government, just as they were likely to tolerate inconveniences in the state of nature. However, when the breach of trust grows sufficiently great, or when government is no longer able to accomplish its primary function of protecting life, liberty, and property, it may be considered effectively dissolved. This is particularly evident when a magistrate alters, abolishes, or replaces the legislature without approval from the people; laws that arise from this body lack popular consent, and thus are to be considered illegitimate and

19. Ibid., II, §135, 27.

20. Ibid., II, §192, 17–18.

21. Ibid., II, §202, 1.

22. Ibid., II, §149, 13–18.

void. Similarly, if a government ruler abolishes the legislature altogether, alters the system of elections, subjects the people to the unlawful influence of a foreign nation, or ignores the implementation of the laws or the execution of justice, the government no longer operates by consent of the governed.

Locke reiterates that because government exists to protect the rights of the people and to promote the common good, any government that abuses these ends or neglects its responsibilities may be justly replaced with another government. Remedial action subsequently undertaken to preserve the individual and society at large is neither unlawful nor rebellious—nor should it be feared. While some might be inclined to incite rebellion without good cause, this would be tantamount to an act of war and thus would be undertaken "only to their own just ruin and perdition."[23] Ultimately, Locke reminds us that in matters regarding the legitimacy of revolution, the people will decide for themselves if the actions are needed, and that God in heaven is the one and only true judge of what is right and just.

Historical Significance

Over the last 300 years, Locke has been revered by historians, philosophers, and political theorists for his efforts in promoting the virtues of liberal government, articulating a universal understanding of human rights, and initiating a Protestant discussion on the tenets of natural law. Several of his important works are taught in universities throughout the United States and Western Europe, including *An Essay on Human Understanding* and his *Letter Concerning Toleration*, but his *Second Treatise of Government* is undoubtedly the most influential. In this volume, Locke's declaration that people are born free and that government exists only by the consent of the governed directly challenged those arguing in favor of a divine right of kings—a position that found few supporters after the turn of the eighteenth century. Moreover, his argument that government has limited authority over individuals became popular among those who urged religious toleration and promoted a vision for civil society wherein government and religion operate in separate spheres of influence. Locke's appeal to the laws of nature established by "one Omnipotent, and infinitely wise Maker" helped to formulate an understanding of universal law that remains influential and relevant today.[24]

23. Ibid., II, §230, 3–4.
24. Ibid., II, §7, 11.

While all of these factors are important to understanding Locke's enduring impact on the university, his influence was secured when ideas from the *Second Treatise* inspired the American War of Independence (1775–1783) and the subsequent revolutions that swept across the globe shortly thereafter. Indeed, it would be difficult to overstate the significance of Locke's influence on the birth of the United States, for he has been heralded as its "philosopher king"—the first philosopher to govern a great nation.[25] His writings on government inspired the initial decision of the colonists to dissolve their political ties with Great Britain, and the written record of wrongs found in the Declaration of Independence was included to prove Locke's point that "revolutions happen not upon every little mismanagement in public affairs . . . [but only after] a long train of abuses, prevarications, and artifices, all tending the same way, make the [tyrannical] design visible to the people."[26]

Furthermore, many of the ideas referenced in the Declaration of Independence, including the natural rights of people, the purpose of government, and the recourse available to the people when government becomes oppressive, are greatly influenced by the *Second Treatise*. For example, the opening sentence of the second paragraph of the Declaration states: "We hold these truths to be self-evident, that all men are created equal, that they are endowed by their Creator with certain unalienable rights, that among these are life, liberty and the pursuit of happiness." This single statement aligns with Locke's premises in Section 4, which states that all people are naturally in a "state of perfect freedom to order their actions . . . as they think fit"; that all people are naturally in a "state of equality, wherein all the power and jurisdiction is reciprocal"; and, in Section 61, that people are "born free, as we are born rational."[27] Jefferson's next assertion that "to secure these rights, governments are instituted among men" aligns with Locke's explanation for why we quit the state of nature and join together to form a political society; the next phrase—"deriving their powers from the consent of the governed"—aligns with Locke's standard of legitimacy for all governments: "politics [cannot] be founded on any thing but the consent of the people."[28]

25. Robert A. Goldwin, "John Locke," in *History of Philosophy*, ed. Leo Strauss and Joseph Cropsey (Chicago: University of Chicago Press, 1987), 476–512.

26. Locke, *Two Treatises*, II, §225, 1–7.

27. Ibid., II, §4; §61, 1–2.

28. Ibid., II, §175, 2–3.

As important as these passages may have been, Locke's influence on the founding of the U.S. Constitution was less direct, and thus his place of influence within canon of political philosophy may have waned over time. However, his proposition regarding the innate equality of people found new life among civil rights leaders during the abolitionist movement in the years preceding the Civil War, and in the struggle for civic and political equality for African Americans in the decades following. Black leaders like Frederick Douglass (1818–1895) and W. E. B. Du Bois (1868–1963) invoked Lockean philosophy to assert that blacks, too, were created equal with inherent rights to life, liberty, and property, and to urge leaders to replace governments that refuse to protect them. Writing in 1845, twenty years before the legal end of slavery, Douglass laments that "[i]n all the broad lands which the Constitution of the United States overshadows, there is no single spot,—however narrow or desolate,—where a fugitive slave can plant himself and say, 'I am safe.'"[29] Nearly sixty years later, Du Bois advocated for full civil and political equality for blacks, arguing that until that is accomplished, equality cannot be realized. Thus, he concludes:

> [B]y every civilized and peaceful method we must strive for the rights which the world accords to men, clinging unwaveringly to those great words which the sons of the Fathers would fain forget: "We hold these truths to be self-evident: That all men are created equal; that they are endowed by their Creator with certain unalienable rights; that among these are life, liberty, and the pursuit of happiness."[30]

Significance for Christians

Christians have long argued that there is a universal standard of right and wrong that applies to all humankind. This standard is most clearly conveyed in the scriptural passages describing God's commandments, confirming for believers that scripture is sufficient "and profitable for teaching, for reproof, for correction and for training in righteousness."[31] Yet, some biblical verses suggest that moral law is also communicated through the creation. Psalm

29. Frederick Douglass, John W. Blassingame, John R. McKivigan, and Peter P. Hinks, eds., *Narrative of the Life of Frederick Douglass, an American Slave Written by Himself* (New Haven: Yale University Press, 2001), 11.

30. W. E. B. Du Bois, *The Souls of Black Folk* (New York: Penguin Group, 1996), 50.

31. 2 Timothy 3:16. Unless otherwise stated, all scriptural passages are taken from the English Standard Version (ESV).

50, for example, declares that the heavens declare God's righteousness, and Romans 1:19–20 explains that "what can be known about God is plain to [non-believers], because God has showed it to them. For his invisible attributes . . . have been clearly perceived, ever since the creation of the world, in the things that have been made." Additionally, Romans 2:14–15 asserts that that even those who are unaware of specific divine commandments nevertheless "by nature do what the law requires . . . [for] they show that the work of the law is written on their hearts." In his *Second Treatise*, Locke similarly posits that people living in perfect freedom in the state of nature are also governed by universal and immutable natural law. This law is not mysterious or esoteric, but is knowable by applying reason and conforming to the divine standard of common equity.

For Christians looking for an explicit description on what is and is not included in the law of nature, Locke offers some basic guidance. The law of nature is designed to protect those things given to people directly from God—specifically, life, liberty, and property—and thus any behavior or action that would deprive another of these things would be considered a violation of God's law. Natural law, which is the only source of law in the state of nature, must be followed by all people in all places at all times; however, even after governments are established, natural law forms the foundation of civil law. According to Locke, "the obligations of the law of nature cease not in society, but only in many cases are drawn closer, and have by human laws known penalties annexed to them, to enforce their observation. Thus the law of nature stands as an eternal rule to all men."[32]

Although the Bible is not intended to be a primer on government, Locke's invocation of equality and freedom align with scriptural teachings as well. Both men and women are described as being made in the image of God, imbued with his characteristics and his nature. Genesis 1:27 (NRSV) states, "So God created humankind in his own image, in the image of God he created them; male and female he created them," and this description is repeated through the Old and New Testaments. Furthermore, the Bible declares that all people are equal in their standing before God—first as sinners, "all have sinned and fall short of the glory of God"—and then as heirs of salvation: "there is no distinction . . . [all] are justified by his grace."[33] The equality that is found in the kingdom of God is described as overcoming earthly inequalities as well. Galatians 3:28 declares: "There is neither Jew

32. Locke, *Two Treatises*, II, §135, 23–27.
33. Romans 3:22–23.

nor Greek, there is neither slave nor free, there is no male or female, for you are all one in Christ Jesus"; and Colossians 3:11 reiterates that "there is no Gentile or Jew, circumcised or uncircumcised, barbarian, Scythian, slave or free, but Christ is all, and is in all."

In scripture, the salvation found in Jesus Christ is described as a liberating event. Jesus declared that he was sent by God "to proclaim liberty to the captives and recovering of sight to the blind, to set at liberty those who are oppressed."[34] Christ is also described as a liberator in Galatians 5:1–2, "[f]or freedom Christ has set us free; stand firm, therefore, and do not submit again to a yoke of slavery," and 2 Corinthians 3:17, "where the Spirit of the lord is, there is freedom." While the traditional interpretation of these passages describes liberation in spiritual terms—that is, humanity's liberation from the bondage of sin—other passages, such as those found in 1 Corinthians 7:21, have been interpreted as endorsing political freedom: "Were you a bondservant when called? Do not be concerned about it. (But if you can gain your freedom, avail yourself of the opportunity.)" It is unlikely that the intended recipients of Paul's epistles who were living under Roman rule could have envisioned a revolution like the one initiated by the American founders; however, some believe that Paul alludes to such a day in Romans 8:19–21: "For the creation waits with eager longing . . . for the creation was subjected to futility, not willingly, but because of him who subjected it, in hope that the creation itself will be set free from its bondage to corruption and obtain the freedom of the glory of the children of God."

To say that the Bible endorses Locke's view of government would be somewhat misleading, for the Bible talks more about one's responsibilities toward the kingdom of God than one's role in earthly kingdoms. Nevertheless, Locke's principle that God remains in control of his creation, including human government, is communicated throughout scripture in passages such as Daniel 2:21: "[God] changes times and seasons; he removes kings and sets up kings," and Colossians 1:16–21: "For by him all things were created, in heaven and on earth, visible and invisible, whether thrones or dominions or rulers or authorities—all things were created through him and for him." Additionally, the Bible supports the idea that government's purpose is for our protection. For instance, Paul declares in Romans 13 that political rulers are God's servants—full-time ministers who are appointed for our good—and, accordingly, they are due our financial support (in the form of taxes) and our obedience. This teaching is repeated in Paul's letter

34. Luke 4:18, quoting Isaiah 49:8–9.

to Titus: "Remind them to be submissive to rulers and authorities"; and Peter's first epistle: "Be subject for the Lord's sake to every human institution, whether it be to the emperor as supreme or to governors as sent by him to punish those who do evil and to praise those do good."[35]

Admittedly, passages that emphasize the need for submission make it difficult to justify revolutions against oppression. However, Locke encourages obedience to legitimate governments and describes rebellion against good regimes as acts of war. Nonetheless, scripture declares that our ultimate obedience is to God, not people. When human authorities are acting in accordance with God's will, as revealed in the laws of nature, then we are to obey. However, when rulers command that which God forbids, we are told to disobey government and submit to God instead.[36] Locke's assertion that people may disassociate from governments ruled by tyrants and despots would align with this teaching. Ultimately, the beneficence of God described throughout scripture and his promise to give us a future and a hope (e.g., Jeremiah 29:11), suggest that we ought to seek to live under a government that protects our rights and promotes our well-being.

Conclusion

Locke's premise that all people are born free and equal is one of history's most revolutionary ideas. It has been used to augment the teaching of scripture, which describes the equal standing that people have before God and the equality they have in Jesus Christ, and it has been used to correct the injustices of those who believe that some people are innately superior or inferior to others. Furthermore, Locke's corollary proposition that government exists only by consent of the governed has radically transformed human institutions. Oppressive rulers now have a more difficult time claiming absolute or divine authority over the people, and revolutionary movements, starting with the American Declaration of Independence, have helped to curb totalitarian impulses and political injustices around the world.

35. Titus 3:1; 1 Peter 2:13–14.

36. Exodus 1:17 describes the conflict between Pharaoh's command to kill all of the male Hebrew babies and God's prohibition against murder: "But the midwives feared God and did not do as the king of Egypt commanded them, but let the male children live" (ESV).

CHAPTER 7: ECONOMICS

Adam Smith, *The Wealth of Nations*

BY ROGER B. CONOVER

Introduction

IN CURRENT DISCUSSIONS OF economics and politics in the United States, a battle rages over the configuration of a society of great individual liberty. For those applying a deontological ethic, the presence and increase of individual liberty is the good, the goal itself. For others of a more consequentialist bent, the question is whether such a society is able to produce, in a sustained manner, outcomes which best achieve some measure of social welfare or well-being.

Adam Smith's 1776 work, *The Wealth of Nations*, is frequently called upon in support of arguments for individual liberty, laissez-faire economics, and market capitalism.[1] It contains plenty of material to choose from regarding what Smith calls "natural liberty,"[2] and also the benefits, in terms

1. Adam Smith, *The Wealth of Nations, with introduction by Alan B. Krueger*, ed. Edwin Cannan (New York: Bantam Dell, 2003). Cannan's 1904 editorial work presents the fifth edition of Smith's work corrected and checked against the first and following editions. Formally titled *An Inquiry into the Nature and Causes of The Wealth of Nations,* numerous versions of this work are available online and in print. For citation here, Smith's book and chapter numbers are cited first, and then the page numbers from the Bantam version are cited in parentheses. Throughout this chapter, quotations will be rendered in American English to avoid distraction.

2. Smith, *The Wealth of Nations*, II.2 (414).

of material output, from the freedom to participate in production and trade. Unfortunately, those who select individual quotations from Smith often fail to capture the full meaning of the text; they practice poor exegesis.

In *The Wealth of Nations*, Smith undertakes a thorough analysis of economic interaction and presents a nuanced understanding of economic systems. His discussion is structured in the language of economic activity and output, but it is rooted in a commitment to a conception of individual liberty bounded by moral sentiment and law. He draws broadly on historical data and business examples of his day, and above all on the use of reason, to accomplish his task. The book is clearly a product of the Enlightenment era.

The Wealth of Nations is an examination of the "nature and causes" of wealth and income on both the micro (business and individual) level and the macro (national) level. More importantly, it strives to describe the relationship between these levels, and the impact of business and individual decisions on national production and consumption. By describing in detail the environment and institutions of commerce and trade, by attempting to deal with the *whole* of the political economy of his day, Smith lays out the framework that comes to define the discipline of economics and sets the agenda for research for centuries to come.

As Christians, we recognize that in *The Wealth of Nations*, Smith engages a number of issues that both resonate with us and challenge us.[3] He speaks of individual liberty, of justice, and of values. He believes that self-interest is the usual reason that people make the choices that they do in society, and yet believes that this yields society-wide benefits. At the same time, he castigates employers, workers, and politicians alike for their common tendency to exploit opportunities to use power to enrich themselves at the expense of the whole of the society. He condemns the love of money and the economic system of his day built upon it, but advocates a model of an economy that promotes creativity and efficiency, as well as avarice and greed, to build even greater wealth.

In section two of this chapter, I present a summary of the content of *The Wealth of Nations*. I consider the influence of Smith's book on the university in section three. In section four, I reflect on a number of issues of concern for Christians that are addressed by the book. Section five concludes.

---

3. It should be noted that the purpose of this chapter is neither to provide a critique of market capitalism, nor an apologia.

A Summary of The Wealth of Nations

The Wealth of Nations is an important book in Western economics for its critique of the prevailing conception of what constitutes wealth, its historical analysis, and its systematic presentation of an alternative economic model. Central to Smith's analysis is the observation that money (i.e., "gold and silver coins") is not the fundamental component of wealth. Coins, like any other commodity, can be purchased. The baker, for example, can purchase coins with bread, although this is the reverse of how people normally think of such a transaction. Smith believes that this misconception about money leads the policy makers of the day to misunderstand the nature of the economy. Coins must be purchased, but bread *can be made*. He argues, "The *annual labor* of every nation is the fund which originally supplies it with all the necessaries and conveniences of life which it annually consumes."[4]

Book One

Book One deals extensively with labor and labor productivity. In it, Smith describes industrial and agricultural activities of production, prices, and the distribution of the created value as the payments to the various inputs, including labor, "stocks," and land.

Labor is central to Smith's understanding of economic functioning. He asserts that, "Labor . . . is the real measure of the exchangeable value of all commodities. . . . It was not by gold or by silver, but by labor, that all the wealth of the world was originally purchased."[5] This includes the labor necessary to acquire the tools, the skills, and the resources necessary to produce the goods. He then defines his view of the worth or value of a good as, "When the [market] price of any commodity is neither more nor less than what is sufficient to pay the rent of the land, the wages of the labor, and the profits of the stock employed in raising, preparing, and bringing it to market, according to their natural rates, the commodity . . . is then sold precisely for *what it is worth, or for what it really costs the person who brings it to market.*"[6]

---

4. Smith, *The Wealth of Nations*, Introduction (1), emphasis added.

5. Ibid., I.5 (43).

6. Ibid., I.7 (81), emphasis added. Note that this definition of what a thing is worth is based on the exchange value, not on any sense of what the thing is "worth" to the person who uses it.

Expansion of the wealth of the nation, therefore, requires increasing the output available to the population (i.e., output per capita). Improvements in the productive capacity of labor are critical to expanding the supply of these "necessaries and conveniences." Of prime importance for improving productivity in Smith's thinking was the "division of labor." This division entails dividing up the set of activities necessary to complete a product for sale or exchange. Smith contends that the process of specialization is the source of "the greatest improvement in the productive powers of labor."[7]

This model of specialization and exchange is the principle framework that Smith constructs for understanding economic interaction.[8] He says, "Among men . . . the most dissimilar geniuses are of use to one another; the different produces of their respective talents, by the general disposition to truck, barter, and exchange, being brought, as it were, into a common stock, where every man may purchase whatever part of the produce of other men's talents he has occasion for."[9] This disposition to exchange allows people to avoid doing everything they would have to do on their own to subsist (e.g., growing food, hauling water, making clothes, and shelter).

The ability to exchange is limited by the size of the society, the nature of the production task, and transportation costs. But within those limits, people take on different kinds of work, specializing in one type of activity and exchanging the surplus that they produce for what else they need. In Smith's model, there would be free and general participation, and limited power for anyone in the economy to dictate a person's choice of employment or the prices for either inputs or outputs.

Book One includes a discussion regarding different types of labor and the differences in wages that would be paid. These differentials may be due to the "agreeableness of the occupation," the "easiness and cheapness, or the difficulty and expense of learning the business," or other reasons associated with the nature of the work.[10] However, it is important to note that Smith is not naïve about the difference between his vision of a well-functioning economy and the reality that his model abstracts from. He cites the lack

7. Ibid., I.1 (9).

8. Developing a "model" in economics is now the standard methodological approach to understanding the more complex economic reality the model describes. Whether formal or informal, a model is recognized to be an abstraction, a representation of reality. It is understood *not* to be a complete, or "true," representation.

9. Smith, *The Wealth of Nations*, I.2 (26).

10. Ibid., I.10 (139 ff).

of the ability of labor to move freely between towns due to local or trade (union) regulations and wage legislation established by the government as other causes of wage disparities.[11, 12] Indeed, for Smith, the free movement of labor is a moral issue as well as one of productivity, since "The property which every man has in his own labor, as it is the original foundation of all other property, so it is the most sacred and inviolable."[13]

He also recognizes that neither the "masters" nor the workers operate from pure motives.[14] "Masters are always and everywhere in a sort of tacit, but constant and uniform, combination, not to raise the wages of labor above their actual rate. . . . Such combinations, however, are frequently resisted by a contrary defensive combination of the workmen, who sometimes, too, without any provocation of this kind, combine, of their own accord, to raise the price of their labor."[15]

In his conclusion to the last chapter of Book One, Smith begins to unfold his proposed solution to this situation. Surprisingly, perhaps, it is not to restrict and regulate economic activity, but to *expand* it. By allowing more workers to participate, it is more difficult for them to combine without provocation, and by expanding competition, masters find it more difficult to collude. In the absence of these powerful interests, with increased freedom to participate and free movement of labor and resources, Smith expects that the individual interests of the participants in the market will lead to an allocation of those resources. This will yield substantially more output and a more "natural" distribution of the created value than would be possible under a controlled and restricted system.[16]

Book Two

Book Two treats the issue of capital more closely, how it is accumulated, and how it is used. In this book, Smith also provides a history of "money."

11. These trade regulations specifically limit the number of workers who could pursue a particular trade in a town. See ibid., I.10 (181 ff).

12. Smith notes that in determining these policies, the government finds "its counselors are always the masters"; see ibid., 1.10 (195).

13. Ibid., I.10 (168).

14. "Masters" here is not an arbitrary hierarchical term. They are masters of their trades who take on apprentices and other workers.

15. Smith, *The Wealth of Nations*, I.8 (94–95).

16. Cf. ibid., I.7 (82).

It is important to understand the way that Smith conceives of capital, since the term is not always well understood.

"Stocks" are the possessions that one has to live on. They may only be sufficient to meet the immediate consumption needs of a person or family. However, if the person saves enough of a stock to be able to live off of, "he naturally endeavors to derive a revenue from [that] part of it . . . . His whole stock, therefore, is distinguished into two parts. That part which he expects is to afford him this revenue is called his capital. The other is that which supplies his immediate consumption."[17] It is from this perspective that Smith praises frugality, since, "Parsimony, and not industry, is the immediate cause of the increase of capital. Industry, indeed, provides the subject which parsimony accumulates; but whatever industry might acquire, if parsimony did not save and store up, the capital would never be the greater."[18]

Smith describes in detail how this capital can be used. He categorizes some of the capital as fixed, such as machinery, factory buildings, land improvements, and human capital (education and skills). This type of capital is used without changing owners to produce goods and generate revenue. Circulating capital, including money, is categorized separately because for this type of capital to generate revenue, it must change hands. For Smith, capital accumulation is not the main objective of production, but rather, "To maintain and augment the stock which may be reserved for immediate consumption, is the sole end and purpose both of the fixed and circulating capitals. It is this stock which feeds, clothes, and lodges the people."[19]

Smith sees that the expansion of capital is important to the improvement of the capacities of labor and the opportunities for its diversification. He is also clearly anti-Luddite in his understanding of the relationship between capital and labor. It is Smith's contention that, "The quantity of industry [work], therefore, not only increases in every country with the increase of the stock which employs it, but, in consequence of that increase, the same quantity of industry produces a much greater quantity of work [output]."[20]

His discussion of money then extends into a discussion of banking and the issuance of what becomes paper money. The banking system that Smith envisioned was one of numerous small banks, any of which might

17. Ibid., II.1 (353).
18. Ibid., II.3 (431).
19. Ibid., II.1 (360).
20. Ibid., II. Introduction (351).

fail if poorly managed, but only to the detriment of the bank and a small number of depositors, and not the society as a whole. This would promote prudent and cautious banking practices.

It is at the conclusion of his discussion on free and unregulated banking that Smith concludes, "In general, if any branch of trade, or any division of labor, be advantageous to the public, the freer *and more general* the competition, it will always be the more so."[21] In Smith's vision of a market economy, both domestic and international, competition will be in the public interest if it is not only free, but general as well, with a multitude of active participants. Indeed, recent banking events in the United States have shown that free markets that are not general are subject to serious failures. Smith is clear that he does not believe that free markets and "natural liberty" should be unbounded, but that, "those exertions of the natural liberty of a few individuals, which might endanger the security of the whole society, are, and ought to be, restrained by the laws of all governments; of the most free, as well as of the most despotical."[22]

Book Three

The history of economic development in Britain and Europe is the focus of Book Three. Here Smith examines the relationship between the agricultural sector and the expanding industrial sector. He also examines the effects of historical policies regulating the development of towns.

The growth of industry was a disruptive force in the mid-1700s. New economic interests were being formed, with landowners and merchant-traders finding that they were sharing more of the overall (higher) economic activity with the rising industrialists. In this Book, Smith is attempting to allay concerns that the development of industry would cause a real decline in agriculture. He observed that, "The gains of both are mutual and reciprocal, and the division of labor is in this, as in all other cases, advantageous to all the different persons employed in the various occupations into which it is subdivided. . . . The greater the number and revenue of the inhabitants of the town, the more extensive is the market which it affords to those of the country."[23] In this argument, we see the foundation of what comes to be

21. Ibid., II.2 (421), emphasis added. In economics, the term "competition" means increased participation, not increased antagonism and destructive behavior.

22. Ibid., II.2 (414).

23. Ibid., III.1 (481).

called the theory of absolute advantage, which he expands on in the next Book in the context of international trade.

Book Four

Beginning with the observation that, "Political economy . . . proposes two distinct objects; first, to provide a plentiful revenue or subsistence for the people, or, more properly, to enable them to provide such a revenue or subsistence for themselves; and, secondly, to supply the state or commonwealth with a revenue sufficient for the public services,"[24] the Fourth Book analyzes economic systems that have been used in various countries and times. In particular, Smith challenges the commercial, or "mercantile," economic system. In this context, he includes an extensive discussion on the role and development of colonies by the European powers.

In Book Four, Smith gathers together a number of threads that he has been weaving. The mercantilist system is the prevailing paradigm that influenced economic decisions and generated policy in the mid-1700s. Under this system, "wealth and money, in short, are, in common language, considered as in every respect synonymous."[25] Economic activity and national policies were constructed to acquire and horde money (gold and silver), generally through the promotion of exports (the sale of goods and thus the importation of gold) and the restriction of imports (the exportation of gold). Smith briefly outlines a number of the rationales of his day used to support this system, and then responds with a thorough critique. For Smith, mercantilism limits the *real* wealth of the nation, that is, the total production of the country, as well as liberty and freedom of action.

In his attack on the mercantilist system, he returns to the fallacy that the accumulation of gold (or silver) should be the objective of the country. Smith shows that the policies designed to restrict imports and expand exports in fact reduce the total value of the annual produce, and thus the real wealth of the country. In his analysis, he covers particular and general import restrictions, export subsidies, and the diversion of trade caused by agreements that favor some countries to the exclusion of others, all of which create monopoly positions for home country producers. Indeed, "Monopoly of one kind or another, indeed, seems to be the sole engine of

24. Ibid., IV. Introduction (537).

25. Ibid., IV.1 (539). It should be of more than passing concern that this perspective continues to be so pervasive today.

the mercantile system."[26] As he earlier argued with respect to towns and rural areas, Smith concludes that, "If a foreign country can supply us with a commodity cheaper than we ourselves can make it, better buy it of them with some part of the produce of our own industry, employed in a way in which we have some advantage."[27]

Smith's discussion of the economic development of the European colonies focuses on the different policies under which those colonies functioned. Without undertaking an extensive review, we observe that Smith concludes, "The political institutions of the English colonies [including land tenure laws, moderate taxation, and more liberal trading policies] have been more favorable to the improvement and cultivation of [the] land, than those of any of the other . . . nations."[28] This focus on institutional differences contrasts with the religious thesis later put forth by Weber and discussed elsewhere in this volume.

Book Five

Finally, the expenses and revenues of the sovereign (or state) are discussed in Book Five. The discussion includes a historical survey of government spending and the ways in which revenues have been raised at different times in different countries.

Some activities fall naturally to "the sovereign," such as defense, justice, and public works. Historically, Smith observed, it was no longer possible to draw into occasional service members of the community to defend themselves, and a professional army needed to be established and funded for the benefit of all. Smith also discussed the need to protect "every member of society from the injustice or oppression of every other member of it," and the expenditures necessary to ensure this.[29] Other categories of public expense listed by Smith include public works in support of general commerce, such as roads and bridges, expenditures in support of particular trades, and education. However, Smith argued that the costs should be borne by the most affected, when possible, as in the case of the support of specific industries.

26. Ibid., IV.7.3 (800).
27. Ibid., IV.2 (573).
28. Ibid., IV.7.2 (725).
29. Ibid., V.1.2 (901).

Regarding spending on education, Smith has a great deal to say about the nature and quality of the education that public and private schools provide, which will be discussed later. But here, Smith expresses particular concern for the workers in industry whose mindless, repetitive jobs are the product of the very division of labor that he extolled as the great engine of wealth creation in the beginning of Book One. He is deeply concerned that "[The worker's] dexterity at his own particular trade seems, in this manner, to be acquired at the expense of his intellectual, social, and martial virtues. But in every improved and civilized society, this is the state into which the laboring poor, that is, the great body of the people, must necessarily fall, unless government takes some pains to prevent it."[30] Smith recognized that there are serious individual costs to the division of labor, even though this manner of organizing work yields great social benefit. He therefore finds it appropriate to finance individual education out of public revenues. Of course, by recognizing this cost, Smith raises the question of what other human costs may be associated with this structure of production.

Smith also discusses methods of raising revenue by the government, including the imposition of a variety of taxes and through government borrowing. Before presenting a detailed analysis of taxes on rents, profits, wages, and consumption, Smith outlines what he believes to be some generally desirable characteristics of a system of taxation, including proportional taxation, clear levies payable at regular dates, and efficient tax mechanisms.[31]

Influence on the University

Smith's impact has lasted over 235 years, and he continues to be quoted (and misquoted) extensively today. In this section, I consider two different ways that Smith has and continues to influence the university. First, Smith directed some of his analysis and critique in *The Wealth of Nations* directly at the university. Second, Smith's work brings together a number of ideas into a single pool. Some of these ideas are new; others are not. Yet the clustering of these ideas in *The Wealth of Nations* provides a catalytic environment that gives rise to both the theoretical underpinnings of modern Western economic society and the academic discipline of economics.

30. Ibid., V.1 (987–88).
31. Cf. ibid., V.2.2 (1043–44).

In the context of his discussion of the division of labor in the university, Smith observes:

> some [productive improvements are developed by] those who are called philosophers, or men of speculation, whose trade it is not to do anything, but to observe everything, and who, upon that account, are often capable of combining together the powers of the most distant and dissimilar objects. . . . Like every other employment, too, it is subdivided into a great number of different branches, each of which affords occupation to a peculiar tribe or class of philosophers. . . . Each individual becomes more expert in his own peculiar branch, more work is done upon the whole, and the quantity of science is considerably increased by it.[32]

The modern university certainly manifests this division of labor. Tremendous gains in scientific, literary, and philosophical knowledge have been facilitated by this level of specialization, both within and through the university.

However, there are both costs and benefits to specialization. It becomes increasingly difficult for the highly specialized philosopher/academic to "not do anything" and to observe and combine dissimilar objects. While Smith demonstrated that he was a true master of combining ideas, the same structure of the university that rewards specialization often fails to promote cross-disciplinary or integrative research. Indeed, the experts in one branch often vigorously resist and are offended by any intrusion by uninformed colleagues from other disciplines.

Smith also had deep concerns over the lack of incentives for good teaching at the university.[33] He says, "In the university of Oxford, [circa 1776] the greater part of the public professors have, for these many years, given up altogether even the pretense of teaching."[34] In the same section, Smith has equally incendiary opinions regarding his expectations of faculty governance or university administrations to oversee and promote good teaching.

The second way Smith has impacted the university, and perhaps the greatest contribution of *The Wealth of Nations*, derives from the fact that it forms a unique "hourglass" in the development of economic thought. Numerous observations on economic life are condensed into a coherent and

32. Ibid., I.1 (xxx).
33. Cf. ibid., V.1.3.ii (especially 962–86).
34. Ibid., V.1.3.ii (964).

internally consistent description (a model, in a most general sense) with a specific objective (growth in material output). This model then challenges the existing perspective on the economic affairs (that of mercantilism), and provides a rational alternative (free and general market interaction). But the model only suggests the structure by which this would improve the economic conditions of society. It is left to future economists to work out most of the formal details of the model, and to politicians to implement policies consistent with the ideas.

By bringing together a variety of ideas into a single, extensive work, Smith provided a vast supply of research topics that have been developed further through the centuries. Some of these ideas existed already; many became formalized later, but their appearance together in *The Wealth of Nations* set in motion changes in thinking and policy that resulted in modern western economic society. The specialized research effort around these ideas became the academic discipline of economics. And certainly many of the ideas of this field, such as cost-benefit analysis, have significantly influenced thinking in other fields in the academy and in society. As a measure of "impact," the ideas are still being worked out more than two centuries later.

Why The Wealth of Nations Matters to Christians

Smith has engaged a number of issues that both resonate with and challenge Christians in *The Wealth of Nations*.[35] Some of these issues have even caused significant divisions among Christians, in part from different values, in part from different definitions of key ideas, and in part from poorly formed understandings of the complex dynamic system that is any economy. In order to improve our conversations, we must recognize that matters of value and values are central to the discussion; our ethical frameworks influence our analyses; issues of what is being measured (output, well-being, or "utility") and how to measure it affect our conclusions of how well structured and suitable an economic system is; and finally, our definitions of self-interest, justice, and other concepts are critical to how we evaluate the economy.

If I might generalize, there are a number of Christian theological themes that are relevant to our consideration of *The Wealth of Nations*.[36] We

35. Smith does include a section on religion and the role and abuses of the established clergy. See ibid., V.1.3.3 (1023).

36. A full consideration of the similarities and differences between Catholic Social

value the individual as created in the image of God, and value individual freedom as enhancing the opportunity to express our creative capabilities. We also recognize that we were created for relationship with God, with other human beings, and with the created order. Even more, we are commanded to love God and others.

So we care about the physical and the institutional conditions within which individuals live, and we value justice. We find conditions of physical deprivation and poverty abhorrent because they condemn human beings to life in less than humane conditions, and so we recognize that the material means of life matter. Yet we also understand that the quantity of goods cannot be the only measure of the well-being of the individual, nor of the community.[37]

As we have seen, Smith has touched on a number of these issues. In particular, in evaluating his use of increasing output per person as a measure of improvement, it is necessary to recall that, for Smith, it is the capacity of labor to produce that determines whether the nation is "better or worse supplied with all the necessaries and conveniences."[38] That is, Smith was not arguing that a freely operating market economic system would improve people's lives in an ultimate sense; he was discussing the physical conditions of the country at the time. It was not the focus of *The Wealth of Nations* to challenge any institutional inequality that might be brought about by a thoroughly free market system, since that system was just nascent.[39] His aim was to address the fundamental shortcomings of the mercantilist system which were preventing improvements in the livelihood of a great proportion of the society.

Smith's presuppositions about human nature and moral responsibility are more fully discussed in his earlier work, *The Theory of Moral Sentiments*. Smith believed that human reason was central to understanding the nature of the economy and the tendencies of people to act within it. But he

---

Thought, the varieties of Protestant social ethics, and Orthodox views is simply not possible here.

37. This is especially true since, using the output measure, it is impossible to distinguish between what people desire and what they *ought* to desire according to a particular value system.

38. Smith, *The Wealth of Nations*, V.1.3.3 (1023).

39. Recall that Smith does discuss income differences among different occupations and between different uses of productive capital in ibid., I.10 (138ff).

believed that human reasoning is fundamentally limited; he had no expectation that human reasoning is able to bring about any natural or divine *telos*.[40]

Additionally for Smith, natural human tendencies promote beneficence and what Smith defines as justice. But he clearly distinguished between the two. He says, "Beneficence is always free . . . [and] the mere want of it exposes to no punishment; because the mere want of beneficence tends to do no real positive evil. [However,] the violation of justice is injury: it does real and positive hurt to some particular persons, from motives which are naturally disapproved of."[41]

With this background, then, we can approach two of the most frequently quoted (and misquoted) passages from *The Wealth of Nations* in which Smith examines human economic interaction and the predominant motivations for it. In the first, he observes that "man has almost constant occasion for the help of his brethren, and it is in vain for him to expect it from their benevolence only. . . . It is not from the benevolence of the butcher the brewer, or the baker that we expect our dinner, but from their regard to their own interest."[42] In the second, Smith states, "[The individual producer] indeed neither intends to promote the public interest, nor knows how much he is promoting it . . . , and by directing [his] industry in such a manner as its produce may be of the greatest value, he intends only his own gain; and he is in this, as in many other cases, led by an invisible hand to promote an end which was no part of his intention [i.e. the increase in total national output]."[43]

That is, for Smith, and for many proponents of individual liberty, there is no imperative for the producer, or the employer, or the worker, or the consumer to be benevolent, only to refrain from deliberately causing injury. There is no binding *command* to love others. From this perspective, no expectation should be held that, among the general society, people will be kind, generous, and loving. The best that can be expected is that, in general, they will be just, as Smith defines justice.

40. Cf. Adam Smith, *The Theory of Moral Sentiments* (Neeland Media LLC. Kindle Edition), Kindle locations 1721–28.

41. Ibid., Kindle locations 1753–85, emphasis added.

42. Smith, *The Wealth of Nations*, I.2 (23).

43. Ibid., IV. 2 (572). This is the *only* use of the term "invisible hand" in the entire work.

For those with a more consequentialist understanding of justice, or with a more universal expectation of response to the command to love, this is hardly enough. The "other-feeling" that Smith discusses in *The Theory of Moral Sentiments* should be what drives social and economic interaction. For them, the equality of humanity should be evidenced in the equality of human conditions on earth.

Yet Smith's focus on historical evidence leads him to view consumption, production, and exchange differently. Writing before the capitalist system had taken hold, Smith believes that it is self-love that is the basis for action for most people.[44] His response is to consider the kind of economic system that would best use this tendency for the greatest national level of general material well-being. His focus on individual freedom as the means for attaining the greatest levels of material well-being should be understood in contrast to the restrictive principles of mercantilism, not in comparison to some heavenly ideal. The "self-love" and "own interest" that is being referenced here is not, for Smith, a preference or a moral imperative, but a practical reality; he was making a descriptive rather than a normative point.

Unfortunately, while Smith's intent is descriptive, when this behavior is presupposed in the course of policy making, it can easily become normative. When policy is designed assuming the behavior, it reinforces the behavior, leading to an *increase* in the behavior. Self-interest can become greed. That is, the descriptive may become the prescriptive, and the dynamic results of the system may be affected by the very assumptions that we make.

Conclusion

In *The Wealth of Nations*, Adam Smith carefully observed economic life in his day and formulated a rational and consistent model of free, general, and open market interaction, with the stated goal of increasing the national level of material output per capita. This model challenged the prevailing mercantilist model and, through time, replaced it in much of the world. While there is much debate over some elements and consequences of this and similar approaches to structuring economic systems, there is little doubt that it generated effective improvements in material well-being compared to the system that it replaced.

44. That is, it is not capitalism that is the cause of self-interested behavior, let alone of greed and avarice. Those latter sins predate economic systems.

The challenge, then, continues to be to evaluate critically the economic and social system, thoroughly understand its functions, and to compare those functions with the objectives that are driven by our belief systems and values. Our theological understanding needs to be brought together with a deep and comprehensive understanding of dynamic social and economic systems. Whether modifications or wholesale changes are being called for, it would be incumbent upon us to undertake as thorough a study as Adam Smith did in *The Wealth of Nations*.

CHAPTER 8: HISTORY

Edward Gibbon, *The Decline and Fall of the Roman Empire*

BY BRADLEY RAINBOW HALE

Introduction

BY THE EIGHTEENTH CENTURY, the history of Rome—its rise, decline, and fall—had been written and rewritten many times. Since the Renaissance, Classical education—the study of the Greeks and Romans—had become foundational for Europe's educated classes, and, by the eighteenth century, underpinned much of European culture and ideology. In their pursuit of wisdom, liberty, and virtue, Enlightenment philosophers and members of the rising middle classes routinely turned to the works of Greek and Roman authors. In addition to Classical learning, artists looked to ancient styles in art, architecture, and literature for inspiration.[1] Thus, when Edward Gibbon sat down to write his great work of history, *The Decline and Fall of the Roman Empire*, he knew that he was treading familiar ground. Later reflecting on this reality in his autobiography, he recognized that he had "chosen an illustrious subject," one that was "familiar to the school-boy and statesman."[2] Yet, neither Gibbon nor his contemporaries considered a new

1. For more on this trend, see Rolf Toman, ed., *Neoclassicism and Romanticism: Architecture, Sculpture, Painting, Drawings* (Cologne: Ullmann, 2011).

2. Edward Gibbon, *Autobiography of Edward Gibbon as Originally Edited by Lord Sheffield* (London: Oxford University Press, 1959), 180.

history of Rome superfluous. In fact, upon the publication of the first volume in 1776, Gibbon's history of Rome met with success, requiring further editions in short order. The remaining volumes, published between 1776 and 1789, also fared well.

The success of the *Decline and Fall* can be credited, at least in part, to the eighteenth-century appetite for Classical learning. It is also, though, a tribute to Gibbon's gifts as a historian, in particular his ability to synthesize and analyze a vast array of material and to present it in an elegant narrative. As historian Peter Gay has written, "Gibbon did not have to teach his readers to love antiquity—they did that without him": rather, he "filled out the outlines of their love with his gripping gift for narrative, his blessed specificity."[3] Gibbon's knowledge and love of his subject as well as his extensive study gave him insight into a complicated history and enabled him to write it with accuracy and clarity. The result of Gibbon's efforts was the production of "a monument of historical literature,"[4] and perhaps even "the greatest of all Enlightenment histories."[5]

Whether or not Gibbon was a philosopher himself, the European Enlightenment of the eighteenth century undeniably shaped his thinking and his understanding of history. Not only did the Englishman live through most of the eighteenth century (1707–1794), he was personally acquainted with some of the greatest philosophers of his day, such as Voltaire and David Hume. He also read the great writers and philosophers of his age, including Montesquieu. In the spirit of the Enlightenment, Gibbon bore a strong obligation to clear, careful analysis, free from passions that might impede the search for understanding. For the Enlightenment philosophers, this especially meant freedom from religious prejudices that thwarted the candid and rational pursuit of knowledge. Gibbon agreed, and believed, in fact, that through much of its history, Christianity had had a pernicious effect on learning. Accordingly, it behooved thinkers, whether historian or philosopher, to free themselves from religious constraints.[6]

3. Peter Gay, *Style in History: Gibbon, Ranke, Macaulay, Burckhardt* (New York: Norton), 38–39.

4. Ibid., 53.

5. Mark T. Gilderhaus, *History and Historians: A Historiographical Introduction*, 5th ed. (New York: Prentice-Hall, 2003), 38.

6. For more on Gibbon's Enlightenment influences, see Peter Gay, *Style in History*, and John Burrow, *A History of Histories: Epics, Chronicles, Romances and Inquiries from Herodotus and Thucydides to the Twentieth Century* (New York: Vintage, 2007). For more on Gibbon's conversion and early life, see David Womersley's Introduction to an abridged

This conception of liberty guided Gibbon in the writing of his master-piece, *The Decline and Fall of the Roman Empire.* The inspiration for writing a history of Rome first came to him, he claimed, while he enjoyed a gentle-manly "grand tour" of the European continent in the 1760s. He traveled through France and Switzerland, where he made friendships that would last for much of his life. As one might expect, though, the highlight of his journey was his sojourn in Italy, especially Rome. Of course, he visited the great city's monuments and ruins, which captivated him and ignited his imagination. "It was among the ruins of the Capitol," he wrote in the closing words of his final volume of the *Decline and Fall,* "that I first conceived the idea of a work which has amused and exercised near twenty years of my life."[7] Thus began his life's work for which he is still known as "the historian of Rome."

The Decline and Fall

Any attempt to summarize Gibbon's impressive work in this brief space would not only be inadequate, but an injustice. Depending on the edition, Gibbon's study can number between six and twelve volumes, comprising a million and a quarter words (give or take).[8] Gibbon's account carries the history of Rome well beyond the end of the western empire in the fifth century, to the fall of the eastern capital, Constantinople, in 1453. Chrono-logically, then, the *Decline and Fall* encompasses approximately 1,300 years of history, beginning with the second century and ending in the fifteenth century with the emergence of the Renaissance. Its geographic scope is also grand, ranging from Rome and its European, African, and Middle Eastern provinces, all the way to China, and it includes accounts of the Byzantine

---

edition of *The History of the Decline and Fall of the Roman Empire,* ed. David Womersley (New York: Penguin, 2005). J. W. Burrow's *Gibbon* (New York: Oxford University Press, 1985) is also a helpful guide to the young Gibbon.

7. Edward Gibbon, *The Decline and Fall of the Roman Empire,* ed. J.B. Bury (New York: AMS Press, 1909), volume VII, chapter lxxi, 338. From here on, this volume shall be abbreviated to Gibbon, *Decline and Fall,* followed by the volume, chapter, and page number in the following manner: Gibbon, *Decline and Fall,* VII.lxxi.338.

8. It is worth mentioning here that there are abridged versions of the *Decline and Fall,* such as David Womersley's, (New York: Penguin, 2005), that provide the reader with the essential chapters, the breadth of Gibbon's exploration, and a good feel for his mastery of language and narrative. This essay utilizes the seven-volume edition prepared by J. B. Bury. The word count is not mine, but is provided by Gilderhaus in *History and Historians,* 38.

Empire, Islam, Persia, and the Mongolian and Chinese empires. Additionally, Gibbon incorporated varieties of history, from political, military, and economic, to cultural, social, and religious. The work also delves into manners, spirit, and values, and even political philosophy.[9]

While an adequate summary may not be possible here, it is certainly feasible to sketch out the overarching narrative and predominant themes of the *Decline and Fall*. As the title suggests, Gibbon set out to understand how the Roman Empire, the greatest empire in human history (at least from the perspective of the eighteenth-century European mind) could have come to an end. Or, as Gibbon put it, his goal was "to deduce the most important circumstances of [Rome's] decline and fall: a revolution which will ever be remembered, and is still felt by the nations of the earth."[10] As with many of his eighteenth-century contemporaries, Gibbon hinted at the prospect of historical laws at work.[11] Yet, in his role as historian rather than philosopher, Gibbon largely resisted the temptation to offer simple or singular explanations for the end of the Roman Empire. For Gibbon, simplicities "were simply not enough."[12] Thus, he posited numerous reasons for Rome's decline, from the ravages of time and nature to the "use and abuse of the materials."[13] Domestic turmoil also took its toll, particularly in the last centuries of the empire. Additionally, decay from within the empire and attacks from outside forces contributed to the empire's ultimate collapse. More than anything else, though, Gibbon attributed the fall of Rome to the "triumph of barbarism and religion."[14] By "religion," Gibbon meant Christianity.

Before he addressed "the triumph of barbarism and religion," though, Gibbon provided a description and assessment of Rome in the second century when the empire appeared to be at the height of its power and glory. As Gibbon wrote in the very first lines of his inquiry, "In the second century of the Christian era, the empire of Rome comprehended the fairest part of the earth, and the most civilized portion of mankind."[15] Furthermore, Rome

---

9. Burrow, *Gibbon*, 22.

10. Gibbon, *Decline and Fall*, I.i.1.

11. See Michael Bentley, *Modern Historiography: An Introduction* (New York: Routledge, 1999), for more on this idea.

12. Gay, *Style in History*, 54.

13. Gibbon, *Decline and Fall*, VII.lxxi.317.

14. Ibid., VII.lxxi.317, 321.

15. Ibid., I.i.1.

had achieved peace as its emperors generally abandoned the expansion of the empire's frontiers in favor of fortification. The Roman world also benefitted from a "long peace, and . . . uniform government"[16] that practiced moderation, exemplified in a policy of religious toleration that encouraged domestic stability and "not only mutual indulgence, but even religious concord."[17] Economic prosperity accompanied the political, religious, and military stability, as citizens could safely conduct commerce on both land and sea. As luxury and wealth grew, so did learning. Rome's greatness had been attained "and preserved by the wisdom of the ages."[18] In brief, Rome had achieved the height of "civilization."

The word "civilization" was new to the eighteenth century. For eighteenth-century thinkers, "civilization" stood in opposition to "savagery" and "barbarism," and represented the apex of human progress and achievement. At the same time, though, "civilization" assumed its own set of hazards, including the possibility that humanity could become separated from natural liberty.[19] For Gibbon, both the optimistic and pessimistic connotations of "civilization" applied to second-century Rome. Rome had, undoubtedly, achieved great progress in its prosperity, government, and religious toleration. However, its peace and prosperity had also "introduced a slow and secret poison into the vitals of the empire."[20] Roman civilization had achieved great affluence, but the empire's inhabitants both "enjoyed and abused the advantages of wealth and luxury."[21] Gibbon also argued that comfort and security had drained Rome of its vigor and energy, and its people lost "the fire of genius." Moreover, Rome's "military spirit evaporated," with Romans increasingly content to entrust the military to mercenaries rather than assume the responsibility of the citizen-soldier.[22] In fact, in the transition from republic to empire, Rome's ethos of civic welfare, once a hallmark of its greatness, began to fade. While it provided security and prosperity, the imperial government also sapped Romans of "that public courage which is nourished by the love of independence, the sense of national honour, the

16. Ibid., I.ii.62.

17. Ibid., I.ii.31.

18. Ibid.

19. Burrow, *Gibbon*, 22. See also Dorinda Outram, *The Enlightenment*, 3rd ed. (New York: Cambridge University Press, 2013).

20. Gibbon, *Decline and Fall*, I.ii.62.

21. Ibid., I.i.1.

22. Ibid., I.ii.62.

presence of danger, and the habit of command."[23] As a result, Rome's government and politics descended into corruption. In one of the great ironies and tragedies of history, Rome's "immoderate greatness" led to its decline.[24]

Gibbon's sense of history, however, was "too complex to be subsumed by any single formula of decay."[25] Rome's internal deterioration made it vulnerable to external threats, and in the fourth and fifth centuries, northern European peoples, such as Visigoths and Vandals, endangered Rome's peace and security. By the fifth and sixth centuries, these "barbarian invasions" became bolder, culminating in assaults on the city of Rome itself.[26] Gibbon lamented the defeat of civilization at the hands of barbarism, but, with hindsight, Rome's loss seemed unsurprising. Of course, to Gibbon, as well as many of his eighteenth-century contemporaries, "barbarian" indicated "backward," at least in their conception of history as linear progress toward civilization.[27] Barbarians, unlike their civilized and urbane counterparts, were unsettled and unsophisticated herders. However, unlike the civilized and soft, Barbarians possessed a fierce devotion to freedom. According to Gibbon, the Germanic tribes of northern Europe, the Barbarians, prized many of the virtues that the Romans had squandered. They possessed a "manly spirit of freedom" as well as drive, energy and vitality, the qualities of character that had made Rome great.[28] Thus, in this contest between "barbarism" and "civilization," especially in the arena of virtue, the advantage fell to Europe's uncivilized peoples.

Thus, Rome had been "undermined by a slow decay" and "invaded by open violence." For Gibbon, though, Christianity posed a more insidious threat to the Roman Empire. "The pure and humble religion," the historian explained, had "gently insinuated itself into the minds of great men, grew up in silence and obscurity, derived new vigour from opposition, and finally erected the triumphant banner of the cross on the ruins of the Capitol."[29] In time, the new faith grew from an obscure religion to become the official religion of the empire, achieving a "remarkable a victory over

23. Ibid.

24. Ibid., IV.xxxviii.173.

25. Burrow, *Gibbon*, 39.

26. For more on this topic, see Bryan Ward-Perkins, *The Fall of Rome and the End of Civilization* (New York: Oxford University Press, 2005).

27. Burrow, *Gibbon*, 74.

28. Gibbon, *Decline and Fall*, I.ii.64.

29. Ibid., II.xv.1.

the established religions of the earth."[30] While many devout Christians of the eighteenth century would have considered Christianity's victory a benefit to humanity, Gibbon emphasized its deleterious effects on the Roman Empire. Christianity imperiled or destroyed many of the great attributes of the empire, including its religious tolerance, its public and martial virtues, and its unity. Thus, as one modern historian has written, Christianity became the "villain" in Gibbon's drama of Rome's tragic fall.[31]

In his two most tendentious, even notorious, chapters, the fifteenth and sixteenth, Gibbon explained how Christianity arose from its position of weakness to dominance. Among the reasons Gibbon enumerated for Christianity's success at Rome's expense was the new religion's intolerance, which presented a challenge to the empire's unity and civic virtues. Gibbon admiringly observed that Rome's moderate religious climate had allowed "even hostile nations" to embrace, or at least respect, "each other's superstitions."[32] Christianity's "exclusive zeal for truth," however, made "religious harmony" difficult if not impossible and was entirely foreign to the Roman Empire.[33] Pagan practices, which Christians believed were demon worship and an affront to the one, true God, pervaded Rome's civil ceremonies. Thus, not only did Christians constantly have to be on their guard against temptation and corruption, but their "inflexibility" and "intolerance" set them against Roman civilization. In Gibbon's estimation, this represented a refusal to abide by "the moral consensus of humanity and the values embodied in human society."[34] As such, Christianity arrived in Rome as "an alien and destructive force,"[35] upsetting Rome's religious and civic equilibrium.

Christianity's emphasis on the soul's ultimate fulfillment in another world also undercut Rome's civic strength. Gibbon conceded that the "promise of eternal happiness" had been "advantageous" in winning "great numbers of Romans" over to Christianity.[36] However, the focus on the next life also disparaged the Roman principle of civic responsibility. "Public virtue" or "patriotism" derived from the citizen's investment in

30. Ibid., II.xv.3.
31. Gay, *Style in History*, 40.
32. Gibbon, *Decline and Fall*, II.xv.3.
33. Ibid., II.xv.7.
34. Burrow, *Gibbon*, 56.
35. Ibid., 53.
36. Gibbon, *Decline and Fall*, II.xv.24.

"the preservation and prosperity of the free government."[37] Romans bore a responsibility to their fellow citizens and to Rome itself, manifest in their commitment to sustain their earthly government. At least during the Republic, they had gone to war as citizen soldiers and they participated in the civic and religious rituals of their society. Christians, by contrast, had no such allegiance to civil society. In fact, Gibbon argued that they "were animated by a contempt for their present existence, and by a just faith of immortality."[38] What is more, armed with their expectation of God's ultimate justice, Christians eagerly awaited the day when divine wrath would judge Rome, which they considered nothing but a new incarnation of Babylon. Thus, as far as Gibbon was concerned, Christians' hope in a future life dealt a severe blow to Roman notions of public virtue and citizenship.

Even the virtues that Christians embraced were frequently antithetical to Rome's civic ethos. Gibbon conceded that "the primitive Christian demonstrated his faith by his virtues," but argued that these tended to be of little use to society at large. In fact, many of the most virtuous primitive Christians, according to Gibbon, simply withdrew from society. Having once been "the most abandoned sinners," many of the most pious Christians not only endeavored to lead righteous lives, but in their penitence and self-denial they devoted themselves to "serious and sequestered" lives of chastity and temperance.[39] This impulse could certainly be seen in the later development of monasticism, which Gibbon considered to be a corruption and abuse of the Gospels. As "unhappy exiles from social life," Christian monks disdained "all the forms and decencies of civil society."[40] While Christian ascetics may have constituted an extreme example of this behavior, Gibbon reminded his readers that Christian values were, by and large, at odds with the public good. After all, "it was not in this world that the primitive Christians were desirous of making themselves either agreeable or useful."[41]

Christianity's final triumph, as well as Rome's fate, came with the conversion of Emperor Constantine in the fourth century. Constantine's conversion to Christianity secured the religion's future and sealed the empire's fate. After Constantine sanctioned Christianity, not only could adherents

37. Ibid., I.i.11.
38. Ibid., II.xv.24.
39. Ibid., II.xv.35–36.
40. Ibid., VII.xxxvii.62–64, 67.
41. Ibid., II.xv.37.

evangelize freely, but the threat of persecution no longer deterred converts. Christian leaders, as well as the state, could focus attention on extinguishing heresy. In regard to the emperor, he could enhance his power as defender of truth. The entanglement of Christianity and the Roman state, however, had a corrupting influence on both. Emboldened by Christianity, Constantine and his successors became increasingly despotic. Church leaders became more interested in power and politics than piety. In the end, the establishment of Christianity debased the virtues of both the religion and the empire.

Importance to the University

In regard to historical research and writing, Gibbon did not initiate any new methodologies in the *Decline and Fall*. As one modern historian has put it, "Gibbon did not originate new historical techniques, nor did he fully exploit some of the auxiliary historical sciences being developed in his own day."[42] In fact, one might argue that he attempted to return to an ancient form of historical writing, imitating Roman historians, especially Tacitus. Placing a premium on factual accuracy, he researched thoroughly, focusing on ancient sources. However, unlike modern historians, he "did not himself work with manuscript sources, though he was indebted to and appreciative of those who did."[43] In particular, Gibbon took advantage of the scholarship that had been produced about Rome, especially during the seventeenth century, which had seen "the publication of an immense body of historical documents—laws and bulls, charters and codes, annals and chronicles— and the compilation of histories incorporating them."[44] He also made use of innovations by other scholars in their study of coins, medals, and inscriptions from the Roman world. In many respects, his great contribution to historical method was simply his dogged research and tireless effort to know more about Rome than anyone else.

Gibbon did not, however, simply want to know more facts about Rome. This was the practice of "antiquarians," those who compiled details. As a historian, Gibbon undertook what he and his contemporaries considered "philosophical history," the effort to understand underlying causes and

42. Roy Porter, *Edward Gibbon: Making History* (London: Weidenfeld and Nicolson, 1988), 74.

43. Burrow, *A History of Histories*, 333.

44. Porter, *Edward Gibbon*, 74.

connections of historical events and human actions. "Philosophical history," as defined by historian J. W. Burrow, "reveals connections and penetrates below the surface appearance of things to explain their occurrence. History so treated is the pathology of the human mind in action: it is the history of error, prejudice and illusion that chiefly interest the philosophic inquirer."[45] The historian, for Gibbon, ought to be able to see beyond the obvious and to discern "a tissue of events connected by deeper causes."[46] In this sense, Gibbon, like many modern historians, envisioned the practice of history as a problem-solving discipline. He posed a historical problem or question—in this case, why did Rome fall?—and attempted to answer it using the best available sources and evidence. Guided by historical documents and testimony as well as the narrative of events, a historian might provide insights into the course of human affairs, and even human nature.[47] Thus, while Gibbon may not have introduced any new methodologies, his *Decline and Fall* represented a new way of thinking about the purposes of historical inquiry.

Perhaps the most original contribution that Gibbon made to the historian's vocation is found in his approach to Christianity. As noted earlier, one of the principle goals of the Enlightenment had been to free knowledge from religious constraints and prejudices. In fact, many of the Enlightenment thinkers challenged the notion that theology was the "queen of the sciences," and offered philosophy as a liberating alternative.[48] Reflecting this Enlightenment criticism of Christianity's undeserved reign over knowledge, Gibbon perceived that for much of the Christian experience, history had "obediently served as handmaiden to a glittering superstition."[49] Freeing himself from this subservience, he distinguished between the role of the historian and the theologian:

> The theologian may indulge the pleasing task of describing Religion as she descended from heaven, arrayed in her native purity. A more melancholy duty is imposed on the historian. He must discover the inevitable mixture of error and corruption which she

45. Burrow, *Gibbon*, 23.

46. Burrow, *A History of Histories*, 333.

47. Gay, *Style in History*, 48–49.

48. For more on this topic, see Robert Darnton, *The Great Cat Massacre and Other Episodes in French Cultural History* (New York: Basic Books, 1984), especially the chapter entitled, "Philosophers Trim the Tree of Knowledge."

49. Gay, *Style in History*, 31.

> contracted in a long residence upon earth, among a weak and de-
> generate race of beings.[50]

Gibbon thus rejected the Christian historians' assumption that their vocation was to uncover and explain the workings of divine providence.[51] For
Gibbon, the historian's task was not to affirm Christian truth or the workings of providence, but to explore human motives, actions, and affairs.

Importance to Christians

Having liberated history from theology, Gibbon thus liberated himself to
fulfill the Enlightenment standard and to study the history of Christianity
without preconceptions. This did not, however, mean a frontal attack on
the faith, an activity popular among some Enlightenment philosophers.[52]
In fact, Gibbon appears to have made allowances for "first causes," or divine
causes in the story of Christianity. He conceded that the truth of Christian
doctrines and the designs of providence could explain why Christianity
emerged victorious over paganism. Thus, in addressing the historical problem of Christianity's rise, Gibbon admitted that "an obvious but satisfactory
answer may be returned; that it was owing to the convincing evidence of the
doctrine itself, and to the ruling providence of its great Author."[53] His con-
cessions to first causes and the "convincing evidence of the doctrine itself,"
though, seem perfunctory if not disingenuous. While it is true that Gibbon
had converted to Christianity twice—from Protestantism to Catholicism
and back—his theology largely reflected Enlightenment skepticism about
doctrine rather than a commitment to orthodoxy. But this seems to indicate a doctrinal ambivalence rather than any particular commitment. Thus,
it is difficult to accept Gibbon's suggestion that the "obvious" explanation
for Christianity's rise could ever be "satisfactory."

　　This is made even clearer as Gibbon clearly defined the historian's
purview as the study of secondary causes rather than first causes. In explaining how "the Christian faith obtained so remarkable a victory over
the established religions of the earth,"[54] the historian's obligation was not

50. Gibbon, *Decline and Fall*, II.xv.2.

51. Porter, *Edward Gibbon*, 117.

52. Voltaire famously said, "Ecrasez l'infame!" or "Crush the wicked thing!" Quoted
in Gilderhaus, *History and Historians*, 35.

53. Gibbon, *Decline and Fall*, II.xv.3.

54. Ibid., II.xv.3.

to uncover the mysteries of God, but to understand the role of humans. With study, research, and reason, a historian could discern human actions and decisions, and perhaps even motivations. Even if these "efficaciously assisted the truth of the Christian religion,"[55] secondary causes could be affirmed with documentary and historical evidence. Thus, the historian's task clearly remained focused on the mundane, not the heavenly. Only such an inquiry could allow a "candid but rational inquiry into the progress and establishment of Christianity."[56] Humans, not heaven, constituted the subject of historical inquiry.

In spite of Gibbon's efforts to delineate the occupations of the theologian and historian, the *Decline and Fall*, not surprisingly, generated a wave of criticism from "all stripes of religious opinion, from High Church dogmatists to dissenters."[57] Gibbon's opponents attacked not only the historian's scholarship, analysis, and sources, but also his religion and moral character. Assuming that he had written his history in an "age of light and liberty,"[58] Gibbon apparently failed to anticipate the outcry that a candid appraisal of Christian history might provoke. According to his autobiography, the criticism caught Gibbon off guard, and he claimed that if he had foreseen the response of "the pious, the timid, and the prudent," he might "have softened the two invidious chapters."[59] In 1779, he responded to his detractors with his *Vindication of some passages in the 15th and 16th chapters of The Decline and Fall of the Roman Empire*. As one might expect, he made his stand on the ground he knew best, the history of Rome. For the most part, instead of addressing questions about his own faith and his morals, Gibbon focused primarily on the accuracy of his research and writing. This response, as well as the eloquence and clarity of the work itself, succeeded in justifying the *Decline and Fall* to most of England's reading public, even if he did not satisfy his most vehement critics.[60]

Gibbon's understanding of history as an earthbound study of human actions and ideas rather than of divine agency ultimately prevailed, and continues to govern the discipline of history. Modern historians have "abandoned attempts to determine ultimate or final causes, that is, God's

55. Ibid., II.xv.57.

56. Ibid., II.vx.1.

57. Womersley, introduction, *Decline and Fall*, xix.

58. Gibbon, *Autobiography*, 180.

59. Ibid., 185.

60. Womersley, introduction, *Decline and Fall*, xix.

role in the historical and natural worlds."[61] Even Christian academic historians eschew "providential history," or the attempt to reveal God's plans and purposes in history.[62] This does not mean that they have given up on the effort to relate their faith to their scholarship, and there is an ongoing conversation among Christian historians about the nature and character of "faithful history."[63] Some Christian historians have suggested that faith might influence the choice of topic or shape research questions, but that the research and writing of history must conform to the professional standards and practices of their secular colleagues.[64] As such, as one former president of the Conference on Faith and History has noted, "Christians can't footnote divine revelation or propose that they see God's will in the workings of history."[65] Others, however, challenge the willingness to adopt secular methods and principles so unhesitatingly.[66] While there are Christian historians who suggest that their teaching and writing might create occasions for reflection on morality and virtue, they have colleagues who warn about the dangers of "preaching through history."[67] There is little consensus on the meaning of "faithful history," but whatever the approach, Christian historians generally agree that it is not the historian's task to uncover how the hand of God has guided human history. Like Gibbon, contemporary Christian historians draw a line between the responsibility of the theologian and the "melancholy duty" of the historian.

61. Gilderhaus, *History and Historians,* 29.

62. Robert Tracy McKenzie, "The Vocation of the Christian Historian: Re-Envisioning our Calling, Re-Connecting with the Church," *Fides et Historia,* 45:1 (Winter/Spring 2013) 11.

63. Donald Yerxa, "That Embarrassing Dream: Big Questions and the Limits of History," *Fides et Historia,* 39:1 (Winter 2007) 54.

64. George Marsden, *The Outrageous Idea of Christian Scholarship* (Oxford University Press, 1997).

65. Rick Kennedy, "Introduction: The Sacred Calling of History," *Fides et Historia* 35:2 (Summer 2003) 2.

66. Christopher Shannon, "After Monographs: A Critique of Christian Scholarship as Professional Practice," in John Fea, Jay Green, and Eric Miller, eds., *Confessing History: Explorations in Christian Faith and the Historian's Vocation* (Notre Dame, IN: University of Notre Dame Press, 2010), 168–86.

67. McKenzie, "The Vocation of the Christian Historian," 11–12. See also Thomas Albert Howard, "Virtue Ethics and Historical Inquiry," in Fea, Green, and Miller, *Confessing History,* 83–100.

Conclusion

Today, historians recognize Gibbon as one of the greatest of historians, to be studied especially by those who wish to pursue historical research and writing as a vocation. The road to this status was not inevitable or easy. Gibbon fell out of fashion in the nineteenth century as the French Revolution, Napoleonic Wars, and subsequent rise of the nation-state in nineteenth-century Europe all challenged Enlightenment assumptions about history and historical writing. Furthermore, nineteenth-century historians, influenced at least in part by the Romantic movement, began to challenge the apparent inability of their eighteenth-century counterparts to sympathize with their subjects and to understand historical actors on their own terms, rather than measuring them by the standards of the eighteenth century.[68]

Gibbon fared much better in the twentieth and twenty-first centuries, however. Admirers such as Winston Churchill helped to rehabilitate Gibbon's reputation as a historian and literary figure. In the arena of contemporary scholarship, while historians do not always agree with Gibbon's conclusions, they find it difficult to write about the end of the Roman Empire without making some reference to "the historian of Rome." As the eminent Classical scholar, Peter Brown, suggested, historians of Rome all work "in Gibbon's Shade."[69] Moreover, historians of all fields, not simply ancient history or the Enlightenment, study Gibbon's work as they develop their own understanding of what it means to write history. Gibbon did not pioneer a new understanding of history on his own. However, his *Decline and Fall of the Roman Empire*, with its attention to historical scholarship, accuracy, and elegance, unquestionably played a crucial part in the development of the modern discipline of history.

68. For more on Gibbon's legacy, see Bentley, *Modern Historiography*; Burrow, *A History of Histories*; and Gilderhaus, *History and Historians*.

69. Peter Brown, "In Gibbon's Shade," *The New York Review of Books* (April 15, 1976) 14–18. See also Burrow, *A History of Histories*, 344.

CHAPTER 9: BIOLOGY

Charles Darwin, *On the Origin of Species*

BY JOSHUA MORRIS

Introduction

ON THURSDAY, NOVEMBER 24, 1859, the world was changed forever. This may seem like an odd proclamation, since this date does not conjure the vibrant imagery or even the vague recollection that dates like July 4, 1776, January 1, 1863, or December 7, 1941, do for most.[1] However, many would argue that the book published on that day impacted human history as profoundly as the events that occurred on the dates mentioned above. Not only did the publication of Charles Darwin's *On the Origin of Species by Means of Natural Selection, or the Preservation of Favoured Races in the Struggle for Life* revolutionize the field of biology, but it also has had lasting effects on nearly every academic discipline.[2] The impact of *Origin of Species* has been

---

1. July 4, 1776, is the day that the American Colonies declared their independence from British Rule. January 1, 1863, is the date that Abraham Lincoln issued the Emancipation Proclamation. On December 7, 1941, the Japanese Government attacked Pearl Harbor. Admittedly, these are examples from the United States, but they illustrate watershed moments that impacted people around the world.

2. This was the original title of *Origin of Species*. The title was shortened for the sixth edition. See the original Charles Darwin, *The Origin of Species by Means of Natural Selection, Or the Preservation of Favoured Races in the Struggle for Life*, 6th edition, with additions and corrections (London: John Murray, 1872).

so great that some have placed Darwin among the most influential people in human history.[3]

While *Origin of Species* is filled with numerous novel observations and interpretations, the only truly original concept presented by Darwin is that of natural selection. The ideas of common ancestry and the transmutation of species (evolution) had been proposed decades earlier, but they were not widely accepted by the scientific community of the time. The notion of natural selection proved to be key because it allowed Darwin to support, crystalize, and integrate these controversial scientific theories (common ancestry and the transmutation of species) into a coherent model for the diversification of life on earth. This amalgamation of information into a palatable and well-supported theory is truly what made *Origin of Species* so revolutionary.

Charles Darwin's career began at a time of conflict and change for the scientific community. Born in 1809 to a wealthy British doctor, Darwin was tasked to follow in his father's footsteps before natural history caught his attention. As a part of his training at Cambridge, Darwin not only learned natural history through his studies of botany, zoology, and theology, but also he studied geology under a prominent catastrophist geologist, Adam Sedgwick.[4] Influenced by the Church of England and the Royal Society, a majority of the British scientific community of this time saw the pursuit of science as an act of worship to God. In fact, Christian theology was so intertwined with science that scientific theories that did not match up with the contemporary biblical interpretation were shunned in both academic circles and in popular culture.[5]

3. Michael H. Hart, *The 100: A Ranking of the Most Influential Persons in History* (New York: Citadel, 2000).

4. Historical information about Darwin, his work, and its influence for the chapter was taken from: Janet Browne, *Charles Darwin: Vol. 1, Voyaging* (London: Jonathan Cape, 1995); Janet Browne, *Charles Darwin: Vol. 2, The Power of Place* (London: Jonathan Cape, 2002); Peter Bowler, *Evolution: The History of an Idea*, 3rd ed. (Berkeley, CA: University of California Press, 2003); Charles Darwin, *The Autobiography of Charles Darwin 1809–1882*, with the original omissions restored, edited and with appendix and notes by his granddaughter Nora Barlow (London: Collins, 1958); Charles Darwin, *Journals of Researches Into the Natural History and Geology of the Countries Visited During the Voyage of H.M.S. Beagle Round the World, Under the Command of Captain Fitz Roy, R.N.*, 2nd ed. (London: John Murray, 1845); Richard Keynes, ed., *Charles Darwin's Zoology Notes & Specimen Lists from H.M.S. Beagle* (Cambridge: Cambridge University Press, 2000); and Edward Larson, *Evolution: The Remarkable History of a Scientific Theory* (New York: Modern Library, 2004).

5. The Royal Society of London for Improving Natural Knowledge (The Royal Society)

A great example of a view that was shunned because of this interplay between religion and science was the theory of the transmutation of species. Jean-Baptiste Lamarck championed the idea that species progressively changed over time in 1809.[6] However, the idea was not initially recognized since it conflicted with the accepted convention that species were "fixed" as a part of the Divine Plan.[7] Carolus Linnaeus, considered by most to be the father of modern taxonomy, was an integral advocate for the fixed species model nearly a century earlier. However, in the late eighteenth century, some scientific observations began to conflict with the "fixed species" view. As geologists discovered and began to categorize fossilized remains, they began to discover animal species that were no longer in existence. Some scientists (like Lamarck) proposed a completely alternative hypothesis to the fixed species view in response to these discoveries, while others argued that extinction was merely a form of adaption and that the laws that govern these events were still a part of the Divine Plan. Since the "fixed" view was deemed to be more compatible with contemporary biblical interpretation, it was widely accepted and became very influential. Following the scientific convention, Darwin rejected the transmutation of species early in his career. However, his experiences as the naturalist on the *HMS Beagle* caused him to reconsider these views.

Not long after completing his studies at Cambridge, Darwin joined the crew of the *Beagle* as it set off to survey and explore South America. During this nearly five-year expedition, Darwin served as both the naturalist and the geologist. As the *Beagle* voyaged throughout the southern hemisphere, Darwin collected geologic samples and fossils, observed and collected wildlife samples, and made observations of indigenous people groups. Upon his return, Darwin was credited with the discovery of multiple new species. The scientific academy was so impressed by the breadth and quality of his work that he immediately gained notoriety as a leading naturalist. However, recognition as a scientist was not the only thing the voyage of the *Beagle* afforded Darwin. It also gave him a new outlook on natural law.

---

is a British scientific advisory board that was established in 1660 by King Charles II. The purpose of the Society is to champion and oversee scientific inquiry in Great Britain.

6. J. B. Lamarck, *Zoological Philosophy, An Exposition with Regard to the Natural History of Animals,* originally published in 1809, trans. Hugh Elliot for Macmillan, London, 1914 (rpt. Chicago: University of Chicago Press, 1984).

7. By Divine Plan, I refer to religious belief that God determines all things, including biological phenomena.

Based upon his observations, Darwin began to reconsider his earlier views on evolution. During the expedition, Darwin studied Lyell's *Principles of Geology* extensively, as he found its uniformitarian stance useful in interpreting most of his geologic observations.[8] Darwin also began to suspect that species diversified over time, originating from a common ancestor. This change of heart was mostly due to some intriguing observations that occurred when the *Beagle* stopped in the Galapagos Islands. While in this archipelago, Darwin observed the behavior of and collected multiple different specimens of birds found on each of the islands. When the birds were finally categorized, twenty-five new species were identified. However, Darwin was struck by the resemblance among each of the finches in the Galapagos, and the stark similarity between these finches and those collected on the mainland. Darwin was also intrigued by the volcanic nature of the islands, as this suggested that the islands were a relatively recent geologic formation. In addition, Darwin observed a remarkable link between the body structure of each finch and the environmental behaviors that he witnessed. Each bird seemed to be perfectly adapted to the microenvironment in which it lived. These observations of remarkable similarity between closely related species and their nearly perfect adaption to the environment caused Darwin to rethink the fixed species model and led him to favor the idea of "common descent with modification."[9] The thought that each species of finch adapted over time from a common ancestor was more realistic than twenty-six divine acts of creation, especially in light of the geologic age of the Galapagos Islands. Because Darwin was so enamored with this theory, he spent the next few years searching for a mechanism that could drive the evolution of species over time.

Observing that animal breeders were able to produce progeny with certain traits by selectively breeding parents with those traits, Darwin began broad studies in animal husbandry. After extensive observations and experimentation, he confirmed that specific traits could be artificially selected based upon careful breeding. During this period, Darwin also read Thomas Malthus' *An Essay on the Principle of Population*.[10] In this groundbreaking work, Malthus argued that, if left unrestrained, the human popu-

8. Charles Lyell, *Principles of Geology*, 4th ed. (London: John Murray, 1837).

9. Darwin, *Origin of Species*, vi.

10. T. R. Malthus and G. T. Bettany, *An Essay on the Principle of Population: A View of its Past and Present Effects on Human Happiness; with an Inquiry into Our Prospects Respecting the Future Removal or Mitigation of the Evils which it Occasions* (rpt. London: Ward, Lock, and Co., 1892).

lation would breed beyond its ability to gather and produce resources. This lack of resources would ultimately lead to a struggle for survival. This idea of a "struggle for resources" struck Darwin because it coincided nicely with his observations from the previous decade. Not completely convinced that the scientific community would accept his arguments, Darwin spent the next twenty years observing, studying, experimenting, and writing in an attempt to provide as strong an argument as possible for his new theory. Finally, under pressure from the discovery of a competing yet similar theory from Alfred Russell Wallace and because of the constant urging from his friend Charles Lyell, Darwin published *Origin of Species* in November of 1859. While the initial response to the book was mixed, it has become one of the most influential scientific books ever written.

Summary of the Book

The first edition of *Origin of Species* contained fourteen chapters in addition to a brief preface and introduction. Another chapter was added to the sixth edition in response to popular criticism leveled against natural selection. Since the sixth edition is considered the complete version of *Origin of Species* it will be referenced in this section of the chapter.

Darwin begins *Origin of Species* with three quotes that highlight the harmony between natural law and a rational creator, a concept that was central to the natural theology that governed the scientific practice of the day. After outlining the contents of the book, he then provides a historical sketch that acknowledges the progression of evolutionary theory and references the relevant literature on the topic. Darwin then introduces the book by highlighting his credentials as a scientist and as an author.

Chapter I provides a detailed and exhaustive history of animal husbandry and plant breeding. In this section, Darwin provides multiple examples that illustrate that discriminatory breeding can lead to a diverse set of progeny, each arising from a common ancestor. He then suggests that the diversification that arises from artificial selection happens most often because of the accruing of small incremental changes. However, Darwin also proposes that large-scale changes can occur, albeit rarely.

Now that Darwin has established that diversification can and has occurred, he uses Chapter II to question the definition and classification of living species. Arguing that variation is seen both within species and above the species distinction, Darwin contends that the variation among individuals is a central theme of nature. As a way to strengthen his point, Darwin highlights the constant change that occurs within classification schemes as scientists disagree on the importance of certain distinctions.

In Chapter III, Darwin introduces the concept of a competition-based resource allocation system within nature. In this system, the ability to gain the resources required for survival and reproduction is directly tied to individual fitness. Based upon this point, he contends that natural selection provides the mechanism for population based change because the completion and resulting reproductive fitness would cause beneficial traits to be preserved via the survival of the fit individuals and their progeny. Deleterious traits would then be lost, as less fit individuals lose the struggle for survival.

Darwin continues his discussion of natural selection in Chapter IV. He begins by highlighting the idea that the accumulation of small incremental changes within a population can eventually lead to large-scale change within that group. He begins by comparing natural selection's power to induce change to that of artificial selection. Darwin also highlights how the selection of mates by animals helps to facilitate the natural selection process. He then discusses how natural selection could induce variation as well as extinction, and that the combination of the two is necessary for speciation. In this chapter, Darwin asserts that, given sufficient time, natural selection could lead to a universal descent with modification.

Chapter V discusses the inheritance of selected traits. Although the mechanism of heredity was unknown at this time, Darwin argues that acquired characteristics are, in fact, passed on from generation to generation. In this chapter, he also suggests that the genetic machinery somehow allows useful traits to be kept, while unused traits are often lost.

Darwin then devotes the next four chapters to possible objections to his theory. Since his theory proposes a very gradual descent with modification, he devotes most of Chapter VI to the apparent lack of transitional species found in nature. Darwin resolves the dilemma by arguing that the lack of fitness and small population sizes of these transitional species would lead to a relatively fast extinction. Since these species would be quite transient, he contends that there would be few remnants in the fossil record. Darwin also uses this chapter to discuss his thoughts on the evolution of complex organs, which he argues also occurs as a gradual process.

Since multiple critiques of natural selection had been proposed since the first edition, Chapter VII (in the sixth edition) was used to respond to these concerns. Much of the chapter reacts to a popular criticism, which questions the ability of natural selection to induce change from intermediate forms that would have had far less fitness than the parental population. Darwin counters by proposing multiple scenarios that highlight how incremental change could still lead to the fitness necessary for diversification.

Chapter VIII focuses on the evolution of insects as it relates to instincts. Darwin felt that this was an important addition to *Origin of Species,* as the major examples used (slave-making ants and honeybees) highlight how natural selection could cause changes in instincts and behaviors in a highly organized social structure.

Darwin tackles another important objection to his theory in Chapter IX. In this chapter, he reacts to the observation that hybrids are often sterile. Many critics believed that sterility observed in hybrids was "created" to stabilize species in nature. While Darwin agrees that sterility is often seen in hybrid species, he provides a few examples of plant species where hybrids are in fact fertile. He then uses the content of this criticism to argue for his observations on natural variety found within species presented in Chapter II.

The book shifts its attention to geology in Chapters X and XI. In Chapter X, Darwin revisits the points of contention from Chapter VI, again justifying his theory with regard to the lack of transitional species. This time, citing arguments from Lyell, he claims that the absence of transitional species in the fossil record is not unexpected because of the extreme imperfection of the fossilization process.[11] Darwin also discusses what is now known as the Cambrian Explosion, the sudden appearance of multiple different forms of life at a specific point in the fossil record. While Darwin acknowledges that he does not have a sufficient answer for this problem, he suggests that further discoveries should yield a wider abundance of transitional species. Darwin uses Chapter XI to analyze whether the fossil record supports a descent from common ancestry model or a special creation of individual species model for the origin of life. As expected, he argues that the variable rates of change seen for different animal groups, combined with the patterns of extinction observed in the fossil record, are best explained by his theory.

Darwin then explores what he considers to be bio-geographical evidence for his theory in Chapters XII and XIII. In Chapter XII, Darwin argues that the distribution of biodiversity is best accounted for by descent

11. Lyell, *Principles of Geology.*

with modification rather than from special creation. Darwin observed that in locations with similar climates, like parts of South America, Africa, and Australia, the natural inhabitants are strikingly different. However, the biodiversity found in each of these continents is very similar to locals close in proximity, but with very different climates. In his view, this observation is best explained by his theory.

Darwin continues this argument in Chapter XIII, where he describes observations of how mammals fill specific niches in certain island settings, while on other islands, reptiles and birds fill the same niche. Darwin found both of these observations compelling because special creation would cause the same type of organisms to inhabit the same types of niches in similar climates. Since he saw that the adaption was location dependent, this would suggest that diversification was occurring in that location based upon the common ancestor(s) present.

Chapter XIV deals with classification, morphology, and homology. Darwin again questions the current classification system and then discusses the similarities between morphologic structures in very different species. He asks, "What can be more curious than that the hand of a man, formed for grasping, that of a mole for digging, the leg of the horse, the paddle of the porpoise, and the wing of the bat, should all be constructed on the same pattern, and should include the same bones, in the same relative positions?"[12] Darwin also points out that embryos from the same order have very similar structure. He then discusses how the presence of rudimentary organs, such as remnants of a pelvis and leg bones found in some snake species, supports his theory.

The final chapter reviews the main points from the book and also discusses Darwin's hope that this work will be influential in changing the field of natural history. Obviously, Darwin's wish came true, but possibly on a much grander scale than he anticipated.

Importance of Book for the University

The effects of *Origin of Species* have been undeniably far-reaching. Not only has the book significantly changed the field of biology, but it has also had a profound impact on nearly every academic discipline and on Western civilization as a whole. The influence of *Origin of Species* has been so great that it would be impossible to discuss exhaustively its full effects. Therefore,

12. Darwin, *Origin of Species*, 382.

this section will focus on the major points of impact that *Origin of Species* has had on both academia and culture as a whole.

Influence on the Field of Biology

First and foremost, publication of *Origin of Species* had an almost immediate effect on the biological sciences. Not only did it essentially create the new field of evolutionary biology, but it also changed the scientific paradigm on the diversification of species. While the theory of the transmutation of species from a common ancestor did not immediately gain universal acceptance, it has become one of the central tenants of current biology. However, the credence given to this theory has not always been closely tied with the acceptance of natural selection. Since its inception, the principle of natural selection has been one of the most widely scrutinized, undergoing numerous critiques and experimental challenges. During most of the late nineteenth and early twentieth centuries, other evolutionary theories were more widely accepted by the scientific community. However, unlike most of these aforementioned scientific theories, natural selection has stood the test of time. Further research has shown that natural selection is necessary but not completely sufficient to describe the origin and diversification of life.[13] Even so, natural selection has become one of the central doctrines of modern biology. While the broad acceptance of natural selection by the biological community has placed Darwin among the scientific elite, many have argued that its discovery was not his greatest scientific accomplishment. Rather, most scientists have agreed that the impacts that *Origin of Species* has had on the process, definition, and philosophy of science is far more profound.

Natural Theology to Scientific Naturalism: What is the Nature and Purpose of Science?

As described in the introductory section of this chapter, science in the early nineteenth century was practiced under the paradigm of natural theology. However as the scientists of the eighteenth and nineteenth century studied

13. For example, the concept of "punctuated equilibrium" is a widely accepted alternative to Darwinian "gradualism"; see Niles Eldredge and S. J. Gould, *Punctuated Equilibria: An Alternative to Phyletic Gradualism,* in *Models in Paleobiology,* ed. T. J. M. Schopf (San Francisco: Freeman, Cooper and Company, 1972), 82–115.

natural theology, they began to collect data that appeared to contradict the biblical interpretation of the time. These "contradictions" began philosophical and theological debates as to the nature and best practice of science. Some scientists and theologians argued that special revelation should be kept as the primary philosophical underpinning for the practice of science. Proponents of this position maintained that, since scripture was divinely inspired and can be literally interpreted, it provides essential information necessary for the interpretation of natural history. Others viewed the Genesis account of creation and the flood narrative as allegory. Thus, the interpretation of natural data could be explored and explained beyond the literal interpretation of the creation and deluge accounts presented in scripture. Advocates for this model proposed that a balance be struck between scientific interpretation and special revelation as each could inform the other. A third group, led by T. H. Huxley, argued for the complete secularization of science.[14] Huxley and his colleagues judged that the practice of science was inhibited by theology, as the two are irreconcilable. Thus, the scientific method was best practiced under the philosophy of scientific naturalism, the belief that the scientific data should only be interpreted with regard to natural laws and other scientific data. This means that, although God may exist, scientific practice should be unencumbered by appeals to the divine will or scripture. While this idea was thought to be overly progressive during Darwin's early scientific career, it began to gain traction in the scientific community as more of academia began to view secularization as progressive.

According to most historians, *Origin of Species* was the proverbial "straw that broke the camel's back." Although Darwin acknowledged references to natural theology in the work, many emphasized his ability to explain the origin and diversification of life on earth naturally rather than providentially. If something as important as the divergence of life on earth can be explained using this evolutionary rationale, then why could not other scientific data be interpreted in the same way? This debate over the nature and purpose of science engulfed the scientific community in the latter part of the nineteenth century. However, through the work of the "X Club," a group of prominent scientists led by T. H. Huxley, the philosophy of science shifted toward scientific naturalism by the start of the twentieth century. This position has become central in modern-day scientific practice

14. Thomas Huxley, "Darwin on the Origin of Species," *Westminster Review* 17 (April 1860) 541–70.

as it has become the foundation of the scientific method. The modern scientific community has become closely tied to this philosophical paradigm and is considered to be both best practice and essential for scientific progress. Popular culture has also embraced this view in response to the modern technologies that it has afforded. Many have also credited Darwin and the work of the "X Club" for the secularization of the university as a whole during the early twentieth century.[15]

"Fall from Grace" vs. Pinnacle of Evolution: What Is the Nature of Man?

The implications of *Origin of Species* were also felt well outside of the halls of academia. One of the major controversies that *Origin of Species* triggered was the result of the brief insinuation that humans could be a product of evolutionary processes, just like the rest of creation. At this time, most held to the Christian ideal that humanity was a special creation, who were divinely appointed, yet fell from grace. Under this theological paradigm, humans were created in the image of God, but reflected that image poorly because of their fallen nature. Thus, humanity and culture were only advanced through the restoration of the fallen nature via relationship with God. The idea that humans were merely the pinnacle of the evolutionary process completely contradicted this belief not only in essence, but also in outcome. If humans were in fact just highly evolved mammals, then what aspects of human nature actually parallel the divine? Under this perspective, the best practice for human advancement would also change significantly. If evolutionary processes were the creative force that forged the human "pinnacle" from lesser beginnings, then the application of the same methods could create a new zenith for the human race. Darwin solidified his stance on the debate in 1871 when he published *The Descent of Man, and Selection in Relation to Sex*. In this work, Darwin directly applied his evolutionary theories to human origins, arguing that all human characteristics slowly evolved from a common, non-human ancestor.[16] However, since evolutionary thought had gained a foothold in parts of academia, the concept of

15. Ruth Barton, "An Influential Set of Chaps: The X-Club and Royal Society Politics 1864–85," *The British Journal for the History of Science* 23, no. 1 (1990) 53–81; cf. Adrian Desmond, *Huxley: The Devil's Disciple* (London: Joseph, 1994).

16. Charles Darwin, *The Descent of Man, and Selection in Relation to Sex*, 1st ed. (London: John Murray, 1871).

human evolution was relatively well received. Those who embraced Darwin's ideas not only did so because of its perceived scientific merit, but they also embraced human evolution as the easiest way to improve society. If human traits could in fact be controlled via selective breeding, then humanity could be advanced in lieu of a dependent relationship with God.

Social Darwinism: How Should Humans Treat Each Other?

As the idea that humans were an evolutionary product that could be further modified via discriminatory breeding began to take hold, it spawned multiple positions that collectively became known as social Darwinism. This concept eventually spawned the eugenics movement of the early twentieth century. First proposed by Herbert Spencer, the argument that a human's position within social hierarchies was a result of the individual's fitness was greatly enhanced by the publication of *Origin of Species*. Under this theory, the "best" individuals would obtain the highest positions in society and by doing so would cause society to advance. In advocating for this form of social elitism, Spencer actually coined the term "survival of the fittest."[17] In the 1860s, Darwin's cousin, Francis Galton, further refined this idea. According to Galton, society should regulate human breeding so that more fit individuals breed with greater frequency than those with less fitness.[18] Acceptance of these beliefs led to the eugenics movements of the early 1900s. Members of these groups sought to genetically improve society by removing those with less fitness. Some countries sterilized criminals and the mentally challenged. Others, like Nazi Germany, chose to enact mass genocide on multiple people groups. While the ideals of eugenics have fallen out of favor because of the atrocities that occurred in Nazi Germany, some of its influence can still be seen in today with the development and use of reproductive screening technologies such as selective abortion and PGD.[19]

17. Herbert Spencer, *Principles of Biology*, vol.1 (London: Williams and Norgate, 1864).

18. Robert Bannister, *Social Darwinism: Science and Myth in Anglo-American Social Thought* (Philadelphia: Temple University Press, 1989).

19. PGD refers to the technology known as Pre-Implantation Genetic Diagnosis. The process allows for the selection of specific traits from embryos that have been created via in vitro fertilization.

Importance of the Book for Christians

When analyzing the effects that *Origin of Species* has had on Western civilization, a central theme quickly emerges: secularization. As expected, this influence frequently carries a negative connotation within Christian circles and has caused Darwin to be oft-blamed for the downfall of society. While there is no doubt that Darwin and *Origin of Species* have had a secularizing influence, placing him as the "prime cause" is a bit misguided and fails to recognize the fundamental changes that occurred long before Darwin started his career as a naturalist. These key changes tied with often ignored premises of both Christian theology and science will be the focus of this portion of the chapter as the influence of *Origin of Species* is further discussed. Interestingly enough, Darwin's personal faith journey provides an excellent platform to discuss these issues.[20]

From Orthodoxy to Doubt

As described in his autobiography, Darwin began his scientific career as an orthodox Christian. However, because of the natural occurrences and cultural diversity that he observed while on the *Beagle*, his faith came into question. Upon his own admission, this time of doubt occurred because Darwin was unable to align his studies with his understanding of Christian doctrine. Under the worldview of natural theology, Christian doctrine and scientific inquiry were to work in unison to accomplish the same goal—a better understanding of God. However, as this interplay of ideas progressed, many scientists failed to recognize that this merger of natural and special revelation was going to be extremely difficult, as there can be fundamental disagreements between the two. Most often discussed in relation to Galileo, it is very easy for these two types of knowledge (natural and special revelation) to be in conflict since they are habitually processed with completely different lenses of understanding.[21] Special revelation is grounded in a fixed set of scriptures, with interpretation that is based in tradition. However, natural revelation is in its essence progressive. As humans explore and in-

---

20. Information for this section was modified from Charles Darwin, *The Autobiography of Charles Darwin 1809–1882,* with the original omissions restored, edited and with appendix and notes by his granddaughter Nora Barlow (London: Collins, 1958).

21. Michael Sharrat, *Galileo: Decisive Innovator* (Cambridge: Cambridge University Press, 1994).

terpret the natural world, the ideas that result will inherently develop as more information is gathered. Therefore, if the two are going to be joined, then a difficult balance must be struck, with critical analysis occurring on both sides. Like most, Darwin found this amalgamation to be difficult and began to analyze both Christian theology and the practice of science to determine which of the two was going to become dominant in his understanding of the world.

From Doubt to Disbelief

As was commonplace in post-Enlightenment culture, Darwin turned to reason in an attempt to justify belief in the Christian God. However, once again, he quickly observed a fundamental disagreement between his understanding of Christian doctrine and his observations of the nature of the world. As Darwin witnessed all forms of sickness, predation, parasitism, and death during his adventures on the *Beagle*, his observations of the world could not be harmonized with his perception of the Christian God. The problem of pain and evil haunted Darwin, making belief in a rational and benevolent Creator extremely difficult. Christian culture in the early nineteenth century painted the pre-fall world as a place that completely lacked pain, suffering, and death for all of earth's inhabitants. It also taught that broad acceptance of Christian faith would ultimately lead humanity back to that utopia in the afterlife. However, modern society was becoming increasing skeptical of the church's ability to deliver on this promise and looked for alternative ways to deal with this issue in the present world. This obstacle, together with the human tendency to process absolute good and evil in light of individual pain and suffering, set the course in Darwin's quest for understanding.

Darwin also had difficulty accepting the roots of Christianity, finding no difference between the cultures of the "savages" that he encountered on expedition of the *Beagle* and that of the early Jews. Considering the elitism, classism, and racism that were prevalent in Darwin's day, this view was not uncommon among Christians, especially those with social standing. Darwin said: "During these two years I was led to think much about religion. Whilst on board the *Beagle* I was quite orthodox . . . But I had gradually come, by this time, (i.e. 1836 to 1839) to see that the Old Testament from its manifestly false history of the world, with the Tower of Babel, rainbow as a sign . . . from its attributing to God the feelings of a revengeful tyrant, was no more to be trusted than the sacred book of the Hindoos or the beliefs of any barbarian."[22] These views made it very difficult for Darwin to accept multiple tenets of Christian faith in light of all of the recent progress that Western culture had made toward an ideal society though education and reason. Darwin's inability to reconcile these issues ultimately led him to adopt agnosticism as his religious worldview. Therefore, scientific discovery became the dominant way by which he gained knowledge about the world around him.

Secularization and Society

The progression of Darwin's personal faith journey strangely parallels the evolution of secularization in Western civilization during the early twentieth century. It began as progressive academics found the reconciliation of scientific progress with the traditions of Christian theology increasingly difficult. Thus one had to be deemed as primary so that newly acquired scientific observations could be properly interpreted. This problem was compounded by the prevalent social and academic elitism that instilled a prideful confidence that pain and suffering could be alleviated via human ingenuity, whereas traditional theology had yet "failed" with regard to theodicy. Thus secularization, as outlined by the elite in post-*Origin of Species* academia, offered a new path to better academia and society.

In response to the growing prevalence of secularization, a mass exodus from Christian theology occurred, hurling society toward a secular worldview and a naturalistic hope for a brighter future. While the new technologies that have been created as a result of this shift have been broadly praised, other outcomes of this movement became quite problematic. The resulting social progress movements that fueled many of the atrocities surrounding the Second World War (especially Nazi Germany) led to a demand for absolute morality in order to enact justice upon those responsible. As a result, a theistic worldview re-emerged in parts of the academy, as absolute morality can only be justified in the presence of a *moral designer*. However, the scientific community as a whole has been quite resistant to this renaissance of religion within the university, citing fundamental worldview differences and a history of incompatible beliefs.[23]

22. Darwin, *Autobiography*, 61–62.

23. For example, see "Nature Methods Editorial, An Intelligently Designed Response," *Nature Methods* 4, no.12 (2007) 983.

Surprisingly, some Christian groups share a similar sentiment to that of the scientific community with regard to the incompatibility of science and religion. These groups often prioritize the Theory of Evolution as the central dogma of all scientific practice and believe that any and all aspects of the Theory, including natural selection, are in complete contradiction with biblical interpretation. This all-exclusive assessment of the Theory of Evolution is often held as a response to the evolutionism that is prevalent among many atheists.[24] However, this view fails to recognize that acceptance of the Theory of Evolution (or some conglomeration of its tenets) neither requires the adoption of ontological naturalism as a worldview, nor conflicts with widely accepted interpretations of the biblical creation account.[25, 26]

This comparison of Darwin's personal struggle and the movement to secularize society highlights three central questions for Christians to ponder in the post-*Origin of Species* era: 1) How should Christians respond to societal change and new information without sacrificing central tenets of their faith? 2) How do Christians reconcile the problem of evil in light of societal ills and changes? 3) What is the process by which Christians identify and correct socially-derived doctrine that is incompatible with the basic tenets of the faith? While the answers to these questions are difficult, they must be addressed for Christianity to stay scientifically as well as socially relevant in the postmodern period. Perhaps the answer lies in the re-emergence of the theistic worldview within parts of the academy. This suggestion would then task the Christian members of the academy to reflect scientifically and critically as well as biblically upon their theological worldview and the betterment of humanity.

24. Evolutionism is a term used to describe a worldview that uses the Theory of Evolution, which supports naturalism, since natural phenomena are thought to be sufficient to explain life.

25. Ontological Naturalism is the worldview that believes that nothing exists outside of mass, matter, and naturally occurring phenomenon.

26. For example, see Augustine, *The Literal Meaning of Genesis*, translated and annotated by John Hammond Taylor, S. J., 2 vols. (New York: Newman, 1982); and David Young, "The Contemporary Relevance of Augustine," *Perspectives on Science and Christian Faith* 40, no. 1 (1988) 42–45.

Conclusion

Darwin's work as a scientific naturalist not only revolutionized the field of biology, but it has had lasting effects on both the university and culture. While Christians have often been skeptical of *Origin of Species* because of its secularizing influence on Western civilization, Darwin's work cannot be ignored because it has become foundational to modern science. The lessons learned from his life and work also become important as Christianity deals with the ever-changing landscape of the postmodern world.

CHAPTER 10: PSYCHOLOGY

Sigmund Freud, *Interpretation of Dreams*

BY THERESA CLEMENT TISDALE

"It contains, even according to my present-day judgment, the most valuable of all the discoveries it has been my good fortune to make. Insight such as this falls to one's lot but once in a lifetime."

—Sigmund Freud (Preface, *Interpretation of Dreams*[1])

IN 1931, SIGMUND FREUD wrote these words in the preface to the third, revised, English edition of his book, *Interpretation of Dreams*.[2] Though published in November of 1899, both author and publishing house, Franz Deuticke, agreed that the book should bear the date 1900 so that it would be forever linked with the dawn of a new century. "Psychoanalysis," wrote Freud in 1923, "may be said to have been born with the twentieth century;

1. This statement appears only in the preface to the third English edition of *The Interpretation of Dreams*; it does not appear in the third German edition. For full bibliographical information for *The Interpretation of Dreams*, see the following footnote.

2. Sigmund Freud, *The Interpretation of Dreams*, vol. 4 of *The Standard Edition of the Complete Psychological Works of Sigmund Freud*, trans. and ed. James Strachey (London: Hogarth Press, 1953), ix-627. The following year, his publisher asked Freud to write a condensed version for lay readers, resulting in publication of *On Dreams*, vol. 5 of *The Standard Edition*, 629–86. This chapter is based on an edition published by Avon Books (New York, 1965), which is a reprint of the original work included in *The Standard Edition*.

for the publication in which it emerged before the world as something new—my *Interpretation of Dreams*—bears the date '1900.'"³

Sigmund Freud was perhaps one of the most compelling and controversial figures of the twentieth century. He is compelling because his body of work spanned five decades (with the authorized English translation comprising twenty-four volumes) and has had a profound impact on every major academic discipline, most particularly psychology. He is controversial because of his (then and perhaps now) scandalous and radical views about sexuality, aggression, religion, and the human condition. His ideas have been considered especially egregious by Christians (and perhaps other devout religious persons) because of his often quoted indictment that "religion is the universal obsessional neurosis,"⁴ and "God is nothing more than an exalted, Oedipal father."⁵ Freud considered religion to be the only truly formidable enemy of science in a contest over which discipline had the most explanatory power regarding reality and could thereby capture the prize of the human mind and imagination.

Thinking Christians need to be aware of what people and ideas are shaping culture and society and to recognize points of resonance and dissonance. Engagement and ongoing dialogue are crucial in order to have input, influence, and impact in the increasingly complex world in which we live.

Freud revised *Interpretation of Dreams* eight times. The final edition was published in 1930, nine years before his death. Freud linked the book's publication with the introduction of psychoanalysis to the world, but his ideas were not enthusiastically received. In the first eight years only six hundred copies were sold. Although disappointed, Freud's enthusiasm for the topic was not diminished. This slow start was later eclipsed by success. The book has remained continuously in print for over a hundred years and has been the focus of many publications over the years.⁶ In 2000, the cen-

3. Freud, *A Short Account of Psycho-Analysis*, vol. 19 of *The Standard Edition*, 191.

4. Freud, *Obsessive Actions and Religious Practices*, vol. 19 of *The Standard Edition*, 126; Freud, *An Autobiographical Study*, vol. 20 of *The Standard Edition*, 65; and Freud, *The Future of an Illusion*, vol. 21 of *The Standard Edition*, 42.

5. Freud, *Totem and Taboo*, vol. 13 of *The Standard Edition*, 147; and Freud, *The Future of an Illusion*, vol. 21 of *The Standard Edition*, 22.

6. Ernst Kris, "New Contributions to the Study of Freud's *The Interpretations of Dreams*—A Critical Essay," *Journal of the American Psychoanalytic Association* 2, no. 1 (1954) 180–91; Leo Rangell, "Historical Perspectives and Current Status of the Interpretation of Dreams in Clinical Work," in *The Interpretation of Dreams in Clinical Work*, ed.

tenary was marked by numerous articles and essays reviewing the work for its past, present, and future significance, and it was named by some as the book of the century.[7] The purpose of this essay is to provide context, summary, and commentary on this psychoanalytic classic with particular attention to how Christians may interact with this compelling and controversial book and the man whose innovative ideas launched a movement that significantly shaped Western civilization.

The Man behind the Method

No theory or idea evolves in a vacuum; it is usually the product of a person or persons who have been shaped by a host of complex factors. Some are individual, interpersonal, and environmental (e.g., historical, social, economic, political, racial, ethnic, and religious). Freud was shaped by all of these in myriad ways, so to better understand his book *Interpretation of Dreams* some context may be helpful.

Sigismund Schlomo Freud was born on May 6, 1856, in Freiberg, Moravia, which is now the Czech Republic (a predominantly Catholic country). In 1859, the family moved to Leipzig for about a year before settling in Vienna in 1860, where Freud lived until 1938, when he fled Vienna for London following the *Anschluss*—the annexation of Austria by Nazi Germany.

Freud was named for his grandfather Rabbi Schlomo, but later changed his name to Sigmund Freud in 1877. His father Jakob was a wool merchant of modest means. His mother Amalia was his father's third wife

---

Arnold Rothstein (Madison, CT: International Universities Press, 1987), 3–24; Marshall Edelson, "Language and Dreams—*The Interpretation of Dreams* Revisited," *Psychoanalytic Study of the Child* 27 (1972) 203–82; and Leonard Shengold, "The Metaphor of the Journey in *The Interpretation of Dreams*," *American Imago* 23, no. 4 (Winter 1966) 316–31.

7. Ramon Greenberg and Chester A. Pearlman, "*The Interpretation of Dreams*: A Classic Revisited," *Psychoanalytic Dialogues*, 9, no. 6 (1999) 749–65; Richard D. Chessick, "Review of *The Interpretation of Dreams*: Sigmund Freud, trans. Joyce Crick," *Journal of American Academy of Psychoanalysis* 29 (2001) 184–87; Ilse Grubrich-Simitis, "How Freud Wrote and Revised his *Interpretation of Dreams*: Conflicts Around the Subjective Origins of the Book of the Century," *Psychoanalysis and History* 4, no. 2 (Summer 2002) 111–26; Valerii Leibin, "The Interpretation of Dreams as Part of Freud's Psychobiography," *Psychoanalytic Review* 90, no. 6 (2003) 811–28; and Lewis Aron and James L Fosshage, "The Interpretation of Dreams: A Centennial Celebration," *Psychoanalytic Dialogue* 9, no. 6 (1999) 721–24.

and was twenty years younger than her husband. She was near in age to her husband's two sons by his first marriage. The complex dynamics of this blended family may have stirred some internal dynamics in Freud that later found their way into his theory of the Oedipus Complex.[8]

Freud was Amalia's first born. He had seven younger brothers and sisters, but was clearly his mother's favorite. She called him "my golden Sigi."[9] Freud's intelligence and gifts were readily apparent. He was reading Shakespeare at eight and Goethe by ten. He was given his own room in the household so that he could study and practice his music undisturbed.

Juxtaposed with these high ambitions of his own and his parents, Freud encountered limitations because of his Jewish heritage.[10] His intentions to study law were changed to medicine, and although he wanted a research career (teaching was not open to Jews), he pursued clinical practice so that he might be financially able to marry his fiancée Martha Bernays, the granddaughter of a Chief Rabbi. During their four-year engagement, Freud wrote her more than 400 love letters.[11]

Freud studied medicine at the University of Vienna, became a doctor, and practiced neurology. He was mentored by French neurologist Jean-Martin Charcot, and partnered with Josef Breuer in studying and treating hysteria. Freud and Breuer published their work *Studies on Hysteria* in 1895.[12] In Paris Freud studied hypnosis with Pierre Janet.

As Freud began his independent practice in Vienna he focused on mental and nervous disorders. He had been using hypnosis in his practice, but increasingly abandoned this in favor of free association as he realized his patients experienced some improvement when able to talk freely and openly about their symptoms.

8. George E. Atwood and Robert D. Stolorow, *Faces in a Cloud: Intersubjectivity in Personality Theory* (Northvale, NJ: Jason Aronson, 1993).

9. Ernest Jones, *The Life and Work of Sigmund Freud*, vol. 1: *The Formative Years and the Great Discoveries, 1856–1900* (New York: Basic Books, 1953), 3.

10. Emanuel Rice, "The Jewish Heritage of Sigmund Freud," *Psychoanalytic Review* 81, no. 2 (Summer 1994) 237–58.

11. Jones, *The Life and Work of Sigmund Freud*, vol. 1.

12. Josef Breuer and Sigmund Freud, *Studies on Hysteria*, vol. 2 of *The Standard Edition*, xxix-335.

Although Freud published some important papers in neurology,[13] he is best known for his corpus of works on psychoanalysis,[14] the inaugural book being *Interpretation of Dreams*. His ideas and work drew followers with whom he had both close and contentious connections. He remained married to his wife Martha for fifty-three years, and they had six children. The youngest, Anna, followed in her father's footsteps in a psychoanalytic career. In 1930, Freud was awarded the Goethe Prize for literature, Germany's highest and most prestigious literary honor.

In 1923, Freud was diagnosed with throat and mouth cancer, brought on by his lifelong habit of smoking cigars. Over a seventeen-year period he had thirty-three operations and at one point needed a partial prosthetic jaw. Although in enormous pain, he continued to work and write until his death. His physician Max Schur had years earlier agreed that, when the time came, he would administer morphine to Freud to ease his passing.[15] Freud died in London on September 23, 1939.[16]

Book summary

A book that was revised eight times over a thirty-year period and translated from German to English is a challenge to summarize. What is offered here is an overview of the last (eighth) revision with some effort made to note sections that were substantively changed and why.[17]

Interpretation of Dreams might be referred to as the first fruits of Freud's self-analysis, which took place between 1896 and 1899. Freud began his self-analysis shortly after the death of his father, Jakob. The other significant source and inspiration for his theory on dreams was his work with patients suffering from a host of what were then termed neurotic

13. From 1876 until 1896, Freud was primarily a neurologist and anatomist. He wrote three monographs on infantile cerebral paralysis, and in 1891, Freud wrote his most important neurological work: "On Aphasia."

14. *The Standard Edition of the Complete Psychological Works of Sigmund Freud,* 24 vols., trans. and ed. James Strachey (London: Hogarth, 1953).

15. Peter Gay, *Freud: A Life for Our Time* (New York: Anchor, 1989).

16. Gay, *Freud: A Life for Our Time*; Jones, *The Life and Work of Sigmund* Freud, vol. 1; Ernest Jones, *The Life and Work of Sigmund Freud*, vol. 2: *Years of Maturity, 1901–1919* (New York: Basic Books, 1955); and Ernest Jones, *The Life and Work of Sigmund Freud*, vol. 3: *The Last Phase, 1919–1939* (New York: Basic Books, 1957).

17. Sigmund Freud, *The Interpretation of Dreams* (1900; rpt. New York: Avon Books / Basic Books, 1965).

disorders, which today would include phobias, conversion hysteria (when psychological suffering is converted into somatic symptoms with no discernible organic cause), dissociation, obsessive-compulsive disorder, post-traumatic stress, anorexia, and non-psychotic depression.

As a result of his self-analysis (particularly of his dreams) and his clinical experiences, Freud came to believe that dreams were the creation of the dreamer and that dreaming represented an organized mental activity distinct from the mentation of waking life and one that obeys its own laws. In taking this position he stood in opposition to both conventional wisdom and scientific opinion of his time. On the one hand, he distanced himself from the classical and popular methods of dream interpretation in use since ancient times, which held that dreams were communications from angelic or demonic sources. From this point of view, with the help of culturally embedded symbols and codes, the future could be foretold. On the other hand, he distanced himself from prevailing scientific opinion of his day that dreams had no psychological significance, but are simply disorganized productions generated by mental stimuli (a jumble of firing neurons, if you will). It was the psychoanalytic method of free association that led Freud to the discovery of the purpose and meaning of dreams, hence he declared: "The interpretation of dreams is the royal road to knowledge of the unconscious activities of the mind."[18]

At the time he was writing, Freud recognized the limited understanding of the neurophysiology of dreaming and therefore decided to offer what was possible at the time: a psychological theory and understanding of dreams and their significance.[19] In the process, he also proposed a model for how the mind works and laid the foundation for psychoanalysis, the method of therapy originated by Freud in which free association, dream interpretation, and analysis of resistance and transference are used to explore repressed or unconscious impulses, anxieties, and internal conflicts, in order to free psychic energy for mature love and work.

---

18. Ibid., 608.

19 An unpublished manuscript was found among Freud's letters to Fliess. It detailed his work on establishing a quantifiable foundation for psychoanalysis as a natural science. He recognized that science had not advanced enough for this to be fully developed, and this deficiency led him to establish psychoanalysis in its own right. This manuscript is included in his complete works: Sigmund Freud, "Project for a Scientific Psychology," in *Pre-Psycho-Analytic Publications and Unpublished Drafts (1886–1899)*, vol. 1 of *The Standard Edition*, 281–391.

The book consists of seven chapters that may be grouped in three sections: an historical overview of the early views of the meanings and methods of dreams and their interpretation (Chapter 1), an articulation and explication of Freud's view that dreams have meaning and, through the employment of his discovered method and interpretive technique, how the meaning can be understood (Chapters 2–6), and an essay presenting his general model of the mind and how it works (Chapter 7).

In Chapter 1, Freud summarizes and reviews the most significant scientific writing focused on dreams written before the turn of the twentieth century. The prehistoric view of dreams was in some respects carried forward into classical antiquity: that dreams were revelations or communications from external sources (divine or demonic) and were instructive in foretelling the future or creating mischief, respectively. This conceptualization had implications for views of the world as well as the soul. He noted the distinction by some (including Aristotle) that dreams, as products of the human mind, by definition could not have divine agency. He identified a tension within and between views about the source and resultant purpose of dreams. He eschews consideration of supernatural sources of dreams in favor of views supported by science. In a series of subsections within this chapter, Freud explores prevailing and sometimes competing explanations of dreams proffered by a host of philosophers and scientists. Some interesting topics explored in this section of the chapter include:

- whether dreams are an extension of waking life or are unrelated (Freud posits the material is related),

- whether the material in dreams is in some way derived from past experience in childhood or from more recent experience (Freud posits both, predicated on the view that all material in dreams is based on experience because no mentation, however fragmentary, is ever lost),

- the range of stimuli that may influence dreams, including noise, light, images while falling asleep, impending illness of which there may be no current symptom, subjects of interest in waking life,

- that dreams may be forgotten due to the troubling nature of the content or a lack of significance assigned to remembering; that dreams involve experience, images, and feelings and do not follow the patterns of linear, logical, sequenced, regulated daytime thought (indeed this transition from more to less control may impede sleep),

- that dreams may reveal wishes, desires, or impulses that are unthinkable in waking life, and that a range of theories exist (so Freud posited at the time) that attempt to explain dreams within a wider context.

However, for Freud none of these theories or threads of theories were sufficiently explanatory. He believed a wholly new cloth needed to be woven that would address the psychical significance of dreaming, particularly how dreams related to other mental processes. He was also interested in what biological function dreams may have, and perhaps most importantly, whether and how dreams may be interpreted so as to understand their meaning.

In Chapter 2, Freud articulates his unique theory and method of dream interpretation. He credited his discovery of the *Oedipus Complex* and his understanding of the meaning of dreams to his self-analysis and clinical work. His hope and intention was that his method would not only unlock the mysteries of dreams, but also lead to greater understanding and successful treatment of mental disorders. He begins by noting that two prevailing interpretive methods were either to take the dream as a whole and replace the symbolism with future fact (he uses the example of Pharaoh's dream of the seven fat and thin cows interpreted by Joseph) or to see each element of a dream as separate and decode it according to a fixed key. Freud's method employed elements of the latter.

Psychoanalysis as a method is predicated on the practice of *free association*, by which a patient is encouraged to notice and report whatever comes to mind without censoring, criticizing, or evaluating the content. Freud believed that the restriction, criticism, and censoring of thought, ideas, or dreams significantly blocks the understanding of dreams and psychological symptoms. Free association enhances the emergence of unconscious material into consciousness and thus (to use one of Freud's favorite phrases) *throws light* on the patient's struggles. To facilitate free association, Freud suggested his patients recline on a couch and close their eyes while he sat out of view. Closing one's eyes was later deemed non-essential. When patients relayed dreams, Freud would ask them to engage in free association to each aspect of the dream. These associations might include images, sounds, memories, feelings, poems, works of art, or music.

To illustrate his new method, he relays the details of a dream that was pivotal in developing his theory. So significant was the night on which his reported dream, referred to as "Irma's injection," occurred that he wrote to his friend Fliess that perhaps someday a plaque would be placed on the house inscribed with the words: "In this house on July 24th, 1895 the secret of dreams was revealed to Dr. Sigm. Freud."[20]

As he relays his analysis of this dream, Freud notes that he needed to compare the conscious content of the dream (which he later terms *manifest content*) and the unconscious concealed thoughts lying behind it (the *latent content*). Latent content surfaces from a reservoir of unconscious impulses and/or fragments of memory, which Freud referred to as *dream thoughts*. These are revealed through free association. Freud identified the trigger of a dream as something incidental from the previous day (which he termed *the day's residues*) that links with unconscious dream thoughts that are pressing for expression.

Step by step, Freud guides the reader through his interpretive process. Although he notes that he did withhold some details of his dreams, the extent of his revelations about personal experience was (for his day) a very vulnerable and brave undertaking. Freud wanted to lead by example, forging a path leading to self-discovery through interpreting dreams.

In his concluding remarks in Chapter 2, Freud makes a declarative statement that is the result of analyzing the dreams of his patients and colleagues, but most particularly illustrated in the detailed examination of his own dreams: "When the work of interpretation has been completed, we perceive that a dream is the fulfillment of a wish."[21] In Chapter 3, Freud underscored his admittedly bold statement that dreams are fulfillment of wishes. More specifically, he says that dreams may express wishes of an erotic or aggressive nature, although this may likely be disguised.

To address more fully the idea of disguised wishes, which he introduced in a footnote to a later edition of the book, Freud devoted Chapter 4 to the topic of distortion in dreams. He stated that previous theories of dream interpretation have focused on conscious or manifest content of dreams; however, his focus is on the latent or unconscious content of dreams. Interpretation reveals what lies beneath or behind a dream. He assumed some would wonder how distressing and/or anxiety dreams can be wish fulfillments. In response, Freud stated: "Everyone has wishes that he would prefer not to disclose to other people, and wishes that he will not

20. Sigmund Freud, *The Complete Letters of Sigmund Freud to Wilhelm Fliess, 1887–1904*, trans. and ed. Jeffrey Moussaieff Masson (Cambridge, MA: The Belknap Press of Harvard University Press), Letter 137.

21. Freud, *The Interpretation of Dreams*, 154. In Chapter 5, Freud asserted that a dream may reflect a past wish as well as one from present day.

admit even to himself."[22] Therefore, in conscious life these wishes may be suppressed or denied, and in dreams they may be distorted or disguised.

Freud posited that when dreaming, there are two psychical forces at work: the wish that is pressing for expression, and censorship of the unacceptable wish. This tension results in distortion. Chapter 4 is full of examples and illustrations of distortion in dreams, including the assertion that dreams regularly have more than one meaning. To the thorny question of why what are termed counter-wish dreams occur (dreams that logic would suggest express a wish for an undesirable outcome), Freud replied that some of his patients had a wish for him to be wrong and would therefore thwart his interpretive efforts. To this somewhat humorous possibility is added a more troubling and sobering possibility that, for some, frustration or other undesirable outcome *is* the fulfillment of a wish. This latter type of dream represents a form of mental masochism.

In Chapter 5, Freud deepened the foundation of unconscious latent content by examining the varied sources of dreams. These sources include material from infancy or childhood, recent events, and physical sensations or illness. He also included a section on typical dreams, such as embarrassing dreams of being naked, dreams of a beloved person's death, and examination dreams. Typical dreams are so named because they were dreamt by most people, although similarity of source or sources could not be assumed. Without the free associations of the dreamer, a dream could not be interpreted and thereby properly understood. The import of this section may be in discovering that for more than 100 years people have been dreaming about similar themes, suggesting something consistent about the human condition. As in other chapters, Freud provided a plethora of examples, many from his own life, illustrating the many sources of material for dreams.

Chapter 6 details Freud's understanding of the mental processes involved in converting latent unconscious content (dream thoughts) into manifest conscious content. He called this process *dream work*. Freud reminds the reader that the emphasis on latent unconscious content, rather than manifest conscious content, is what sets his theory apart from others in the near or long past, as does his method of using free association to facilitate the surfacing of unconscious material along with his carefully articulated interpretive method.

22. Ibid., 193.

Freud equated both dream thoughts and dream content to languages with their own syntax and laws, making accurate translation essential to understanding meaning (versus superficial symbolic comparisons, which would be misleading). He equated a dream to a rebus (a medieval picture puzzle) in which each element must be translated and then used to create the whole. Chapter 6 is the most lengthy and dense chapter of the book. It is also full of references to literature, particularly the writings of Goethe, who was among Freud's favorites. Literary examples and numerous dreams are used for illustrative purposes, which help make the concepts more accessible. The sections of this chapter explain the various mental processes employed during dreaming, which include:

- *Condensation*: a process of fusing or combining dream thoughts that share a common theme. Brevity and economy of expression are important, as is having the dream thoughts combined in a way that successfully avoids censorship.

- *Displacement*: another expression of censorship where the dream thoughts that are surfacing in relation to an idea, person, feeling, or memory can be reassigned, even to an opposite expression. This principle underlies the formation of symbols in dreams.

- *Representation* and *Representability*: two sections that address how dream thoughts will be represented in dreams. Dreams do not follow the same rules of logic, syntax, and speech as does waking life. There is no realistic presentation of time. Composites and contradictions may be commonplace. The proximity of images in dreams, scenes that undergo transformation, or multiple dreams on the same night all suggest a relation between the elements. Manifest content will likely be in the form of symbols that may represent more than one idea, and may be presented in a form that has successfully avoided censorship.

- *Symbols in Dreams/Some Further Typical Dreams* and *Some Examples/ Calculations and Speeches in Dreams*: There is a decidedly different tone to these two sections. Freud offers a type of "dream book" that relates recurring symbols and images in dreams (as well as certain recurring associations) to male and female genitalia and sexual activity. In the second section, he added to this "dream book" some interesting examples of interpretations of numbers, calculations, time, and historical events that may all appear in dreams. The sections are replete with examples. However, what is missing is the careful and considered process Freud has earlier articulated whereby each dream element is explored via free association, and the analyst offers interpretations based on the patient's history, associations, as well as what the analyst may know about typical dreams and concomitant collective interpretive ideas. Many of these dreams were provided by friends or colleagues and so were not fully analyzed by Freud using his interpretive method. This I think is a drawback to these sections. The volume of material, the dearth of explanation or elaboration of the process, and numerous conclusions may lead to confusion and misunderstanding of his theory and suspicion about his interpretations.

- *Absurd Dreams*: Freud addressed his critics who used the occasion of absurd content in dreams to dismiss them as "the meaningless product of a reduced and fragmentary mental activity."[23] His reply was that absurdity is only apparent and will disappear when the dream is properly interpreted and the meaning revealed. Absurdity in dreams may reveal a critical, mocking, or ridiculing motive emanating from the patient's dream thoughts.

- *Affects in Dreams*: contains a fascinating discussion of emotions in dreams. The central thesis (a true gem of this whole chapter) is that affect in dreams is a through line that will most reliably lead to a person's dream thoughts. The more intense and dominating an emotion is in dream thoughts, the more it will vie for expression in the dream content. According to Freud, the sources of affect in dreams may be somatic, may derive from something that happened on the dream day, or may emanate from an enduring mood (or affective tendency) on the part of the dreamer. However, because of dream work (condensation, displacement, and representation), the content and affect in dreams may appear contradictory or an emotion may be represented by its opposite in order to avoid censorship.

- Secondary Revision: refers to the process that dream content goes through beginning with the transition from sleep to waking when the dreamer begins to focus consciously on the dream and attempts to recall and reconstruct it. The purpose of secondary revision is to fill in the gaps in the dream structure. This aspect of dream work is the only carry over from previous theories of dream interpretation, which according to Freud, focused exclusively on conscious content and

23. Ibid., 461.

process. Although this part of dream work is conscious, censorship is still operative.

Chapter 7 is the *piece de resistance* of the book. On the foundation of his many years of medical training as a neurologist, his clinical work with patients, and his four-year self-analysis, Freud has constructed not only a method for interpreting dreams, but also a revolutionary understanding of the human mind. This chapter contains six sections devoted to topics such as forgetting dreams, regression, wish-fulfillment, the function of dreams, primary and secondary processes/repression, and the unconscious and consciousness/reality. The reader may recognize in these topics the building blocks of Freud's theory of dreams and of mental life. Through his discovery and application of his method for understanding and interpreting dreams, Freud noticed that dreams bore some similarity to psychological symptoms. This led him to ponder the workings of the mind in both normal and pathological states.

The most striking and lasting concepts and contributions of this chapter include Freud's articulation of primary and secondary processes. Primary process is developmentally earlier, governed by the desire for pleasure and avoidance of what is not pleasurable, and is not limited by time, space, or logic. Opposites can coexist without contradiction. This is the mentation of dreams, fantasies, and symptoms. Secondary processes come developmentally later and are represented by language and governed by (Aristotelian) logic.

Also in this chapter, Freud introduces his topographical structure of the mind: unconscious, preconscious, and conscious. What in this book Freud referred to as censorship (the firewall of sorts between the conscious and unconscious mind) would later be revised when he introduced his structural model of the mind (id, ego, and superego). In this later model, censorship is taken up in the function of the superego to constrain the expression of impulses.

Regression and repression are two other building blocks of Freudian theory. In dreams, regression occurs when an idea is turned back into a sensory image from which it was originally derived. In waking life, regression occurs when thoughts or memories that have been suppressed or are unconscious are transformed into images. This, Freud observed, was the stuff of paranoia and hallucinations in his patients suffering with hysterical symptoms.

In this final chapter, Freud articulated and set forth a substantive scientific theory that was psychological rather than neurophysiological; the latter endeavor he began, but set aside. Freud's work on this, *Project for a Scientific Psychology*, was discovered among the letters he wrote to his friend Fliess, which were published at a later date.[24] Also included in the book are various appendices, bibliographies, and indexes all oriented around the subject of dreams.

A Lasting Legacy

In view of the title of this book, the reader might ask, "Why should Christians care about the work of a man who referred to himself as 'a godless Jew'[25] and 'an unrepentant heretic'?"[26] Are his scathing critiques and negative commentaries on religion enough to banish him from serious consideration by thinking Christians? I hope not, and let me explain why.

Interpretation of Dreams has been heralded by some as "the book of the (twentieth) century"[27] and by others as "one of the greatest books of Western civilization, a permanent member of the so-called Western canon."[28] Arguably, the book launched the fields of psychology, psychiatry, and psychoanalysis, and contributed significantly to others (such as literature, medicine, and neuroscience).

Freud popularized the idea of the unconscious, and that past experiences may live on in present day life without a person being aware of the impact. While he did not purport to have discovered the unconscious (this he credited to poets and philosophers), Freud was the first to develop a theory about how the mind worked and for how it could be known, understood, and studied. It was a foundation for the scientific study of the mind from that time forward.

24. Freud, "Project for a Scientific Psychology."

25. Sigmund Freud, "Letter from Sigmund Freud to Oskar Pfister, October 9, 1918," *International Psycho-Analytical Library* 59 (1918) 61–63.

26. Jones, *The Life and Work of Sigmund Freud*, vol. 2, 46.

27. Ilse Grubrich-Simitis, "Metamorphoses of *The Interpretation of Dreams*: Freud's conflicted Relations with his Book of the Century," *International Journal of Psychoanalysis* 81, no. 6 (December 2000) 1155–83; and Grubrich-Simitis, "How Freud Wrote and Revised his *Interpretation of Dreams*."

28. Chessick, "Review of *The Interpretation of Dreams*," 184.

Dreams, because they were the closest and purest access to unconscious process, were of particular fascination to Freud. Following this "royal road" would lead deeper into the mysteries of mental life. Freud was the first to discover that dreams had meaning and that we dream to deal unconsciously with impulses, feeling, and/or memories that we cannot yet admit into conscious awareness. Dreams, he discovered, are a form of internal communication that need to be interpreted to be understood. He believed that insight into one's inner life would lead to healthier living because increased self-awareness would free the energy used to contend with problems unconsciously to be directed toward conscious, present-day interests and relationships.

To postulate the existence and influence of the unconscious on current mental and behavioral life involved an admission of not knowing and required acknowledging the unconscious as a source of influence in everyday life. This was highly offensive to the Enlightenment sensibilities of his day, which were moving in a direction of positivism and rationality. Freud was brave in making these bold claims, and it cost him dearly in lack of support for his work in general and this book in particular for almost a decade after publication.

Added to the insult to Enlightenment sensibilities was injury to Victorian consciousness. Freud emphasized several controversial theories relating the unconscious to sex, aggression, fantasy, and religion. He broke a major taboo of the Victorian era that prohibited anything but polite social discourse. Hidden or unacknowledged realities became the subject of open, public conversation. In addition to talking about sexual and aggressive impulses and fantasies, he addressed the darker side of human existence, the human tendency to seek pleasure and instant gratification, and the need to tame baser instincts. He was willing to say things that most people did not want to hear, let alone admit to thinking or feeling at a conscious or unconscious level.

Many Christians find Freud and his writings offensive because of his characterization of religion. It was not until I conducted my own research on Freud's life and began reading his work myself that I discovered that what I had been exposed to was largely a caricature of Freud. The impressions I had formed (from second hand source material and also from media presentations) were of a rigid, arrogant, dogmatic man who was hung up on sex and hated religion: a man obsessed with creating a dynasty and intolerant of any disagreement. For many, he was a misogynist at worst, patriarchal at best. Another caricature was that of the removed analyst who would sit behind his patients, offer an occasional "uh huh" and then pronounce at the end of session that the patient (if he were male) was in love with his mother and wanted to replace his father, or (if the patient were female) that she had penis envy. These indictments are a gross misrepresentation and oversimplification of Freud the man and his work as a whole.

Any serious student of the Bible knows the danger of proof texting, of taking a passage or idea out of context, and of not going back to the original language to understand the meaning of a passage of scripture and a particular passage in the whole counsel of the word of God. A parallel I am making is that Freud's work was originally in German, not English; so at best we are starting with a translation that some scholars feel strips the life, beauty, and nuance out of the work as a whole.[29] Another intended parallel is that Freud developed many of his ideas over half a century. Any one particular idea must be seen in the full context and compared with other versions of the same idea across time.

It is true that in much of his work Freud called attention to religion in a negative way, but let us consider one aspect of that more closely. Freud advocated for increasing awareness of one's inner life, and he led the way in this by undertaking his own self-analysis, which he later acknowledged was in many respects prompted by the death of his father. This profound loss brought on a desire for self-examination, though he did not realize it at the time. Freud believed that whatever was discovered through dreams and analysis must be faced squarely without excuse, judgment, or escape. He objected to the use of religion as an escape rather than facing troubling realities (memories, feelings, impulses, and wishes). On this point, I agree with him. In present day language, we might refer to this as using religion as a defense against awareness, as a way to avoid admitting or dealing with wishes, feelings, memories, and thoughts that we do not want to admit. What Freud tragically missed was the experience of religion as a source of hope, joy, and purpose, and of faith as a pathway to redemption.

Freud's influence on the Western world, on the academy, and on society at large, including the church, has been enormous and continues to grow. Grotjahn has observed: "It might be said that Sigmund Freud disturbed the sleep of the world."[30] Freud biographer Peter Gay has observed that in

29. Bruno Bettelheim, *Freud and Man's Soul* (New York: Knopf, 1982).

30. Martin Grotjahn, "Franz Alexander: Western Mind In Translation," in *Psychoanalytic Pioneers*, ed. Franz Alexander, Samuel Eisenstein, and Martin Grotjahn (New

Western civilization we all speak Freud whether we know it or not.[31] Because of the enormity of Freud's influence on Western culture, philosopher and theologian Paul Ricoeur has argued that believers are obligated to interact with Freud's ideas and must be willing to expose religious belief to a hermeneutic of suspicion.[32] Rather than undermining a believer's faith, Bingaman has asserted that this engagement will bring about the death of simplistic faith and a resurrection of a deeper, more robust, and more nuanced faith.[33] In her foreword to Bingaman's book, *Freud and Faith: Living in the Tension*, Diane Jonte-Pace observes of the author:

> First, he urges that believers respond to Freud with both yes-and-no. He recommends a resounding "no" to the enlightenment Freud for whom religion is always immature and neurotic; a "no" to the Freud for whom God is nothing but a projection; a "no" to the Freud for whom God is excluded from ultimate reality. He would say "yes," however, to the Freud who understands and critiques the dynamics of immature faith; "yes" to the Freud who articulates the problematic attraction of the God of consolation and constraint; "yes" to the Freud who finds meaning in imagination and psychical reality. His yes-and-no holds Freud in dialectical tension.[34]

Through interaction with Freud's ideas about, and critique of, religious faith, one will be changed. Bingaman, and Ricoeur before him, believe this will be a change for the better. I agree with them.

After Freud's death, many psychoanalysts began writing about the value and importance of religion and faith to healthy and unhealthy psychological functioning, and this remains a focus in the literature.[35] Analysts in the 1940s, particularly Fairbairn and Guntrip, introduced religious ter-

York: Basic Books, 1966), 390.

31. Gay, *Freud: A Life for Our Time*.

32. Paul Ricoeur, *Freud and Philosophy*, trans. Denis Savage (1965; rpt. New Haven, CT: Yale University Press, 1977).

33. Kirk A. Bingaman, *Freud and Faith: Living in the Tension* (New York: State University of New York Press, 2003).

34. Ibid., x.

35. For early revisions to psychoanalysis after Freud, the work of object relations theorists W. Ronald D. Fairbairn, Donald W. Winnicott, and Harry Guntrip are most notable. Recent scholarship in this area includes Ana-Maria Rizzuto, *The Birth of the Living God: A Psychoanalytic Study* (Chicago: University of Chicago Press, 1979); Randall Lehmann Sorenson, *Minding Spirituality* (Hillsdale, NJ: Analytic Press, 2004); and Marie T. Hoffman, *Toward Mutual Recognition: Relational Psychoanalysis and the Christian Narrative* (New York: Routledge, 2011).

minology and themes into discussions of theory and practice. Fairbairn, who was raised Presbyterian and later converted to Anglicanism, and Guntrip, who was a Congregational minister before becoming an analyst, mainstream for the psychoanalytic community the notion that religion and faith are important developmental realities that must be understood and included in treatment. In the first of many that followed, psychiatrist and psychoanalyst Ana-Maria Rizzuto conducted a thorough qualitative study and analysis of how an understanding of God develops. She, too, noted this as part of healthy development. So the field has and is changing for the better with respect to the dialogue between psychoanalysis and religion.

Some scholars have noted that Freud's rejection of God and religion was likely influenced by multiple complex factors in his life, including: the times in which he lived, socio-political realities, the religious life of his family, and the particular struggles of the patients he saw in his practice whose obsessions and neuroses had a quality to them that threw negative light on faith and religion.[36] In addition, other scholars have noted that Freud's critique of Christianity is likely based in large part on the influence of his Catholic nanny during a time when his Jewish heritage caused him, on occasion, to be marginalized and even the focus of overt discrimination.[37] This is important to keep in mind as a way of remembering the humanness of Freud even while contending with objectionable aspects of his theory.

Increasingly, many Christians are finding Freud's work to provide important insights for personal and spiritual growth and healing. Some Christian psychologists and psychoanalysts have discussed ways in which dreams and the unconscious are important considerations in a distinctively Christian understanding of wholeness and healing. In a contemporary classic, *Dreams: God's Forgotten Language*, John Sanford (a Jungian analyst and Episcopal priest) discusses the relevance of dreams to Christian experience.[38] He invites readers to adopt a biblical perspective that views wholeness as completion rather than perfection. This view of wholeness includes recognition of both conscious and unconscious aspects of experience. Dreams are considered an important source of access to unconscious life.

36. Ana-Maria Rizzuto, *Why Did Freud Reject God? A Psychodynamic Interpretation* (New Haven, CT: Yale University Press, 1998).

37. Paul C. Vitz, *Sigmund Freud's Christian Unconscious* (Grand Rapids: Eerdmans, 1988).

38. John A. Sanford, *Dreams: God's Forgotten Language* (1968; rpt. New York: HarperCollins, 1989).

Following in Sanford's footsteps, psychologist David Benner, in another contemporary classic, *Care of Souls: Revisioning Christian Nurture and Counsel*, devotes an entire chapter to dreams and the unconscious. Dreams, according to Benner, are the "language of the soul."[39] He points out that, for many Christians, Enlightenment and Christian teaching may have subtly or directly associated conscious, rational thought with goodness, and the unconscious with badness (by virtue of its Freudian connection with impulses of a sexual and aggressive nature). Benner suggests a redemptive view of the unconscious and dreams that reclaims the biblical notion of dreams as an important possible source of communication from God (citing Daniel 2), as well as communication between the unconscious and conscious aspects of the self (citing Psalms).

Through examples from clinical practice and ministry, both Benner and Sanford discuss how many Christians may believe that denying or suppressing unconscious realities is the path to wholeness. They relate how, sadly, this is not the case. In fact, what is denied or unacknowledged has the opposite impact of exerting more influence over feelings and actions rather than less. Benner makes the statement:

> One of the most important things we have learned from depth psychology is that there can be no wholeness apart from the redemption of the unconscious. This insight was expressed in Freud's observation that our capacity for freedom of choice and action is limited by our bondage to personality factors that operate beyond our awareness.[40]

Both Benner and Sanford recommend a consistent and disciplined process of prayerfully considering the meaning of dreams as unconscious communications from the self under the sovereign eye of God. They recommend this be done in the company of a trusted and trained pastor or counselor and include keeping a dream journal.

There is much more that could be said about Sigmund Freud, the unconscious, and dreams. Advances in neuroscience are opening new vistas to understanding the complexities of the human mind. Interdisciplinary dialogue is advancing the development of theologically and theoretically rich conceptualizations of human experience. Adopting a yes-and-no response to Freud, who was in many respects ahead of his time, and in other

39. David G. Benner, *Care of Souls: Revisioning Christian Nurture and Counsel* (Grand Rapids: Baker, 1998).

40. Ibid., 161.

respects behind his time, will facilitate the capacity of Christians to hold in dialectical tension sources of truth and revelation while we are still in an age where we only see through a glass darkly.

CHAPTER 11: SOCIOLOGY

Max Weber, *The Protestant Ethic and the Spirit of Capitalism*

BY NORI LOWE HENK

Introduction

WHEN I TEACH MAX Weber's *The Protestant Ethic and the Spirit of Capitalism*,[1] I often begin by making a bold statement: "Protestant Christians make the best capitalists." This is perhaps a simplified statement, but it does get at the heart of Weber's guiding question—what is the social relationship between religious culture and economic culture? I also make it clear to my students that sociologists who study religion are not proving God's existence or asking traditional theological questions about ultimate reality, but are studying the social fact that people's beliefs in God(s) and theological precepts affect their behavior. Making this distinction is especially necessary when teaching at a Christian university. It does not mean that a sociological study like *The Protestant Ethic and the Spirit of Capitalism* has no theological implications because it certainly does. Moreover, I explain, the relationship between religion and society has largely been based on religion's capacity to sacralize the normative social order. This is a key insight sociologists use to evaluate religious influence in our everyday lives.

---

1. Weber's study was originally written in German, and there are two English translations. I use the more recent translation by Stephen Kalberg, Third Roxbury Edition (Los Angeles: Roxbury, 2002).

On the one hand, society can impose a secular law to maintain normative behavior with punitive consequences such as a monetary fines or imprisonment. On the other hand, in a more powerful and persuasive way, religious ideas can be used to normalize behavior on the basis of one's salvation and God's plan in the world. Given Weber's social context, there is perhaps no stronger cultural force than religion to persuade people to behave in highly rationalized, systematic, and orderly ways.

Weber's study of the relationship between the historical rise of Protestantism and modern capitalism points out these central sociological insights and, in fact, is one of the first studies to outline clearly how and why sociological theories differ from traditional theological and philosophical ideas in their understanding of human behavior. In this chapter, I will summarize the main points of the book, the reasons the book is important for university students to study, and the implications the book has for Christians who read it.

Summary of the Book

Within the religious framework of this edited volume, I will start my summary of *The Protestant Ethic and the Spirit of Capitalism* with Weber's discussion of Martin Luther's theological idea of calling. Prior to Luther, the Catholic understanding of calling was a specific task given only to those in religious leadership, such as priests and monks, particularly those called to an otherworldly orientation (e.g., living apart from the world in a monastery). In his translation of the word calling, Luther used the German word *Beruf*. In German, *Beruf* means "calling," but it is the kind of calling that is directed at one's daily work in *this* world. According to Weber, Luther's translation used a word that was not in the Catholic Bible and therefore introduced a new theological idea. The word *Beruf* is found in 1 Corinthians 1:26, 7:20; Ephesians 1:18, 4:1, 4:2; 2 Thess 1:11; Hebrews 3:1; and 2 Peter 1:10. For example, 1 Corinthians 7:20 says, "Let each man abide in that *calling* wherein he was called" (ASV).

What is new about the word *Beruf*, and why is it significant? Luther's German translation of the word changed the idea of calling from the highest calling of the monks and priests to the sacred calling for all believers—befitting of the common phrase attributed to Luther, "the priesthood of all believers." Specifically, Luther's idea of calling was meant to testify to Christians' salvation and God's good will in their everyday life. This focus on "work" rejects the Catholic notion that divinely sanctioned work in this world is a choice or that it should be separated from this world; instead everyday work in this world is "pleasing to God."[2] Weber explains that the word *Beruf* was not initially central to Luther's theology, but over time it became important in defining his theology, especially against traditional Catholic thought, to the point that monastic, "otherworldly" work was seen as less pleasing to God than the work done in this world. According to Luther, this-worldly work is "the only way to please God. This fulfillment, and only this, is God's will. Therefore every permissible calling is of absolutely equal validity before God."[3] Changing the meaning of "calling" to cover all kinds of work in this world paved the way for legitimating a new kind of work within a rational capitalist economy.

I begin with the theological concept of *Beruf* because of the socio-logical implications this idea has in its affinity to capitalism. Perhaps Weber overstates his case, as many scholars point out, but his essential argument in the book is that Protestant nations more easily adopted a modern capi-talist economic system than Catholic nations. I will not heavily critique this macro-level relationship per se, but rather focus on the sociological in-sights Weber offers for the unique, mutual influence between religion and economic behavior. This relationship is neither a simple nor a necessary or deterministic one; rather, historical forces brought Protestantism, with its "this-worldly" orientation, and modern capitalism together in a way that reinforced and benefited both. A general shift in Western countries from economic traditionalism to economic rationalism was happening at the height of the Age of Enlightenment at the same time that the dominant worldview was shifting from a Catholic to a Protestant perspective. Eco-nomic traditionalism spoke of an economic order in which production was about making just enough to live and nothing more. In contrast, economic rationalism was about profit, economic growth, and mass production be-yond satisfaction of basic needs, specifically emphasizing entrepreneurial endeavors, individual utilitarianism, and the development of a strong middle class. The shift from Catholicism to Protestantism led to a theologi-cal preoccupation with discerning God's will for every person rather than only those at the top. Catholic values reinforced economic traditionalism in the sense that religion focused more on otherworldliness and the immedi-ate enjoyment of life, and these values tended to be indifferent to capitalist

2. Weber, *The Protestant Ethic and the Spirit of Capitalism*, 40.
3. Ibid., 41.

ideals and ascetic lifestyles. In contrast, Protestant values inclined toward strictly regimented work, a disdain for wastefulness or pompous shows of wealth, and a general fixation on the individual's religious calling, making Protestantism the "capitalist economy's seed-bed."[4]

When I make the statement that "Protestant Christians make the best capitalists," I am not arguing that Protestants are inherently greedy and love wealth for the pure sake of pursuing profit. But in the spirit that Weber argued, Protestants believe in work that is ascetic[5] in nature—ordained by God possessing "a degree of detached modesty,"[6] and practiced in good stewardship over acquired resources. Money and making money are connected to their vocational calling, and acquisition of capital is "the result and manifestation and competence and proficiency in a vocational calling."[7] The individual calling of ordinary people is a modern manifestation of a capitalistic culture and this ascetic Protestant ethic provides significance to our economic actions, legitimizing and even sacralizing our economic decisions. According to that ethic, every economic action requires intentionality and sacred thoughtfulness. In Weber's theory connecting Protestantism and capitalism, the ethic exists and serves the interest of capitalist goals of acquisition and profit: "to the extent that people are interwoven into the context of capitalism's market forces, the norms of its economic action are forced into them."[8] These norms then define people's behavior, and there are both economic and moral consequences for not following these norms. In other words, Protestantism provided the cultural mindset, ideological structure, and socialization necessary to promote and stabilize a rational capitalist economic system. In Weber's words, there is a social "connection between peoples' capacity to adapt to (modern) capitalism, on the one hand, and their religious beliefs, on the other."[9] *Beruf*, as Luther conceptualized it, became an ideological mechanism to legitimize the kind of work necessary for capitalism to flourish.

4. Ibid., 10.

5. Weber's use of asceticism refers to the delay of worldly desires and humble action in this world, and does not refer to the theological practice of monasticism. An austere and disciplined spiritual lifestyle practiced in this world is important for all Christians to live, rather than just the priests or the monks.

6. Weber, *The Protestant Ethic and the Spirit of Capitalism*, 32.

7. Ibid., 18.

8. Ibid.

9. Ibid., 25.

Weber lingers on this point because profit prior to modern capitalism was seen as abhorrent, evil, unnecessary, and illegal. Pre-capitalist moral ideas about profit were characterized by the Catholic Church in the Middle Ages as "moral turpitude," and even modest profit was seen as morally problematic. As Weber explains, "the acquisition as an end in itself involved a fundamentally disgraceful situation, albeit one that existing realities made it necessary to tolerate."[10] If profit was gained, it was often given back to the church or even to former debtors. To evolve to the point that a dominant religious worldview legitimized capitalist endeavors required a complete historical and moral turnaround. This affinity between cultural and economic forces did not solidify until the turn of the eighteenth century, and the capitalist spirit and the Protestant ethic connected more perfectly in economically struggling nations such as the newly created United States.[11] Prior to modern capitalism, work and life were moderated, with low amounts of work for the greatest possible economic outcome: "A comfortable tempo of life was the order of the day."[12] To accomplish historical change, Weber argues, it was not enough to have an economic goal of profit and acquisition. An ethos also had to be present in the workers and the owners in order to facilitate and maximize acquisition and profit. The "traditional economy" was upset and changed to a modern capitalist spirit: peasants became workers; markets became caterers to consumer needs, low prices, and large sales; and whoever did not follow this modern spirit lost out competitively and was effectively left out of the economic system. The Protestant ethic served to rationalize and smooth over the transition from a needs-based economy to a profit-based economy.

In the last two chapters of *The Protestant Ethic and the Spirit of Capitalism*, Weber notes that three religious beliefs serve to establish and legitimize a highly rationalized economic culture. In addition to the previously discussed ascetic concept of calling, the second and third beliefs had to do with God's perfect will and the theology of the elect. In all three beliefs, it is important to remember an earlier point made, namely that these Protestant beliefs affected all believers. Even though Luther helped to establish the theological idea of calling, Weber finds that Calvinist, Pietist, Methodist,

10. Ibid., 33.

11. The United States represented an idealized situation in which to explore connections between the highly rigorous Puritanical way of life and the establishment of economic rationalism.

12. Weber, *The Protestant Ethic and the Spirit of Capitalism*, 28.

and Baptist groups were far more salient than Lutheranism in incorporating the ascetic version of calling into their belief systems and everyday behavior. All four Protestant groups, and particularly those that shaped the Puritanical worldview, practiced rationalized everyday living with "identical manifestations of the moral organization of life," using "highly influential literary devices employed in the organized care of the soul."[13] Beliefs about the next life "absolutely dominated people's religious thinking at that time" and in turn affected the "practical life of believers."[14]

For Weber, Calvinism, Pietism, Methodism, and the Baptists were groups par excellence in demonstrating the social and economic effects of gaining certitude of one's salvation through "good works." Weber begins with the Calvinist doctrine of predestination, which is the belief that some are predestined to eternal life (the elect) and others to eternal death. God sees great purpose in the elect and gives them his free grace and love without condition, but for those predestined to eternal death, God sees their corrupt lives as beyond his grace and redemption.[15] Weber's purpose in discussing the doctrine of predestination is not theological but sociological—to show that this theology gives precedence to God's sovereignty beyond anyone's action, an idea that both provides certainty in God's nature and uncertainty with one's innate sinfulness. According to Calvinism, we cannot work towards God's favor or overcome our sin through acts of contrition: "from eternity, and entirely according to God's inaccessible decisions, every person's destiny has been decided . . . Because his decrees are firm and unalterable, His grace cannot be lost once granted and cannot be attained once denied."[16]

The psychological consequence of the "invisible" elect, according to Weber, is "a feeling of unimaginable inner loneliness of the solitary individual"—nothing that he or she does can change what God has planned.[17] Yet the response to psychological anxiety is a social one in that individuals

13. Ibid, 53–54.

14. Ibid., 54–55.

15. This sentence is a brief summation of the Westminster Confession of 1647.

16. Weber, *The Protestant Ethic and the Spirit of Capitalism*, 59. Although not all four Protestant groups believe in predestination, all four in some way focus on who constitute the elect, a designation which in turn affects their followers' behavior in systematic and rational ways. Weber clearly believes that Calvinist theology is the most ideal type out of the four to establish the Protestant ethic, however.

17. Ibid., 59.

are compelled to follow strict Christian ethics to reveal to the community that they are one of the elect:

> The world exists, and only exists, to serve the glorification of God. The predestined Christian exists, and only exists, in order to do his part to increase God's glory in the world through the implementation of his commandments. Indeed God wants the Christian to engage in community activity because he wants the social organization of life to be arranged according to His commandments, and thus according to the goal of serving His greater glory. The social work of the Calvinist is in the end for the glory of God. It follows that work in a calling is also affected by this aim, and hence this-worldly work stands in service to the community as a whole.[18]

Christians must trust that they are of the elect while at the same time leave open the possibility that they may be in fact the damned: "thus the chosen are, and remain God's invisible church."[19]

Later Protestant theologians, out of pastoral concern for those who had anxiety over their salvation, would suggest that behavior may in fact reveal one's state of grace. This idea was particularly evident in the Lutheran development of Pietism. In fact one's social position may indicate that one is of the elect. Weber explains that "Work, and work alone, banishes religious doubt and gives certainty to one's status among the saved."[20] In addition, if people are among the elect, then they are capable of having this kind of unshakable faith, and through regenerating God's holiness in their lives, they can increase God's glory in their good works. The elected ones in fact must increase God's glory through such acts; they are to be obedient to God's will, and in this obedience achieve the highest reward, the certainty of grace. The works are not in themselves sacred or perfect—actions are human and therefore cannot be used to obtain salvation—"Nevertheless, good works are indispensable as signs of election."[21] For Weber this rationale forms the foundation for practical action for Calvinists:

> God helps those who help themselves . . . The Calvinist creates for himself the certainty of his salvation. Unlike in Catholicism, the creation of this certainty cannot be built from a gradual accumulation of single, service-oriented good works. It is comprised

18. Ibid., 63.
19. Ibid., 64.
20. Ibid., 66.
21. Ibid., 68.

> instead of the systematic self-control necessary, in every moment,
> when the believer stands before the alternatives: Am I the saved or
> among the damned?[22]

The action in this life was not "planless and unsystematic," but rather it "was molded into a consistent methodical organization of his life as a whole."[23]

The relationship between the Protestant ethic and the capitalist spirit within Protestant communities is clearly found in the pastoral care and discourse over wealth and work. The "enjoyment of wealth" was viewed as morally reprehensible because it "results in idleness and indulging desires of the flesh, and above all in the distraction of believers from their pursuit of the 'saintly' life."[24] Worse than accumulation of wealth for oneself is the waste of one's calling; every moment should be used to make sure one is of the elect, and the loss of time is a moral evil. Work was seen as the highest virtue: "first, work is the tried and proven mechanism for the practice of asceticism . . . work constitutes a particular defense mechanism against all those temptations summarized by the Puritan notion of the 'unclean life' . . . Second, in addition and above all, as ordained by God, the purpose of life itself involves work . . . An unwillingness to work is a sign that one is not among the saved."[25] All are obliged to work no matter what their station in life or economic position.

According to the Puritanism, the differences in economic status were "meant to be" and one should not criticize economic differences. Rather providence has given each person "skills" to fulfill the larger design of the economy (for the greater good and the glory of God), thus leading to an increase in productivity.[26] Still, the aristocracy and the very poor are put at odds with this work ethic, for both classes of people are seen as unsuccessful workers who lack a work ethic. Instead the business owner and the middle class are seen as the most blessed by God because of their combination of hard work and ethical calling. Business entrepreneurs and the middle class are more apt at underscoring their fundamental role in the production of goods, in saving and investing within a capitalist system, and in living a modest lifestyle. The middle class vocational ethos is rooted in one's position as a result of God's grace and blessings. As Weber points out,

22. Ibid., 69.
23. Ibid., 71.
24. Ibid., 104.
25. Ibid., 106.
26. Ibid., 107.

"if he stayed within the bounds of formal correctness, if his moral conduct remained blameless, and if the use he made of his wealth was not offensive, this person was now allowed to follow his interest in economic gain, and indeed should do so."[27] This ethical approach then supported the work required for capitalism to thrive. Economic and religious vocations were effectively united: "work and the industrious pursuit of a trade was their duty to God."[28]

The modern capitalist spirit had a historical affinity to the rational organization of life based on the religious idea of a calling to vocational asceticism. This idea of vocation today does not necessitate a religious connotation, although it started out this way and continues to have an element of asceticism even if it may not be religious in nature. We all have a special function, and we must be resigned to it—the difference being that Puritans desired this ideal of vocation, whereas today, Weber argues, we are forced to see work this way. The religious values of Protestantism helped to "construct the powerful cosmos of the modern economic order. Tied to the technical and economic conditions at the foundation of mechanical and machine production, this cosmos today determines the style of life of all individuals born into it, not only those directly engaged in earning a living."[29] For Weber, mutually reinforcing this relationship between religious culture and economic culture will probably exist until all natural resources associated with capitalism have been exploited. Together the Protestant ethic and the capitalist spirit lead Weber to his concluding point: the product of historical forces of capitalism and Protestantism is an inescapable "iron cage," a highly rationalized social behavior that no longer needs religious justification and will not likely be overcome.

Importance of Book for the University

In the classical canon of white male sociologists, Weber comes after Durkheim and Marx. His theoretical vantage point is clear: Weber holds the middle ground between an idealist thinker and a materialist thinker. He did not prioritize the economic order, nor did he assert that ideas inherently shape society. Instead the material world and the ideal world reinforce each other within the plausibility of elective affinity. Moreover, Weber laid

27. Ibid., 120.
28. Ibid., 121.
29. Ibid., 123.

the foundation for value-free social science. *The Protestant Ethic and the Spirit of Capitalism* was not meant to inspire social activism or prognostic thought, but to take a scientific, historical, and social-comparative approach to understanding how the mechanisms of capitalism are regulated by rationalization, rooted in a highly differentiated society, and made plausible through a particular cultural and historical framework. Finally, his major contribution to the field of sociology was establishing concepts and theoretical frameworks to examine why people act the way they do. He understood that people acted with purpose and intention. Some motivations, however, are easily concealed, and these real, underlying driving forces that explain people's behavior are known as idealized reasons. Weber's theories, then, were meant to provide the highest degree of generalizability and visibility through ideal types.

In his book, written at the turn of the twentieth century, Weber has the historical and empirical advantage of pursuing an important sociological question of the day: what led to the dominance of Western culture and modern capitalism? *The Protestant Ethic and the Spirit of Capitalism* represents his attempt to answer this question, one of the largest and most extensive comparative-sociological questions to date. For Weber, the rise of Westernization and particularly capitalism has to do with what he perceives as uniquely rational, systematic, and specialized behavior. Although he does not see this "rise" of capitalism as necessary, he does want to understand how it came to be. One of many variables independent of the economic system of capitalism, for Weber, is the Protestant culture that legitimized rationalization. Weber approaches his analysis knowing full well that 1) religion is often seen as a distinct social force from the economy, or at best that hegemonic economic interests shape religion vis-à-vis a superstructure, and 2) that religion is typically studied from a theological, philosophical, and/or psychological perspective.

The first point is reflective of a Marxist school of analysis that views religion as shaped by material forces rather than an independent social force shaping the economy. Weber deftly shows that the Protestant ethic preceded and helped legitimize modern, rational capitalism, and more importantly he reveals the explanatory power sociology offers by connecting belief systems to everyday behavior in society. Work becomes a central identity and focus of modern life. The ideological structure of calling, salvation, and God's will were central in establishing this pervasive and distinctly Western worldview. The orderly and systematic ways that

Protestants approached their work with a sense of calling paved the way for modern capitalism, and its new kind of profit-based work focused on key elements of rationalization: efficiency, growth, predictability, and scientific control. For Weber, this kind of work absolutely required a culture to sustain and legitimize it. Religious culture therefore supplied the authority to justify capitalist practices and the ideology to normalize and idealize a capitalist approach to work.

The second point raises questions about the relevance of sociology to study topics beyond its usual scope. *The Protestant Ethic and the Spirit of Capitalism* is seen as an exemplar for current sociological studies of religion. Despite the changes we have seen in religion since Weber's time, religion certainly continues to manifest itself as a unique social force shaping moral authority and the moral order of society. Religion continues to offer a universe of meaning, which includes a repository of symbols, beliefs, values, and norms that people use to make sense of their lives. Using Weberian analysis, sociologists try to understand the normative power that religion has in affecting everyday behavior both by reifying the status quo or solidifying a new social order, all of which is justified and idealized using forms of sacralization. In other words, religion has both the hegemonic power to routinize behavior and the critical power to break down traditional structures of authority and radicalize behavior. Furthermore, sociologists seek to understand the unique "affinitive" relationship that religion has in shaping economic, political, familial, and educational institutions, as well as individual behavior and decision making. Weber's study illustrated not only the intellectual value of studying religion from a sociological perspective but also contributed to establishing sociology as an academic discipline.

Importance of the Book for Christians

Weber's biography may help explain why his book is important for Christians to read. On the one hand, Weber's father represented the newly established, wealthy, middle-class bourgeoisie who thoroughly enjoyed his economic position. On the other hand, his mother was a devout Calvinist Protestant, an ascetic who was interested in humanitarian affairs yet disdained worldly affairs. Weber later became critical of his father because of his father's overt bourgeois predisposition, but at the same time found himself ideologically caught between evangelical Christian Reformers and the politically liberal thinking of the day. He did not consider himself a religious person, but he was extremely interested in studying religion throughout his academic career and remained intellectually close to theologians of his time. As a person and as a theorist, he attempted to maintain several tensions in his private, political, and academic life. *The Protestant Ethic and the Spirit of Capitalism* represents Weber's academic approach, a value-free, social-scientific study of religion in relation to the rise of modern capitalism. Similarly, sociologists and students of sociology who have a personal faith must also wrestle between their academic stake in the social sciences and their faith position. Sociologists who study religion specialize in analyzing the human side of religion and religious behavior, but if they are Christians they have the added weight of considering the theological ramifications of sociological insights. I want to begin with the human side of religion and religious behavior as it relates to Weber's book and then conclude with ethical implications that the book has for the Christian community.

The value of Weber's study for Christians lies in his adept ability to underscore the fact that religious people's belief in God inevitably shapes their daily behavior. This point may or may not be a surprise to the reader, but religious behavior extends beyond Sunday morning. If you are a practicing Christian, chances are your belief system influences who and whether you marry, how you raise your children, how and whether you vote, your friendships, your free time, and, according to Weber, your work life and economic decisions. When considering work, most people prioritize pay, job security, flexibility, advancement, and opportunity, but having work that is meaningful, important, and satisfying may be number one on their list. For many of us, work is our identity. It is more than what we do; it is who we are.

Within the Christian community, the idea of vocation and calling is vibrant and self-evident. We say we are "called" to this work for the "glory of God," not by our will but by God's will. Work is not just about making ends meet; it provides meaning to our daily lives. We are just as likely as Luther to seek out biblical passages to gain encouragement and direction about our work lives. Work is seen as good. To the extent that our work is tied to our salvation and/or God's presence in the world, work can be a sign of God's good will in our lives. The belief that Protestant Christians cannot earn their way to heaven remains an orthodox view, but good works still preoccupy us in our attempts at a holy and perfect life. The sacralization processes are evident in the way that our decision-making must honor

God. My university's motto is indeed "God first," and faculty are compelled to teach the idea of "God honoring diversity." God is first in our lives, which means that everything after God is based on our personal relationship to him. Christians may even go as far as to say "God first, nation second," or they may believe in a Christian nation, a "city on a hill." To many varying degrees, our social lives are overlaid with a sacred, moral order.

Similar to Weber's analysis of the middle class, a Christian's view of acquiring money is typically modest and humble. Regardless of how much money they have, Christians believe it is not theirs but God's. Christians are not supposed to love money more than God, but this is a difficult arrangement. Money is necessary in order to live in this world, but we are not to be attached to it. A dispassionate view of wealth remains part of the Protestant ethic today. Yet being an American Christian may yield significant social and economic rewards; in fact, current sociological studies point to social advantages that Christians have in the U.S., such as social mobility and economic opportunities. America is a highly productive nation, the richest country in the world if one were to use the Gross Domestic Product (GDP) as the basis of wealth. The Protestant ethic has provided a foundation for economic success in this Judeo-Christian society. Still, Weber's analysis of modern capitalism concluded with this point: today religion has ceased to be the most important socializing and idealizing force for capitalism.

My last point, then, is to assert the problem of religion in the world today. Weber begins a new conversation in sociological circles with his predictions about religion's decline and the disenchantment with the sacred, and his articulation of a proto-theory of secularization. An equally investigated theory as the Protestant ethic, classical secularization theory, asserts that religion will eventually lose its social influence as a moral force in society. A technocratic and post-materialist society will require rationalizations more powerful than the mythical, magical, emotional, or super-empirical ideas promulgated by religion. Weber predicted that rationalization would lead to severe disenchantment that only forms of charismatic authority might momentarily overcome. This last point continues to be hotly debated in sociological circles today. Obviously on a micro- and meso-level, religion continues to have pervasive influence at least in various subcultures, but on a nation-state and global level, religion's influence is questionable and clearly changing. This decline in religious influence has led to embattlement and anxiety within Christian communities.

By studying *The Protestant Ethic and the Spirit of Capitalism*, we can begin to understand how our Christian worldview shapes our behavior while at the same time becoming aware of the changing authority that religion has in our daily lives and in the world today. Moreover, Weber leaves the Christian community with some very positive questions that can help us navigate a modern/postmodern world. First, Weber offers an important insight into how Christians might understand religion. Religion has a provocative power in legitimizing the social order of the day. Christians should note this relationship with a high degree of responsibility, nuance, and stewardship. If Christians do have power in society, how should that power be used? What is the highest good that can be achieved as a Christian community? How can their religious worldview either legitimize the status quo or critically challenge it?

Second, Weber pushes Christians to think about what constitutes "good works." A tradition of perfectionism makes it very difficult for Christians to strike a healthy balance between doing "good" in the world and overtly demonstrating that they are good and holy.

Finally, Weber sets the social boundaries for understanding how Christians relate to the economy. In other words, he differentiates between what is God's will and what is human action. After reading *The Protestant Ethic and the Spirit of Capitalism*, Christians must explore perhaps the most difficult question of all: what should the moral and ethical relationship be between Christianity and capitalism?

CHAPTER 12: EDUCATION

John Dewey, *Democracy and Education*

BY ANITA FITZGERALD HENCK

Introduction

John Dewey's *Democracy and Education* was first published in 1916, serving as a contemporaneous treatise promoting the importance of a progressive educational system that would prepare youth for their future role as United States citizens. He explained, "The devotion of democracy to education is a familiar fact. The superficial explanation is that a government resting upon popular suffrage cannot be successful unless those who elect and who obey their governors are educated."[1]

However, *Democracy and Education* is more than a century-old manual on the role of schooling in a democratic society. In this text, Dewey promoted the importance of purposeful education that is rooted in core, principled values whose applications would continue to evolve and change over time in a transformational society. This work is both an overview of Dewey's philosophy of education and an introduction to his support for

---

1. John Dewey, *Democracy and Education* (1916; rpt. Hollywood, FL: Simon and Brown, 2011), 7.2 (50). Because *Democracy and Education* is available in the public domain and has been published in many versions, to aid in finding referenced work, Dewey's chapter and section number are cited first, and then the page numbers from Simon and Brown's reprint are cited in parentheses.

pragmatic epistemology, through which he advocates the value of practical education grounded in the liberal arts.

Dewey wrote *Democracy and Education* in the early twentieth century while a professor at Columbia University, after serving for many years at the University of Chicago, where he had developed their progressive University Laboratory School. He is particularly known for his contributions to the philosophy of education and its practical applications, but he additionally helped shape the field of functional psychology, which helped to frame his views on education. He was elected president of the American Psychological Association in 1899 and the American Philosophical Association in 1905. Dewey lived to the age of 92, with *Democracy and Education* written at a mid-point in his life, clearly influenced by the breadth of his professional experiences and the depth of his philosophic thought. This historic framework provides an understanding of Dewey's voice and his perspectives on these important issues.

Meanwhile, a review of the context of United States history concurrent with Dewey's writing is also important to our understanding of the environment in which *Democracy and Education* was written. In the late nineteenth and early twentieth centuries, the U.S. had experienced rapid urban growth due to significant numbers of people moving from rural communities to metropolitan areas, while immigrants from other countries were also establishing residence in large cities. Dewey concluded that the demographic changes of his era would cause significant repercussions for the U.S. educational system because of the need to move from apprentice-type training for unskilled and semi-skilled employment to more formal educational systems requiring increasingly more specialized expertise. Concurrently, public schooling was becoming more available to the general population, aided by the construction and staffing of new schools as well as the expansion of the length of the academic program from grammar school models to the broader availability of public secondary schools. This combination of a society's changing need for how its citizenry was educated and the increased prevalence of public schooling provided a significant crossroads for decisions about how education would be delivered.

This social context and Dewey's breadth of expertise provided the foundation for a classic text that has significantly influenced our understanding of the potential impact of the public education on the nation and its citizens. Thus, the tenets of Dewey's *Democracy and Education*, while never fully implemented, have shaped our thoughts and conversations about the American educational system for nearly a century.

Summary of the Book

Democracy and Education is a dense tome with a wide range of themes and styles—from deeply philosophical reflections to highly practical instructions. The content includes Dewey's philosophy of education, discourse on the role of school in shaping society, and lessons on how to teach various subjects. These few examples and broad characterizations provide a very preliminary summary of Dewey's influential work and its impact on present-day education, for supporters and critics alike.

Democracy and Education's chapter titles reflect an overview of many of Dewey's core principles. These include: "Education as a Necessity of Life"; "Education as a Social Function"; "Education as Direction"; "Education as Growth"; "Education as Conservative and Progressive"; "Thinking in Education"; and "Vocational Aspects of Education," among others in this twenty-six chapter text. Notably, Dewey's fundamental perspectives—the importance of education over schooling and the significance of social influence through the public school system—were not fully consonant with that era's systemic educational values or practices.

The role of education as an agent of social change was not a commonly supported perspective in Dewey's time despite its centuries-old discourse, including the work of ancient philosophers such as Plato and Aristotle. In some sectors, the agenda of social change was viewed with suspicion or concern. This was particularly true for those who historically benefited from a strongly class-oriented model of society and perceived that they might be adversely affected when rising lower and middle classes were advantaged by the impact of education on their quality of life and finances. Thus, *Democracy and Education* contributed to important discussions—from the early 1900s to the present—about the role and delivery of education in a democratic society, as well its impact on social constructs and values.

There are multiple ways and many lenses through which Dewey's work has been examined over the century since its first publication. For purposes of this essay, *Democracy and Education* will be summarized through two broad themes. The first is the role of public education in transmitting societal values, and the second relates to educational pedagogy and content.

Role of Public Education in Transmitting Societal Values

Dewey addressed the role of schooling in society when he wrote, "The conception of education as a social process and function has no definite meaning until we define the kind of society we have in mind."[2] For Dewey, the democratic principles of equality and individual rights for all citizens, for which the United States declared its independence from the sovereignty of England, had important implications for the broad design of educational systems. Thus, he endorsed a system that was progressive and accessible to all within the increasingly diverse society. Dewey espoused providing public education for the entire population—not just a hierarchical elite— believing this was consonant with national values and provided significant benefits for society at large.

In contrast to Plato's views on democratic education, which were rooted in the social class structures of his era, Dewey clarified, "[I]n the degree in which society has become democratic, social organization means utilization of the specific and variable qualities of individuals, not stratification by classes."[3]

Dewey advocated that a society's vision of the purposes of education had significant influence on its delivery and content. He wrote:

> Obviously a society to which stratification into separate classes would be fatal, must see to it that intellectual opportunities are accessible to all on equable and easy terms. A society marked off into classes need be specially attentive only to the education of its ruling elements. A society which is mobile . . . must see to it that its members are educated to personal initiative and adaptability. Otherwise, they will be overwhelmed by the changes in which they are caught and whose significance or connections they do not perceive. The result will be a confusion in which a few will appropriate to themselves the result of the blind and externally directed activities of others.[4]

Yet, this potential for education as a force for social mobility created complexity and uncertainty. Some groups of people had a natural reason to resist change. The privileged upper-class—ensconced in socially dominant roles—could be threatened by the rise of those financially and socially less

2. Ibid., 7.5 (55).

3. Ibid., 7.3 (51–52).

4. Ibid., 7.2 (50).

prominent. Offering accessible education for all citizens could represent an eventual loss of their privilege while providing new opportunities for youth from undereducated families of farmers or semi-skilled laborers. Thus, some citizens found this new role for education to be synchronous with the core values of this developing nation of ruggedly independent citizens, while others saw it as being particularly challenging to their way of life.

Further, by advocating a progressive philosophy that moved from schooling students to educating them and from replicating culture to being an agent of cultural change, Dewey asserted some significant amendments to both the values and practices of the day. Dewey noted this dilemma when he wrote, "Particularly is it true that a society which not only changes but which has the ideal of such change as will improve it, will have different standards and methods of education from one which aims simply at the perpetuation of its own customs."[5] Thus, the challenge to be intentional in planning for the education of youth—in relation to content, pedagogy, and anticipation of the societal impact of this new way of operations—was a new direction from past practices.

Dewey also spoke of the significant social change for individuals and families moving from homogeneous smaller groups that were geographically contiguous to a more racially, religiously, and culturally diverse society, particularly as urban areas grew in population. He emphasized the role of schools as a unifying social construct for this period when he wrote, "The intermingling in the school of youth of different races, differing religions, and unlike customs creates for all a new and broader environment. Common subject matter accustoms all to a unity of outlook upon a broader horizon than is visible to the members of any group while it is isolated. The assimilative force of the American public school is eloquent testimony to the efficacy of the common and balanced appeal."[6]

The absence of a national provision for the delivery of education was a challenging conundrum within the discussion of the role education played in the development of a common social good. The country's decentralized delivery of public education resulted in disconnected systems. In a more geographically mobile society, the lack of connectivity through similar values and educational practices from one region to another would continue as a complicating challenge, even to the present day. As youth moved with their family from one neighborhood to another within an urban area, or

5. Ibid., 7.0 (47).
6. Ibid., 2.4 (16).

across vast expanses of this developing country, they found loosely coupled systems of education, each often vastly different than their last schooling experience.

In short, Dewey's work was rooted in deeply held values of the importance of education for the citizens of a democratic society, of education as an agent of social change, and of the need for schools to be in continuous improvement to be responsive to the needs of society. He inextricably linked the values on which educational systems were predicated with its delivery through educational pedagogy and content.

Educational Pedagogy and Content

Dewey supported the concept of pragmatic education, believing that a responsibility of educators was to prepare youth by teaching them to question, reason, and engage for continuous learning. This advocacy was a contrast to the less formal parent-to-child mentoring process common in agrarian communities or semi-formalized apprentice model for learning a trade in more populated areas. Moreover, his proposal was substantially different from the typical schooling of the era that relied on rote memorization of arithmetic, literature, science, and history facts. Believing this progressive and pragmatic approach was central to the development of a healthy democracy, he wrote: "[A]s civilization advances, the gap between the capacities of the young and the concerns of adults widens. Learning by direct sharing in the pursuits of grown-ups becomes increasingly difficult except in the case of the less advanced occupations . . . Intentional agencies—schools—and explicit material—studies—are devised . . . Without such formal education, it is not possible to transmit all the resources and achievements of a complex society."[7]

As he further expanded this new pedagogy, Dewey promoted the influence of proactive development of mental processes and also emphasized the importance of student experiences as an integrative part of the learning environment. As Dewey explained, "The idea that mind and the world of things and persons are two separate and independent realms—a theory which philosophically is known as dualism—carries with it the conclusion that method and subject matter of instruction are separate affairs."[8] Instead, Dewey advocated for integration between the two realms of ideas and facts

7. Ibid., 1.3 (8).
8. Ibid., 13.1 (92).

in a way that allowed a student to engage actively with the subject matter, with the teacher serving as guide to the introduction of new content. Dewey explained, "In schools, those under instruction are too customarily looked upon as acquiring knowledge as theoretical spectators, minds which appropriate knowledge by direct energy of intellect . . . Something which is called mind or consciousness is severed from the physical organs of activity."[9]

In calling for a new approach to educational delivery, Dewey exhorted, "Were all instructors to realize that the quality of mental process, not the production of correct answers, is the measure of educative growth, something hardly less than a revolution in teaching would be worked."[10] This call for a "revolution in teaching," when juxtaposed with the increased social complexity of the early twentieth-century United States, was an invitation for significant change. It would require a student's deeper understanding of content through exploration of the classic dualities of theory versus practice, thinking versus doing, and training versus lifelong learning. Specifically, Dewey advanced the importance of creating a participatory learning environment, asserting that, "where children are engaged in doing things and in discussing what arises in the course of their doing, it is found, even with comparatively indifferent modes of instruction, that children's inquiries are spontaneous and numerous, and the proposals of solution advanced, varied, and ingenious."[11]

However, advocating for a more responsive educational system—where the child was an active participant and the teacher had a responsibility to foster active student engagement—also challenged a more hierarchical society in which children were to be "seen but not heard." Drawing from his expertise in functional psychology, Dewey reported, "Experience has shown that when children have a chance at physical activities which bring their natural impulses into play, going to school is a joy, management is less of a burden, and learning is easier."[12] This was significantly different from any practice in the U.S. at the time. Dewey described his model in the following contrast:

> Processes of instruction are unified in the degree in which they
> center in the production of good habits of thinking . . . The

9. Ibid., 11.1 (78).
10. Ibid., 13.2 (98).
11. Ibid., 12.1 (86).
12. Ibid., 15.1 (108).

essentials of method are therefore identical with the essentials of reflection. They are first that the pupil have a genuine situation of experience—that there be a continuous activity in which he is interested for its own sake; secondly, that a genuine problem develop within this situation as a stimulus to thought; third, that he possess the information and make the observations needed to deal with it; fourth, that suggested solutions occur to him which he shall be responsible for developing in an orderly way; fifth, that he have opportunity and occasion to test his ideas by application, to make their meaning clear and to discover for himself their validity.[13]

Yet, this new direction also required changes in curricular design and school administrative practices. Dewey noted, "Exorbitant desire for uniformity of procedure and for prompt external results are the chief foes which the open-minded attitude meets in school . . . Probably the chief cause of devotion to rigidity of method is, however, that it seems to promise speedy, accurately measurable, correct results. The zeal for 'answers' is the explanation of much of the zeal for rigid and mechanical methods."[14]

Many of Dewey's proposed pedagogical changes were implemented at the University of Chicago Laboratory School that he founded. However, there were also many misunderstood aspects of his proposals, particularly related to the role of student-centered learning. His views were widely mischaracterized as students deciding what they would and would not do, rather than being understood as challenging the teacher and system to capture the attention and interest of students before engaging in the deep work of preparing students to question, reason, and learn. This contrast from teacher-centric memorization, with students having little voice in seeking clarity and engaging with course content, was a model ready for change. However, Dewey, as change agent, was often misunderstood.

Importance of the Book for the University

A book written by a university educator about education and society has the potential to provide insights of enormous importance and influence to the academy. Dewey's Renaissance-man qualifications, coupled with his enthusiasm for education for the common good of society, result in a rich array of insights and challenges for readers of *Democracy and Education*.

13. Ibid., 12.Summary (90–91).
14. Ibid., 13.2 (98).

While a century-old text, his work is timeless due to his challenge that education cannot be stagnant, but must be adaptive in order to encourage student engagement and be responsive to societal needs. Thus, if Dewey's ideas were implemented, education would be ever changing and ever new.

Of equal importance to universities are discussions about Dewey's views on the nature of curricular and co-curricular content in preparing an educated citizenry. Dewey spoke specifically to the value of a liberal arts education, as distinct from professional training. He wrote, "As societies become more complex in structure and resources, the need of formal or intentional teaching and learning increases. As formal teaching and training grow in extent, there is the danger of creating an undesirable split between the experience gained in more direct associations and what is acquired in school. This danger was never greater than at the present time, on account of the rapid growth in the last few centuries of knowledge and technical modes of skill."[15] A century later, this challenge has only increased.

It seems ironic, a century after these words were penned, that many university professors in traditional academic settings would mourn the loss of emphasis on the liberal arts education so valued by Dewey—learning how to think and reason by broadly studying across disciplines—in exchange for a more narrowly focused undergraduate degree emphasizing professional preparation. Dewey had observed that there are "two types of education: the base or mechanical and the liberal or intellectual."[16] In the early twenty-first century in the United States, there is a proliferation of post-secondary institution-types. These range from classic brick-and-mortar public universities to financially struggling private liberal arts colleges, from burgeoning two-year community colleges to four-year technical universities, from fully online for-profit universities staffed by an array of part-time faculty to free educational opportunities with notable professors through MOOCs (Massive Open Online Courses). Somewhere in the midst of this rapid change, Dewey's framework for the balance between the education of an individual and the needs of an educated citizenry provides an important context for reviewing the status of the current post-secondary educational opportunities in the United States.

Dewey had declared, "[T]he educational process is one of continual reorganizing, reconstructing, transforming."[17] Yet, traditional educators

15. Ibid., 1.Summary (9).
16. Ibid., 19.1 (139).
17. Ibid., 4.3 (30).

view present-day rapid changes across the profession as standing in stark disparity to the concept of valuing of education for the common good. Many fear that the present-day emphasis on undergraduate degrees serving as employment passports evidences that the United States educational system has regressed to a version of an apprentice model. With an emphasis on rote content and focus on narrow academic preparation across a few disciplines, educational purists mourn the return to an emphasis on schooling instead of an advancement of the goal of learning.

The academy is in the midst of a time of tumultuous change and significant debate on future educational delivery systems. While higher education is a renewable model—with continued population growth and a proliferation of non-traditional-aged learners—it also is in a time of re-invention of its role in society. Certainly, the question of schooling versus education is at the root of the present-day dilemma. Dewey's *Democracy and Education* has much to contribute to the discourse, from cycle to cycle, as society changes and new trends emerge.

Dewey wrote, in emphasizing the role of education as preparation for a lifetime, "It is not of course a question whether education should prepare for the future. If education is growth, it must progressively realize present possibilities, and thus make individuals better fitted to cope with later requirements . . . Growing . . . is a continuous leading into the future."[18] This is an important societal role for the present-day academy.

Importance of the Book for Christians

Dewey's views on the importance of education in the development of a democratic society provided some historic challenges for U.S. Christians. Dewey was not well received by the Christian community of his day and has often not been well regarded by evangelical Christian groups even to the present time. He was widely believed to be an atheist, so his perspectives and recommendations have been viewed with suspicion. While Dewey did not ignore mention of religion in *Democracy and Education*, his perspectives were shaped by multiple concerns. On the one hand, for Dewey, religion was yet another subject to be taught in school, not unlike mathematics, science, and art. This perspective concerned those who believed that religion had a more fundamental role of shaping societal values within the public school system. On the other hand, he saw organized

18. Ibid., 5.1 (34).

religion as an option among other social organizations that shaped their members. Dewey wrote, "Each such group exercises a formative influence on the active dispositions of its members. A clique, a club, a gang, a Fagin's household of thieves, the prisoners in a jail, provide educative environments for those who enter into their collective of conjoint activities, as truly as a church, a labor union, a business partnership, or a political party. Each of them is a mode of associated or community life quite as much as is a family, a town, or a state."[19] He advocated a separation of church and state, with faith-based values entrusted to religious organizations, while clearly recognizing the unique socializing function of organized religion. Neither perspective earned him the respect or trust of faith communities.

Dewey's observation that "Continuity of life means continual readaptation of the environment to the needs of living organisms"[20] makes sense in the context of his advocacy for preparing citizens of a relatively young nation to be educated to lead in a democratic society. It is understandable, as a developing nation defines its values and develops the concomitant support systems, that growth and adaptation would occur. Yet, another way to view Dewey's propositions aligns him philosophically with Charles Darwin's theories of evolution, which have largely been condemned by conservative Christians. In fact, the broader context of the Dewey quote cited earlier in this paragraph is as follows: "[C]ontinuity of the life process is not dependent upon the prolongation of the existence of any one individual . . . And though, as the geological record shows, not merely individuals but also species die out, the life process continues in increasingly complex forms. As some species die out, forms better adapted to utilize the obstacles against which they struggled in vain come into being. Continuity of life means continual readaptation of the environment to the needs of living organisms."[21] In reality, civilizations grew, declined, and died out; peoples moved across oceans and began new societies and cultures; and schooling moved from tutors for the wealthy to one-room schoolhouses for the rural poor to land grant universities. Change—or social evolution—has been an important part of the development of this country and its progress. Yet, unfortunately, much of Dewey's work has been overshadowed in Christian circles by his disconnect from faith communities and his adaptation of Darwin's terminology in providing social commentary.

19. Ibid., 2.4 (15–16).
20. Ibid., 1.1 (5).
21. Ibid.

This is unfortunate because even Dewey's supporters would not uphold his proposals *in toto*; as autonomous thinkers, they would still find points of distinction from his perspectives. In turn, there are several places where Dewey's values are consonant with the Christian faith community. For example, his advocacy for the equality of all people should resonate strongly with the Apostle Paul's call for unity amongst diverse parts of the church when he charged the Galatian church, "There is neither Jew nor Gentile, neither slave nor free, nor is there male and female, for you are all one in Christ Jesus."[22] The new social order Dewey espoused, in fact, called for education for all peoples, irrespective of their background—a very Christ-like perspective.

Dewey had much to contribute to our understanding of the interrelationships between schools and societies and the necessity of change for survival. Nonetheless, his works have not been widely appreciated by faith communities and, in particular, in evangelical circles.

Conclusion

In *Democracy and Education*, Dewey promoted the importance of the relationship between education and the health of a democratic culture. In differentiating between schooling and education, Dewey advanced the concept of continuous or lifetime learning for all citizens of the United States. While these concepts were important in the early 1900s, they are significantly more important in the context of the rapid rate of change of the twenty-first century in the United States. The nation's educational system continues to be reframed and redesigned, while the social values shaping it continue to be debated as points of deep ideological difference. Inequities in the funding of schools are largely linked to socioeconomic factors within communities and across the U.S. In turn, this process continues to contribute to a stratified educational system, with differing resources being integrally tied to the property values in children's home neighborhoods. These variations are viewed from distinctively different perspectives. On the one hand, imbalances in educational funding are viewed as inequities and points of deep despair for some; on the other hand, relative differences in resources relate to the "do it yourself" mindset brought by early immigrants, with effort equating to success.

22. Galatians 3:28, *New International Version Bible*.

Debates continue over the autonomy of local communities versus the need for a more nationalized curriculum and financial model for a society of mobile citizens. Yet, even as he penned *Democracy and Education*, Dewey acknowledged, "[W]e are doubtless far from realizing the potential efficacy of education as a constructive agency of improving society, from realizing that it represents not only a development of children and youth but also of the future society of which they will be the constituents."[23]

With current national discussion of improved planning for a Common Core curriculum across primary and secondary education, two of Dewey's principal values are central to the discourse. The first is the need for an integrated curriculum across the disciplines, providing more depth of understanding and less emphasis on rote learning. The second is the importance of connectivity between curricula across the nation, in response to a more geographically mobile society. With 100 years of discourse since the first publishing of *Democracy and Education*, some issues remain constant and a part of lively national debate.

While the United States has yet to realize the full breadth of Dewey's impact, the influence of Dewey is profound. Whether a catalyst for conversation or a clarion of values, Dewey has profoundly shaped our understanding of education and his influence continues today.

23. Dewey, *Democracy and Education*, 6.3 (46).